THE COMMANDERS

THE
COMMANDERS
★★
CIVIL WAR GENERALS
WHO SHAPED THE AMERICAN WEST

ROBERT M. UTLEY

UNIVERSITY OF OKLAHOMA PRESS : NORMAN

Library of Congress Cataloging-in-Publication Data

Name: Utley, Robert M., 1929– author.
Title: The commanders : Civil War generals who shaped the American west / Robert M. Utley.
Description: Norman : University of Oklahoma Press, 2018. | Includes bibliographical references and index.
Identifiers: LCCN 2017033391 | ISBN 978-0-8061-5978-2 (hardcover : alk. paper)
Subjects: LCSH: Indians of North America—Wars—1866–1895—Biography | United States. Army—Officers—Biography. | West (U.S.)—History, Military—19th century. | Command of troops—History—19th century. | Generals—United States—Biography.
Classification: LCC E83.866 .U869 2018 | DDC 355.00978/09034—dc23
LC record available at https://lccn.loc.gov/2017033391

1 2 3 4 5 6 7 8 9 10

For Jerry Greene
ever helpful friend

CONTENTS

═ ★★ ═

ILLUSTRATIONS

═══ ★★ ═══

FIGURES

MAPS

Cartography by Peter H. Dana

PREFACE

The inspiration for this work comes from a book by Thomas Ricks, *The Generals* (2012), an analysis of U.S. Army generals from World War II until that time. On a more modest scale, I attempt to do the same thing here for a cadre of Civil War generals who served in strategic positions in the American West after the war. In combat and command positions, these generals distinguished themselves in the Civil War. In the shrunken postwar Regular Army, they brought the same talents to the West—a field of operations starkly different from the wartime theaters and battlefields. The Indians of the plains and mountains did not fight like the Confederate armies. Adaptation to unconventional war proved difficult for most. Did they make a difference in the opening of the West?

Those chosen for my examination served at the department level, the crucial unit between the division commander and the troops in the field. Each approached his duties in a different way. Some took to the field and led combat commands. Others preferred to command from department headquarters, overseeing more active officers who were leading the field operations. Only one, George Crook, adapted to the changed circumstances. He had learned Indian fighting in the West before the Civil War. So had Generals Augur and Ord, yet they failed to adapt. Despite the army's inability to free itself from orthodox measures, it drove the Indians to collapse within twenty-five years.

In the chapters that follow, after sketching the postwar army, I narrate the history of each of the seven generals, both in the Civil War and in the West. I evaluate each as a department commander, both in Indian affairs and in management of the department. Finally, I appraise them all in a concluding chapter and end by ranking them according to their effectiveness as department commanders.

I have studied and published works on the frontier army for half a century. It is one of several subjects to which I have devoted my professional career as a historian. Much of what is contained in this volume is distilled from the knowledge and insights that I gained in this endeavor. The books most notable in underlying the substance of this book are *Frontiersmen in Blue: The United States Army and the Indian, 1848–1865* (1967), *Frontier Regulars: The United States Army and the Indian, 1866–1891* (1973), *The Indian Frontier, 1846–1890* (1984, 2003), and *Cavalier in Buckskin: George Armstrong Custer and the Western Military Frontier* (1988, 2001). My works on Indians, most importantly biographies of Sitting Bull and Geronimo, have contributed to my understanding of the soldiers who fought them.

Three friends and colleagues who have broadened my view of the frontier army and its leaders should be mentioned: Paul Andrew Hutton, Jerome A. Greene, and Paul Hedren. They have not reviewed this manuscript, but they are published experts in this field. I want to credit their contribution to my career.

Chuck Rankin at the University of Oklahoma Press has been more instrumental in shaping this book than the ordinary press editor. The concept of the book owes much to his thought and urging. His recommendations played a major role in determining the content, and his editing skills greatly improved the narrative. Thanks, Chuck.

Finally, as in my previous books, Peter Dana has crafted his usual excellent maps. The shaded relief maps are a product of his exceptional cartographical mastery and computer skills.

Scottsdale, Arizona
October 2016

THE COMMANDERS

Lieutenant General Philip H. Sheridan,
commanding Military Division of the Missouri, 1869–1883;
commanding U.S. Army, 1884–1888.
Author's collection.

CHAPTER ONE

THE POSTWAR U.S. ARMY

S pring 1866. The Civil War had ended a year earlier at Appomattox Courthouse, Virginia, yet only now had all the members of the Volunteer Army that had fought the war been mustered out of federal service and sent back to their states. The Regular Army, in its prewar form, waited impatiently for Congress to fix the size and composition of the postwar army. Not until the end of July 1866 did Congress send an act to President Andrew Johnson for his signature.[1]

The three generals who had emerged from the war with the greatest combat record and highest public esteem were Ulysses S. Grant, William T. Sherman, and Philip H. Sheridan. Three days before Congress passed the army act, it also passed an act elevating Grant to four-star rank as General of the Army.[2] That slipped Grant's three stars as lieutenant general to Sherman. Sheridan retained his two-star rank as major general.

Instead of fixing a numerical size, the army act authorized the president to vary the number of men in a company between 50 and 100. When the War Department set the number of privates per company at 64, the postwar army emerged with a strength of 54,000. This figure would not endure, however, even with the increased demands of Reconstruction in the South and settlement and development in the West. An economizing Congress pared the strength in 1869 to 37,313 and in 1870 to 30,000. In 1874 Congress set a figure of 27,000 officers and enlisted men, which remained stable.[3]

The 1866 act also specified the composition of line and staff. In reducing the army strength in 1869, however, Congress left the army with ten cavalry regiments, five artillery regiments, and twenty-five infantry regiments for the next three decades. The Ninth and Tenth Cavalry and Twenty-Fourth and Twenty-Fifth Infantry were composed of black soldiers with white officers. To lead this army Congress reduced the number of generals to one full general (William T. Sherman, Grant having been elected president), one lieutenant general (Philip H. Sheridan), three major generals, and eight brigadier generals. When Sherman and Sheridan retired, their grades also retired.

The act provided that the officers of the line would consist half of regulars and half of former volunteer officers who wished to apply for a regular commission. Two of the generals treated in following chapters fell into this category: Nelson A. Miles and Alfred H. Terry.

Complicating the issue of rank was the system of brevets. In the absence of medals to recognize outstanding battlefield performance, brevets were awarded in the next higher rank than then occupied. A captain displaying "gallant and meritorious conduct" could be breveted major. Few generals during the war failed to win brevets in the Volunteers, and many did in the Regular Army. Customarily, as a courtesy, officers were addressed by their brevet rank and wore the uniforms, or at least the insignia, of their brevet rank for the first few years after the war. The system became so confusing that the War Department issued orders to abolish the practice, but officers continued to be addressed by their brevets even while ridding their uniforms of evidence of brevet rank.[4]

Existing brevets, of course, endured throughout the postwar decades. For years, the system sparked controversy in the officer corps. As Colonel John Gibbon advised General Sherman in 1877, "So long as the present system of brevets is maintained the delusion will be kept up, not only in the minds of the officers themselves, but of the people at large, that our army is largely composed of generals and colonels; and I can see but one remedy for the evil, a total abolishment of *all* brevets in the Army, a return to a solid basis in military rank, by its complete annulment of all brevet commissions."[5]

The staff, separate from the line, experienced few changes under the 1866 act and subsequent acts. In fact, the department chiefs (all but two of whom were brigadier generals) were a power unto themselves, protecting and enhancing their turf, cultivating congressional committees, and recognizing no other authority than the secretary of war, to whom they reported directly without officially acknowledging the existence of a commanding general.

The staff consisted of the Adjutant General's Department, which processed and dispatched commands and kept the archives; the Inspector General's Department, which kept tabs on the army leadership as well as arms, clothing, quarters, and all other matters essential to an army's functioning; the Judge Advocate General's Department, which reviewed the operation of military courts and advised the secretary on all legal matters; the Quartermaster General's Department, which had charge of housing, supplies, and transportation both of personnel and materiel; the Subsistence Department, charged with feeding the army; the Medical Department, responsible for health and hygiene of the army; the Pay Department, whose paymasters circulated among the posts dispensing pay; the Corps of Engineers, which constructed works and mapped the country; the Ordnance Department, which armed the troops; and the Signal Corps, which experimented with flags, telegraphy, meteorology, and other means of communication.

The staff chiefs also had subordinates assigned to the lower division and department commands. These officers reported to their respective line commanders, but their principal loyalty was to their staff chief in Washington. In the lower commands, therefore, the line general, contending with mixed loyalties, often lacked the power to control his own logistics—a crippling effect in field operations.

Despite isolation from the staff departments and arrogation of the power to order troop and personnel assignments to the secretary of war, the commanding general still exercised large influence on subordinate commands. This was especially true during the tenure of William T. Sherman, who served from 1869 to 1883. Such was his wartime stature and friendship with subordinate generals that he exerted immense influence on their thinking and actions while constantly feuding with the secretary of war.

Sherman explained his dilemma in a letter to Sheridan in 1872:

> As you say [General John] Pope ought not to fuss about Staff. He has a staff and I have none. He can give an order and enforce its execution, and I can not give an order. . . . I am sometimes consulted, but my inferiors in rank can take my advice or not as they please, whilst I possess no military status. I will endeavor to help department and division commanders in the maintenance of discipline; and in preserving the semblance of an army. Maybe

after General Grant's reelection he may feel disposed to give us some of his sympathy and help. But I know that leading politicians are jealous of military fame and will secretly aid to destroy General Grant, so as to prove that military men do not make good Presidents.[6]

So disgusted with his status did Sherman become that in 1874, over the vigorous protests of Sheridan, he moved his headquarters to St. Louis and essentially abdicated command. With the impeachment and ouster of Secretary of War William W. Belknap in 1876, however, the new secretary, Alfonso Taft, persuaded Sherman to return to Washington and granted him authority over the adjutant general and the inspector general. Subsequent secretaries continued the system.[7]

Two divisions and seven departments made up the organization of the army in the American West. The Military Division of the Missouri, commanded from his Chicago headquarters by Lieutenant General Philip H. Sheridan, encompassed the plains and mountains east of the continental divide.

The division was organized into four departments: the Department of Dakota, headquartered in St. Paul (Minnesota, Dakota, and Montana); the Department of the Platte, headquartered in Omaha (Iowa, Nebraska, Utah, and part of Dakota and Montana); the Department of the Missouri, headquartered at Fort Leavenworth (Missouri, Kansas, Colorado, and New Mexico); and the Department of Texas, headquartered in San Antonio (Texas and the Indian Territory).

The Division on the Pacific, headquartered in San Francisco, comprised all the territory west of the continental divide. While Sheridan enjoyed a long tenure, the Division of the Pacific had a succession of leaders, notably John M. Schofield and Irvin McDowell. The Division of the Pacific embraced the Department of California, also headquartered in San Francisco (California and Nevada); the Department of the Columbia, headquartered at Portland, Oregon (Oregon, Washington, Idaho, and Alaska); and the Department of Arizona, headquartered at Prescott (Arizona).

Pay and promotion preoccupied the officer corps. In each session of Congress, members sought and sometimes succeeded in reducing officer pay. Worse than low pay was no pay. At midnight on March 3, 1877, the congressional session expired before appropriations could be made for the

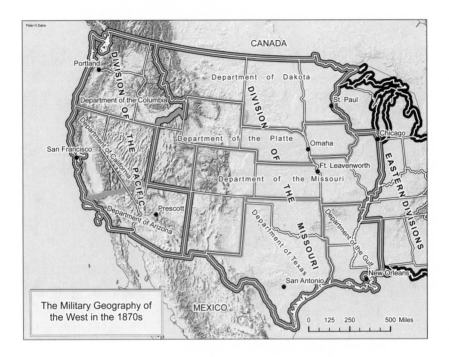

The Military Geography of
the West in the 1870s

army. Not until a special session opened on October 15 was a bill passed
and pay restored.[8]

Commented the *Army and Navy Journal*: "On the postponement of the
extra session of Congress to the 15th of October the officers of the Army
and Navy may say to the Administration, as the frogs did to the boy in the
fable, 'this may be fun for you, but it is death to us.'"[9]

The promotion system rewarded some officers and penalized others.
Strict seniority governed promotion from lieutenant through colonel. Junior
officers assigned to their regiment advanced from lieutenant to captain
only when senior officers transferred or died. This meant that in regiments
with a high turnover a lieutenant might reach captain quickly, whereas in
regiments with low turnover a lieutenant might serve in grade for years—as
many as twenty—before donning a captain's shoulder straps. In 1876 the
Battle of the Little Bighorn removed so many officers from the Seventh
Cavalry's rolls that promotion came quickly.

Promotion from major through colonel occurred within the arm (infantry,
cavalry, artillery); so when a major's vacancy occurred in one of the cavalry

Major General Irvin McDowell, commanding
Division of the Pacific, 1876–1882.
*Brady Collection, U.S. Signal Corps (photo B-5799), National Archives
and Records Administration, Washington, D.C.*

regiments, the senior captain of cavalry moved up to major in the regiment where the vacancy existed. The system prevailed through the grade of colonel.

All general officers were appointed by the president, often without regard to seniority. A vacancy in a general officer's grade triggered a storm of influence-peddling as candidates, including colonels, mustered all the influence that they could find from friends in the army or in Congress or even from prominent civilians. The system, of course, led to rivalries, sometimes bitter, among colonels and generals.

Despite the enmity between staff and line, line officers, confronted with the prospect of years in the same grade and life in an isolated frontier post, mustered all the influence that they could find to wangle a staff appointment. Staff officers lived a much more comfortable and stable life than line officers, for a staff assignment meant living in or near a city and avoiding repeated transfers.

Officers who had led the Volunteer Army during the Civil War found themselves commanding a far different enlisted complement. The Regular Army could not recruit the motivated young men who had rushed to save the Union. Recruits came from every background, beginning with a lower order of intelligence. As Brigadier General Edward O. C. Ord observed in 1872, while the government had developed a greatly improved rifle, "I rather think we have a much less intelligent soldier to handle it."[10] Some were fugitives from justice, others from a shrewish wife, still others from poverty, and many were hopeless drunks (as were some of their officers). Most listed their occupation as "unskilled laborer." The "foreign paupers" decried by a New York newspaper were a burden to the army but included some (mainly Irish and German) who rose to be first-rate noncommissioned officers. Not to be discounted, in addition, were the young men who sought adventure and proved to be good soldiers.

The army suffered a high desertion rate and a low reenlistment rate. This dismal record was attributed to various causes. Execrable living conditions at the frontier posts were one. "Fatigue" labor substituting for soldiering was another. Tyrannical noncommissioned officers accounted for many desertions. Each year 20 to 40 percent of the enlisted ranks deserted, died, or were discharged. The consequence was an army of untrained and inexperienced soldiers.

One exception was the four black regiments. The army offered stable employment to a downtrodden people as well as a uniform that civilian blacks could look up to. These regiments boasted high reenlistment rates and low desertion rates. They suffered discrimination from the high command and passed years in the most undesirable parts of the West. Yet most made good soldiers. The only drawback was their inability to do paperwork, throwing most of that chore on their officers.[11]

The postwar army benefited from greatly improved arms. The rifled musket of Civil War times was altered to receive metallic cartridges. No longer did soldiers have to load their weapons with the awkward, time-consuming paper cartridge and ramrod. Metallic cartridges, quickly slipped into the breach, permitted greater rapidity of fire, greater accuracy, and greater velocity and fire power. The cavalry also rode with metallic ammunition, although they failed to decide between two contenders: the old single-shot Sharps and the Spencer, a seven-shot repeater loaded from a tube drilled into the stock. Some regiments carried a mix of the two, as well as pistols. Not until the early 1870s did metallic cartridges appear for pistols. Until then troopers used the cap-and-ball six-shooter of Civil War times.

In 1872 Brigadier General Alfred H. Terry headed a panel of officers charged with selecting a single rifle and carbine for issue to the troops. They chose the single-shot 1873 Springfield rifle and carbine, .45 caliber, that loaded from the breech. Officers complained that the rapid-fire Winchester failed to be included, especially after George Armstrong Custer's disaster dramatized the superiority of the Winchester in the hands of the Sioux. But the Ordnance Department refused, on the grounds that the Winchester had far less range and penetrating power than the Springfield.

The Terry board did not consider sidearms. By 1873, however, the Colt six-shooter had emerged as the favorite, although a Remington .44 caliber and a Smith and Wesson, as altered by Major George W. Schofield, attained some popularity.

Cavalrymen were also issued a saber. It made a fine ornament on dress parade but was almost never carried in the field. It was cumbersome, noisy, and useless to horsemen, who never got close enough to an Indian to use it.

Artillery took the form of Gatling guns and Hotchkiss howitzers. The Gatling fired 350 rounds a minute from ten revolving barrels. Standard infantry ammunition was fed through a hopper. Most officers considered the Gatling useless. It quickly overheated and jammed with black powder refuse. Also, the Gatling was difficult to transport in rough country and slowed the march of any command that took it. More effective was the light mountain howitzer, a steel-tubed two-pounder that could readily be transported and fired rapidly at ranges up to four thousand yards.

Soldiers went west after the war clad in the huge stocks of clothing left over from the war: dark blue blouses and light blue trousers trimmed with the color of their arm of the service—blue for infantry, yellow for cavalry, and red for artillery. Although the quartermaster general wished to rid his warehouses of surplus clothing, he dealt with constant complaints from the men who had to wear them. They particularly abhorred the ungainly high-crowned hat with a wide brim turned up on one side and decorated with an ostrich feather. The French-style kepi offered little protection from the elements but was the preferred headgear in garrison. The Civil War clothing also suffered from improper fitting, leaving the wearer to have it tailored at his own expense. Civil War contractors, moreover, had turned out shoddy clothing that deteriorated under frontier conditions. All uniforms were wool, hot in the summer and cold in the winter.

Civil War stocks were not exhausted until the late 1880s, but certain sizes ran short, leading the army to adopt new uniform regulations in 1872. Reflecting Prussian influence as a result of the Franco-Prussian War, the new uniforms produced a far more handsome soldier. Spiked helmets with horsehair plumes and large amounts of gold braid and brass buttons characterized dress uniforms, while undress proved more satisfactory.

Still, in the field, officers and men dressed as they pleased. In 1876 a reporter described the appearance of the Fifth Cavalry at Fort Fetterman, Wyoming, on the way to join General Crook's column:

> They came along in thorough fighting trim.... To the fastidious eye ... there was something quite shocking in the disregard of the regulation uniform ... and the only things in their dress which marked them as soldiers were their striped pants and knee boots.... Their blue Navy shirts, broad brimmed hats, belts stuffed with cartridges, and loose handkerchiefs knotted about the neck, gave them a wild bushwhacker appearance which was in amusing contrast with their polished and gentlemanly manners.[12]

The Fifth Cavalry would not have appeared in this manner if they were marching in a winter climate. The Clothing Bureau experimented with various forms of winter gear, but the men themselves improvised. In a Dakota winter they turned out in blanked-lined buffalo overcoats with buffalo skin footgear and headgear. The desert climate also posed a challenge. Finally the army settled on white canvas for fatigue but the old uniform for duty. The one exception was the British-style white pith helmet. The field troops did not like that either.

Gerald Russell typified the soldier who had risen from the ranks of the prewar army and become an officer during the war. Like many, he was an Irishman who had fled to the United States because of the potato famine. The surest employment for an Irish immigrant just off the boat was the U.S. Army, in which he enlisted in 1851. Assigned to the Regiment of Mounted Riflemen (later the Third Cavalry), he served on the Texas and New Mexico frontier, advancing to sergeant by 1862. After being commissioned a second lieutenant in his old regiment, now the Third Cavalry, he distinguished himself in the Vicksburg campaign and in 1867, back on the frontier, was promoted to captain. Like many of his countrymen who had risen from the ranks, he never shed the rough edges of ten years as an enlisted man. As captain of a troop of the Third Cavalry at Fort Selden, New Mexico, he greeted a newly arrived contingent of recruits with words that introduced them and others like them to the world of the frontier enlisted man:

> Young Min! I conghratulate yiz on bein assigned to moi thrupe, becos praviously to dis toime, I vinture to say that my thrupe had had more villins, loyhars, teeves, scoundhrils and, I moight say, damn murdhrers than enny udder thrupe in the United States Ormy. I want yiz to pay sthrict attention to jooty—and not become dhrunken vagabonds, wandhrin all over Gods Creashun, spindin ivry cint of your pay with low bum-mers. Avoide all timptashuns, loikwoise all discipashuns, so that in toime yiz kin become non-commissioned offizurs; yez'll found your captin a very laynent man and very much given to laynency, fur oi niver duz toi no man up bee der tumbs unless he duz be late for roll-call. Sarjint, dismiss de detachmint.[13]

For the recruits, Fort Seden represented the kind of home that they would occupy during their five-year enlistment. In southern New Mexico near the Rio Grande, surrounded by desert sands, Fort Selden was built of adobe long since fallen into disrepair and inhabited by desert insects, enclosing crowded barracks with rude wooden bunks supporting straw mattresses. As cavalry, the men had to maintain their horses in addition to the many chores that substituted for true soldiering. They dined largely on beef, bacon, beans, hardtack, and coffee, prepared by untrained cooks detailed from the troop. Governed less by Captain Russell than by noncommissioned officers, some tyrannical, the soldiers did not always heed their captain's warnings about "discipashun." Most frontier posts boasted a "hog ranch" just beyond the boundary, dedicated to relieving the soldiers of their paltry pay—this and more for thirteen dollars a month.

To vary the terrible table fare, both officers and enlisted men could resort to the post sutler, who charged exorbitant prices for such delicacies as tinned oysters. Post gardens were tilled at some posts but were mainly private gardens maintained by officers. At Fort Rice, Dakota, in 1873, an officer in the mold of Captain Russell exclaimed: "The damn hoppers came along, by God, and ate my garden, by God, then the birds ate the hoppers, by God. And we killed and ate the birds, by God, so that we were even in the long run, by God."[14]

Despite the best efforts of the post surgeon, poor sanitation and hygiene plagued the frontier stations. Water, usually of dubious purity, came from runoff in cisterns or the nearest spring or well. At Fort Sully, Dakota, for instance, water wagons drawn by mules had to make the half-mile journey to the Missouri River to keep the post supplied; there was no other source. In the absence of plumbing, pit toilets had to do. "Honey wagons" made the rounds each morning collecting waste. Not until the late 1880s did permanent posts begin to receive plumbing.

Most garrisons had their complement of women. Officers brought their wives and children with them, at great expense because the army made no provision for them. They made life more bearable by organizing social events. Many of the wives also indulged in gossip and feuding, which soured the harmony of officers' row. One officer entitled the first chapter of his book "Ladies in the United States Army to the Prejudice of Good Order and Discipline."

Tucked away in a remote corner of a post was "Soap Suds Row," which housed the laundresses. Each company rated four, who received rations and a scant wage. Many were married to noncommissioned officers. Like the wives along officers' row, however, they feuded with one another and caused so much discord that the War Department abolished their jobs.[15]

Most recruits entered the army expecting to be assigned to the frontier and campaign against Indians. Often Indian tribes met their expectations, and the soldiers found themselves marching off to war. More often a soldier served his entire enlistment without ever seeing an Indian. Most campaigns failed in their objectives. Indians refused to fight the soldiers unless enjoying overwhelming odds; instead they simply vanished. The troops could prevail only by taking the Indians by surprise, which was rarely allowed to happen. Columns of troops moved ponderously, slowed by wagon trains bearing supplies. Indians had no trouble eluding such expeditions.

The generals who had to conduct campaigns against Indians apparently gave no thought to devising a strategy for contending with tribesmen. Throughout the postwar decades, scores of lightly garrisoned forts supposedly protected nearby communities. When Indian wars broke out, the troops assembled in columns to advance on the enemy. The generals debated whether to consolidate the garrisons in a few posts from which they could be organized quickly for a campaign. But settlers demanded the visible presence of soldiers as well as the market that they provided. Not until Indian hostilities receded in the late 1880s did the War Department succeed in reducing the number of forts.

Largely under the influence of General Sherman, the army sought to professionalize during the postwar era. Schools sprouted for special training, and professional journals proliferated. Yet neither in the schools nor in instructional manuals was the unconventional warfare practiced by Indians addressed. West Point had no courses addressing the subject. The emphasis was on the next conventional war, to be fought by orthodox strategy and tactics. The strategists believed that Indian warfare would soon vanish. The next campaign or two would be the last, as the tribes were concentrated on reservations. This thinking, of course, ignored the fact that for a century the prime mission of the army was fighting Indians.

As a result, Indian campaigns were conducted according to orthodox concepts. Few succeeded because the Indians fought, if at all, by their own very different methods. In the hostile western landscape, offensive columns contended with the daunting challenge of keeping their own men and animals supplied. This meant remaining with their wagon trains or establishing supply depots from which to operate. The mix of the army's conventional methods with the Indian's unconventional methods left the army unprepared for the conventional wars of the nineteenth century: the War of 1812, the Mexican War, the Civil War, and the Spanish-American War.

Ironically, the postwar drive to professionalize partly owed its origins to the alienation of the army from the people. The public condescended to the soldiers and their families, isolated and hardly visible on the remote frontier. As the *Army and Navy Journal* editorialized, "the present trouble with the Army is that it is separated from the knowledge and affections of the people who pay the taxes, and is only seen from year to year in the form of heavy appropriations."[16] Brigadier General John Pope constantly voiced this serious problem. In 1878 he told a congressional committee that it was essential that the army's "relation to the people and to the government should be made closer and more harmonious. Unless this can be done it always invites and will always provoke criticism and unfriendly action."[17]

Faced with public and congressional contempt, if not hostility, the army turned in on itself. One way to relieve their frustration, officers discovered, lay in the movement toward greater professionalization. The special schools and the literature provided an outlet for improving themselves professionally and taking greater pride in their profession.

Even so, it was a profession drifting toward radical change. The Spanish-American War and the Philippine Insurrection marked the last days of the frontier army. In the early twentieth century the reforms of Elihu Root created a different army, organized to fight two world wars. Truly has the period between 1865 and 1900 been labeled "The Twilight of the Frontier Army."

Brigadier General Christopher C. Augur, commanding
Department of the Platte, 1867–1871;
Department of Texas, 1871–1875, 1878–1883;
Department of the Missouri, 1883–1885.
Brady Collection, U.S. Signal Corps (photo BA-350),
National Archives and Records Administration, Washington, D.C.

CHAPTER TWO

CHRISTOPHER C. AUGUR

Despite his brushy sideburns sweeping into an immense mustache, C. C.
Augur was the least visible of the postwar department commanders.
Even so, he was the steadiest, most competent, most reliable, most
attentive to duty, and most administratively able. In contrast to some of the
others, moreover, he was thoughtful, modest, unassuming, undistracted by
ego or ambition, loyal to his superiors, and considerate of his subordinates.
As for his attitude toward the Indians within his jurisdiction, he prompted
General Sherman's remark that he "leans to the side of forbearance and
moderation."[1] Finally, Augur was one of several department commanders
who preferred to command from his headquarters rather than leading
troops in the field. Nevertheless, he left his desk often enough to acquire
and retain a working knowledge of his posts, troops, Indians, landscape,
communications, government officials, and settlers. In short, C. C. Augur
was a superior department commander.[2]

Born on July 10, 1821, at Kendall, New York, Augur entered West Point
Military Academy in 1839 and graduated in 1843. As a second lieutenant in the
Fourth Infantry, he fought in the first two battles of the Mexican War, Palo
Alto and Resaca de la Palma, on May 8 and 9, 1846. Thereafter he spent the
rest of the war first on recruiting service and then as aide-de-camp to General
Enos B. Hopping and, after Hopping's death, to General Caleb Cushing.

PACIFIC NORTHWEST

Promoted to captain in 1852, Augur took station at Fort Vancouver, Washington Territory. In 1855 he went East to conduct a contingent of recruits

to Oregon. On his return, while stationed at Fort Yakima, Washington, he received his first introduction to Indian warfare—a skirmish with Yakima Indians at Two Buttes, Washington, on November 9, 1855. The conflict heralded the forthcoming Yakima War, but Augur participated instead in the newly erupted Rogue River War to the south in Oregon.

The Rogue River expedition of 1856 featured three columns aiming to converge on the lower Rogue River: Major Robert C. Buchanan coming east from Fort Humboldt; Captain Christopher C. Augur coming east from Fort Orford; and Captain Andrew J. Smith coming downstream from Fort Lane. Captain Smith, a tough dragoon, reached the rendezvous first. Alerted to an approaching band of combative warriors, Smith posted his command of fifty dragoons, thirty infantry, and a howitzer atop a low ridge on May 25, 1856, and had them dig in for defense. During the night he sent a courier to summon Major Buchanan to his relief. Through two days and one night, May 27–28, the Indian warriors pounded Smith's position. On the second afternoon, with a third of his command dead or wounded and ammunition and water running low, Smith confronted a howling assault that seemed likely to overrun his position. At that moment he glimpsed Augur's infantry advancing at double time. Smith led his men in a counterattack down the slope and hit the charging warrior force just as Augur's men struck the rear. The Indians fled in disorder, ending the Battle of Big Meadows.[3]

As a headquarters general after the Civil War, Augur could cite (although he was not given to boasting) his baptism of fire at Big Meadows in 1856.

Captain Augur spent the next five years in routine garrison duty at Fort Hoskins, Oregon. Promoted to major of the Thirteenth Infantry on May 14, 1861, he was assigned to West Point Military Academy as commandant of cadets and instructor of artillery, cavalry, and infantry tactics. It was a prestigious posting, but the Civil War had broken out and he was an experienced officer. On November 12, 1861, Major Augur was anointed Brigadier General Augur, U.S. Volunteers.

CIVIL WAR

General Augur first served in the defenses of Washington and then along the Rappahannock River in Virginia. With the failure of General George B. McClellan's Peninsular Campaign, however, Major General John Pope was brought from the West to command the newly constituted Army of

Virginia. In July 1862 General Robert E. Lee dispatched Stonewall Jackson and later A. P. Hill to confront Pope. Instead of Pope, the Confederates encountered Nathaniel P. Banks at Cedar Mountain, near Gordonsville.

Augur had the misfortune to serve under Banks, whose Civil War career proved less than distinguished. Bereft of military experience or knowledge, Banks was a Massachusetts politician who became one of President Lincoln's first "political generals." On May 16, 1861, with the war scarcely begun, Banks sewed on the two-starred shoulder straps of a major general. On August 9, 1862, Brigadier General Augur commanded the Second Division of Banks's Second Corps. Banks opened the Battle of Cedar Mountain by hurling two divisions against Jackson, pushing him back. But the arrival of Hill enabled Jackson to counterattack and drive Banks in retreat. Augur received a severe wound, which kept him out of combat until it healed. Cedar Mountain earned Augur a brevet of colonel in the Regular Army and promotion to major general of Volunteers. It also helped ensure that he would once again have to serve under Banks.

Only five months after Cedar Mountain, in December 1862, Banks led a force of thirty thousand recruits by sea to Union-occupied New Orleans and supplanted another political general, Benjamin Butler, in command of the Department of the Gulf. Banks sent Augur to command the District of Baton Rouge until an army could be organized to capture the Confederate bastion of Port Hudson, on the east bank of the Mississippi River. Upstream, General Ulysses S. Grant tightened the noose on Vicksburg and wanted Banks to remove this last blockage of the Mississippi River. To Grant's annoyance, Banks dithered in New Orleans, reluctant to undertake the mission.

Finally, however, on May 21, 1863, commanding the First Division of Banks's Nineteenth Corps, Augur launched an attack against an outlying defensive position. He scored a victory that opened the way for Banks's army of more than thirty thousand men to surround the fortress, which bristled with heavy artillery. Banks wanted to overpower the fort in one massive assault, then rush on to Vicksburg. His four division commanders opposed such a direct attack as too costly, but Banks insisted. The divisions were to attack when ready, not at a prearranged time. As a consequence, sporadic attacks throughout the day of May 27 resulted in bloody repulses. Banks now settled for a siege. It lasted until June 13, when Banks, fearing for his political as well as military fortunes, launched another assault. That too failed, with severe losses, so Banks continued the siege for another three weeks. Vicksburg fell to Grant on July 4. The Confederate commander at Port Hudson, seeing no purpose in continuing the battle, surrendered on July 9.

Augur had distinguished himself in the Port Hudson operation and was breveted brigadier general in the Regular Army for his conduct there. He was fortunate to be recalled to Washington to take command of the Department of Washington and Twentieth Corps, thus avoiding having to serve in Banks's ill-fated Red River Expedition. Mustered out in September 1865, Nathaniel Banks returned to Massachusetts and was elected to Congress.

On March 13, 1865, Augur received a brevet of major general in the Regular Army for the catchall phrase that adorned so many high-ranking officers: gallant and meritorious services in the field during the Rebellion. He had earned the recognition. Before being mustered out on September 1, 1866, he served on a board examining officers for assignment and promotion in the Regular Army. On March 15, 1866, he received his own Regular Army assignment: colonel of the Twelfth Infantry. For Augur as a combat commander, the war had essentially ended in July 1863 with the surrender of Port Hudson.

DEPARTMENT OF THE PLATTE

The postwar years opened on a violent note in the West. On the northern plains, gold strikes in western Montana had led to the opening of the Bozeman Trail, which ran from the North Platte River northwest along the base of the Bighorn Mountains to the Yellowstone River and on to the Montana goldfields. The Sioux chiefs Red Cloud, Man-Afraid-of-His-Horses, and others objected to migrant traffic across their Powder River hunting grounds. Objection turned to hostility when the army built three forts—Reno, Phil Kearny, and C. F. Smith—to protect the trail. On December 21, 1866, Captain William J. Fetterman led a contingent of eighty infantry and cavalry out of Fort Phil Kearny to pursue a hovering band of Sioux and blundered into an ambush that wiped out Fetterman and all his men.

The new commander of the Department of the Platte was Philip St. George Cooke. Based in Omaha, Cooke was a well-known veteran of the prewar army in the West and now brigadier general (and brevet major

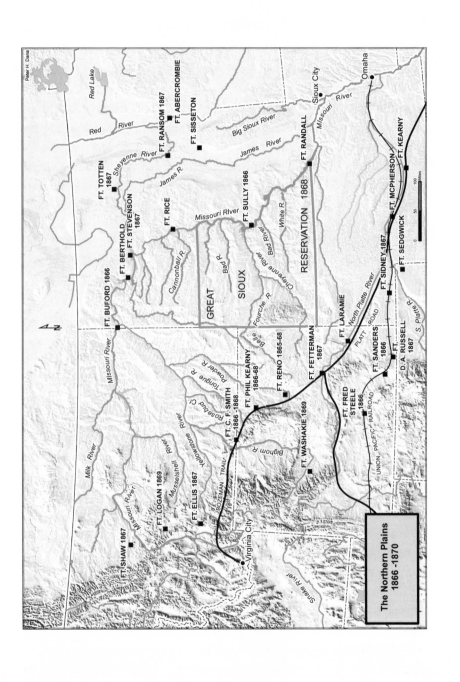

The Northern Plains
1866 -1870

Peter H. Dana

Red Lake

Red River

Red River

FT. RANSOM 1867

FT. ABERCROMBIE

FT. SISSETON

Sheyenne River

Big Sioux River

James River

James River

FT. TOTTEN 1867

FT. STEVENSON 1867

FT. BERTHOLD

FT. RICE

Missouri River

FT. SULLY 1866

Cannonball R.

Bad R.

White R.

Bad River

FT. RANDALL

Sioux City

Missouri River

Omaha

Missouri River

RESERVATION 1868

FT. KEARNY

FT. MCPHERSON

FT. BUFORD 1866

GREAT

SIOUX

Cheyenne River

Belle Fourche R.

FT. SEDGWICK

FT. SIDNEY 1867

FT. LARAMIE

North Platte River

S. Platte R.

D.A. RUSSELL 1867

Missouri River

Tongue R.

Powder R.

FT. PHIL KEARNY 1866-68

FT. RENO 1865-68

FT. FETTERMAN 1867

PLATT ROAD

FT. SANDERS 1866

Rosebud Cr.

FT. C. F. SMITH 1866 -1868

Milk River

Yellowstone River

Musselshell River

FT. LOGAN 1869

FT. ELLIS 1867

BOZEMAN TRAIL

FT. WASHAKIE 1869

Bighorn R.

FT. FRED STEELE 1866

UNION PACIFIC RAILROAD

Missouri River

FT. SHAW 1867

Virginia City

Snake River

N

0   50   100
Miles

general). He had an undistinguished Civil War record, however, seemed older than his fifty-seven years, and provided little support to the commander on the Bozeman Trail, Colonel Henry B. Carrington. When the Fetterman disaster demanded a scapegoat, Cooke pounced on Carrington. General Grant added his own scapegoat, General Cooke. On January 9, 1867, Colonel and Brevet Major General C. C. Augur replaced Cooke as commander of the Department of the Platte. Augur commanded in his brevet rank of major general until elevated to brigadier general in 1869. He spent the balance of his career as a department commander.

With Grant still the head of the army, Sherman as lieutenant general commanded the Division of the Missouri from his St. Louis headquarters. Furious over the Fetterman disaster, Sherman telegraphed Grant: "We must act with vindictive earnestness against the Sioux, even to their extermination, men, women, and children."[4] He softened somewhat later but still instructed Augur to organize a force of two thousand infantry and cavalry, under Colonel John Gibbon, to invade the Powder River country and punish the Sioux. "No mercy should be shown these Indians, for they grant no quarter nor ask for it." Sherman had to place Augur's expedition on hold, however, because a commission appointed by the president was already at Augur's headquarters in Omaha, en route up the Platte to talk with the Sioux.[5]

Chaired by Brevet Brigadier General Alfred Sully and including two former generals, the commission concluded that the Indians of the northern plains wanted peace and should have eighty thousand square miles of the Missouri and Yellowstone basins reserved for them alone. Also, the Bozeman Trail and its forts should be abandoned and military operations should be devoted mainly to guarding construction of the Union Pacific Railroad.

Rather than act on the Sully Commission's conclusions, Congress on July 20, 1867, enacted a measure creating another peace commission. Chaired by the commissioner of Indian Affairs, Nathaniel G. Taylor, a sanctimonious Methodist cleric of rigid certitude, the commission contained a senator, a former general, a prominent humanitarian, and three army generals appointed by the president. President Andrew Johnson named retired General William S. Harney, General Alfred H. Terry, and General Sherman himself. Although retaining his vote on the commission, Sherman frequently absented himself for pressing business in Washington. He chose General

The Indian Peace Commission at Fort Laramie, 1868.
Identifiable are Generals Harney (with bald head and white beard),
Sherman (to Harney's left), Augur (with mutton chops), and Terry (to Augur's left).
National Anthropological Archives, Smithsonian Institution (GN 03686).

Augur to sit in for him. Throughout the existence of the Peace Commission, Augur functioned as a full-time member and cast his vote as such.[6]

Travel with the Peace Commission kept Augur away from his Omaha headquarters, but from a distance he continued to exercise command of the Department of the Platte. He directed the distribution of troops to all the stations and other vulnerable points on the Union Pacific Railroad and made certain that detachments were in position to counter raids from the north on any settlements. Pending negotiations with the Sioux, the Bozeman Trail forts also had to be maintained. The Peace Commission's labors had not discouraged the aggressive young warriors of the Sioux and their Cheyenne allies either along the Bozeman Trail or on the Platte River road.[7]

The commission turned first to Red Cloud's Sioux. Runners had been sent to invite the chiefs to meet with the emissaries at Fort Laramie in

September 1867, but the commissioners had not even reached the fort when word came from Red Cloud that he had to prepare for the fall hunt and maybe would come down next year. Postponing the Fort Laramie meeting, the commission turned to the southern plains, where Cheyennes, Kiowas, and Comanches had been waging war with the army and against encroaching settlers. Meeting the tribal leaders in October at Medicine Lodge Creek, Kansas, the peace-makers succeeded in making what they thought was peace. Although they were later proved wrong, the Peace Commission could present the Medicine Lodge Treaty to Congress as a sign of success. After a visit to Fort Laramie in hope of talking with Red Cloud proved futile (only a few friendly Crows camped at the fort), the commissioners met in St. Louis early in January 1868 to draft their report. All members signed the document, including the generals, who did so reluctantly.[8]

Notwithstanding the report, the Sioux had to be dealt with. As with Medicine Lodge, the commissioners again hoped to meet with Red Cloud and bore a treaty providing for reservations, strung along the Missouri River, where the Indians were to settle and receive government rations. As added enticement, they amended the draft to promise abandonment of the Bozeman Trail forts and designation of a vast block of country in the Powder River region as "unceded Indian territory," closed to all whites. At Fort Laramie in April 1868 the friendly Brule Sioux chief Spotted Tail showed up to sign the treaty, as did some "stay-around-the-fort" people, but not Red Cloud. When the Bozeman Trail forts were abandoned, he would come down and talk.

Red Cloud's attitude frustrated all the advocates of peace as well as those who inclined to war, particularly General Sherman. From history's perspective—and probably from Augur's perspective—Red Cloud and the other Sioux chiefs were justified in clinging to their homeland as long as possible. It supported their way of life and insulated them from the way of life that the white people proposed. Moreover, the Sioux clearly saw that they held the advantage. The government was powerless to make them conform, so they didn't.

Resignedly, the peace emissaries left a copy of the treaty with the post commander at Fort Laramie and returned to St. Louis. Finally, in November 1868, Red Cloud and the other chiefs came to the fort and made their marks on the treaty.

The Peace Commission hoped to resolve the long-festering government policy of presenting the Indians with both peace pipe and rifle. It didn't. In 1868 war broke out on the southern plains. When the commission met in Chicago for the last time on October 7, 1868, the generals outvoted the proponents of the peace pipe on every resolution offered. Sitting in on the meeting was Ulysses S. Grant, the general who soon would be president of the United States. His presence did not harm the generals' cause. For the time being at least, the rifle would prevail over the peace pipe.

C. C. Augur had sided and voted with the other generals on all the issues. His vote rested not alone on loyalty to them. He had mastered the problems confronting the peace commission, as indicated by an untitled six-page essay that he had composed on official stationery, probably late in 1867. The Sioux, he wrote, were fighting for the Powder River country and would never give it up as long as an Indian lives. "They say if they do give it up it will involve their destruction as a people, and they might as well die fighting. This is undoubtedly the tone and feeling of the northern Sioux. Their successes in this country during the past year have emboldened them to hope for success, and with this present feeling I doubt that the really influential chiefs can be gotten in for negotiation."[9]

As for what to do in these circumstances, Augur wrote: "The only course I see is to meet with the chiefs and influential men, and learn what will satisfy them, and then determine whether the government can afford to yield to their terms. If not they will have to be whipped into subjection, an alternative involving much time, much money, and a good many more men than is now generally supposed necessary." Augur was right, although the whipping would not be attempted until 1876.[10]

Elevated to brigadier general in 1869, Augur turned from his peace commission duties to command the Department of the Platte from his Omaha headquarters.

In 1869 the Republican River country of northern Kansas attracted Indians from both north and south. A winter campaign in the south had flushed Cheyennes north into this area, where they joined with Oglala Sioux native to the country and other Sioux riding from the north for the mild climate and ample bison herds. It was a combustible mix, and General Augur organized the Republican River Expedition, consisting of seven troops of the Fifth Cavalry and three companies of Pawnee Indian scouts, with Major Eugene A. Carr commanding. A tough but contentious veteran of the prewar army and a brigadier general during the Civil War, Carr considered himself underrated and deserving of higher rank, as he was. On July 11, 1869, Carr won a signal victory by surprising a Sioux and Cheyenne camp of eighty-four lodges under Tall Bull at Summit Springs, Colorado. The troopers killed fifty-two Indians and took fifteen women and children prisoners. A reorganized command, substituting three troops of the Second Cavalry for three of the Fifth, took the field in September under Lieutenant Colonel Thomas Duncan and on July 26 struck a village of fifty-six lodges on the Arikara Fork of the Republican, drove the occupants in flight, destroyed the village, and rode in futile pursuit for two hundred miles. These operations broke the hold of the Sioux and Cheyennes on the Republican River country.[11]

Spring 1870 confronted Augur with still more Indian problems, compounded by some white problems. In the Sweetwater country near South Pass, miners established a settlement that attracted Indian raids. Farther east, in the Wind River Valley, Shoshones and Arapahos occupied a reservation that Sweetwater miners charged provided a refuge for Arapaho raiders against their stock. On April 2 raiders struck the Sweetwater mines and killed six men. When miners followed the trail and ascertained that it led to the reservation, a party then set out. En route to the reservation they overtook an Arapaho group that was headed to the agency to procure supplies, attacked and killed all of the eleven men, and then let the women and children continue on. The Arapahos protested their innocence of the raid, which may well have been carried out by Shoshones.

Augur ordered two troops of the Second Cavalry to converge on the mines. One, under Captain David S. Gordon, arrived in time to fend off another Indian attack on May 4. In the fight Lieutenant C. B. Stambaugh and a sergeant were killed, together with one Indian warrior. Augur established two posts in this country, Camp Stambaugh at the Sweetwater mines and Camp Brown on the Wind River reservation.[12]

While contending with these troubles, Augur also faced troubles from influential white people. A group of prominent Wyoming entrepreneurs formed an association, the Big Horn Mountain Mining and Exploring Expedition, designed to prospect the western slopes of the Black Hills and the Bighorn Mountains. Said to have recruited two thousand men, the expedition prepared to set forth in May 1870, although the scheme had already come under fire for threatening to invade the unceded Indian territory guaranteed by the 1868 treaty. President Grant became involved. Ultimately orders reached General Augur to prevent the expedition from leaving Cheyenne, using force if necessary. Association leaders seemed to have compromised when they signed a document pledging to avoid the Wind River reservation and confine their operations to the west side of the Bighorn Mountains, but they promptly violated the agreement, entered the Wind River reservation, and pointed north. Augur sent a troop of cavalry to stop them. When they were overtaken, however, the officer discovered that the expedition was already dissolving and simply escorted its former members back to Cheyenne.[13]

In his annual report for 1871—his last at the head of the Department of the Platte—General Augur proudly boasted that not a single white man had been killed in his department in 1871. "This exceptional condition of Indian affairs on the frontier is a subject of unusual satisfaction. Under its happy effects the frontier settlements have been strengthened and extended; new portions of the country have been explored, new mines discovered and worked, and an unprecedented increase of immigration has followed."[14]

On December 11, 1871, General Augur relinquished command of the Department of the Platte to Brigadier General Edward O. C. Ord.

DEPARTMENT OF TEXAS

Less than two months later, General Augur assumed command of the Department of Texas, with headquarters at San Antonio. He had left the Department of the Platte secure and peaceful but now confronted a Texas struggling with Indian hostilities. From the north Kiowas and Comanches swept through Texas and into Mexico, raiding, plundering, and taking captives. From the south Kickapoos and Lipan and Mescalero Apaches living in Mexico crossed the Rio Grande to raid Texas cattle ranches.

Three months after settling in San Antonio, Augur discovered the nature of the hostilities that he would contend with in Texas in the form of a horrific massacre on April 20, 1872, at Howard's Well, a watering place on the San Antonio–El Paso Road west of the Pecos River. Between 125 and 150 Kiowa and Comanche warriors riding south from the Indian Territory fell on a Mexican wagon train hauling military supplies from San Antonio to Fort

Stockton. They killed eleven men and wounded three, then plundered and burned the wagons. Lieutenant Colonel Wesley Merritt and two troops of the Ninth Cavalry, changing stations, came on the scene, followed the trail, and clashed with the warriors. One officer and one Indian were killed, and Merritt took the wounded into Fort Stockton. A paragraph in his report alerted Augur to the enemy he faced in Texas:

> Words fail to convey an idea of the sickening atrocities com-
> mitted by the demons who overpowered the train men. Several
> of them were taken alive, tied to wagons, and burned. An old
> woman was carried some distance from the place of the attack
> and then shot and scalped. Her grand-child had its ears cut off,
> was scalped and had its brains dashed out; while her daughter,
> the mother of the child, who witnessed it all, as also the death
> of her husband at the train, was carried off by the fiends. More
> than one poor wretch crawled from the burning wagons after
> the ropes which bound them were burned off, only to burn to
> blackened unrecognizable masses with their charred hands and
> faces raised in positions of entreaty.[15]

Howard's Well was only the most recent Kiowa and Comanche depreda-tion. They had launched these raids into Texas for years but now raided from two reservations created by the Medicine Lodge Treaty of 1867, the Cheyenne and Arapaho Reservation at Darlington, and the Kiowa and Comanche Reservation at Fort Sill. Although General Sheridan had expanded the Department of Texas to include the Indian Territory, it was off limits to the military. President Grant's "Peace Policy" had placed pacifist Quaker agents in charge of these Indians. Government Indian policy ensured that Indians on their reservations were safe from the army. Pursuing troops had to halt at the Red River, the Kiowa-Comanche reservation boundary. Troops manned Fort Sill, but Colonel Benjamin H. Grierson believed in the Peace Policy and cooperated with the agent. The Fort Sill reservation had become a "City of Refuge."[16]

In his first annual report Augur complained of a daunting military situation. The settlements that were suffering most, he wrote, extended from the vicinity of Fort Richardson through Forts Griffin and Concho to Fort Stockton, then down the Pecos and Rio Grande as far as Fort McIntosh.

The northern line, he pointed out, faced the Indian Territory, home of the reservation Indians, and the Staked Plains, home of the marauding bands that refused to go on the reservations. The other line was exposed to Indians located in Mexico who made their homes a base for operating against the Texas settlements and a market for plunder. The circumstances favored the Indians because troops had to act on the defensive and were constrained in their pursuit of marauding raiders by the reservation on the north and Mexico on the south.[17]

From the moment of his inauguration, President Grant had been repeatedly implored by Texans and their newly admitted congressional delegation to do something about the raiders based in Mexico. Early in 1873 he quietly launched an unorthodox measure: move Colonel Ranald S. Mackenzie, a Grant favorite, and his crack Fourth Cavalry from service in northern Texas to Fort Clark, near the Rio Grande in the south. Mackenzie would then cross the Rio Grande into Mexico and strike the raiders' camps. Shortly after the transfer, in April 1873, William W. Belknap, the secretary of war, and Lieutenant General Philip H. Sheridan, accompanied by Colonel Mackenzie, paused briefly at Augur's San Antonio headquarters before continuing to Fort Clark. They briefed the general on what they expected him to do. How Augur responded to this clear violation of international law is unrecorded, but he did what he was told.

Belknap and Sheridan closeted themselves at Fort Clark with Colonel Mackenzie, a volatile, irascible, hard-driving wartime hero. The only evidence of what took place comes from Mackenzie's adjutant, Lieutenant Robert Carter. He was not present, but his colonel told him about it. In Carter's words, Sheridan directed Mackenzie to "wage a campaign of annihilation, obliteration, and complete destruction" against the offending Indians. That would involve crossing the border into Mexico, so Mackenzie asked for explicit orders. "Damn the orders!" erupted Sheridan, "Damn the authority! You go ahead on your own plan of action, and your authority and backing shall be General Grant and myself. With us behind you in whatever you do to clean up this situation, you can rest assured of the fullest support. You must assume the risk. We will assume the final responsibility, should any result."[18]

On April 20, 1873, Mackenzie addressed a private communication to Augur, setting forth what he needed to prepare for the expedition. He also identified the objective as Lipan, Mescalero, and "Hilleños" Apaches as well as band of Comanches. "It is important that these Indians be attacked as soon as possible for they are making a world of trouble, and there may never be as good an opportunity again."

> I am perfectly willing to take the responsibility after what has been said and know where I can find a trail of stealing parties returning to their camps or feel that I do. My plan would be to send the companies on scouts in different ways and in such manner as not to excite remark and, then get them together quietly where I found such a party had crossed the river and try to arrange so as to reach their camp by daylight in the morning and try to pay them a little for burning those people at Howard's Wells. . . .
>
> I shall expect officially that my action will be disavowed and probably that I shall be put in arrest, but it will quiet this border in a way that it has not been quiet in years.[19]

Although Lipan and Mescalero Apaches had been guilty of raids, the most troublesome were Kickapoos. This must have become apparent to Mackenzie when spies sent across by Lieutenant Colonel William R. Shafter, commander of nearby Fort Duncan, reported on the location of Indian camps as he had promised. Moreover, Mackenzie's strategy of seeking a fresh trail to follow made sense, because that would lawfully mitigate the violation of Mexican sovereignty.

Shafter's spies apparently reported three villages about forty miles up the San Rodrigo River, near Remolino. The closest one belonged to Kickapoos. Fording the Rio Grande on May 17 with six troops of the Fourth Cavalry, about four hundred men, and twenty-five Seminole-Negro Scouts from Fort Duncan, the command raced up the Remolino River and struck the Kickapoo village, about fifty lodges. The horseman charged, shooting down Kickapoos coming out of their lodges, then burning the grass dwellings. Nineteen Kickapoos were killed and forty captured. Mackenzie found two other villages farther up the river, one Mescalero and one Lipan Apache. The occupants had fled, but the troops burned the villages. After two days on Mexican soil, Mackenzie's command crossed back into Texas.

Mackenzie's official report differs in many respects from his private letter to Augur detailing his plans and strategy. Dated May 23, the official report makes no mention of following a fresh trail, indeed not even mention of crossing into Mexico. He treats all three villages as battlegrounds but gives few details other than casualties. Most of the long report dealt with the gallant action of his troops and the brave exploits of each of his officers.[20]

As expected, Mackenzie's violation of Mexican sovereignty angered Mexico, but the precarious Mexican regime of President Sebastián Lerdo de Tejada protested only mildly. As expected (for the spies reported that most of the Kickapoo men had embarked on a hunting expedition), only women, children, and old men fell to Mackenzie's carbines.

Grateful Texans lauded Mackenzie as the hero of a great victory, which in fact was largely a killing of noncombatants, as Mackenzie knew it would be. But Remolino had the intended effect. Cross-border Indian raids subsided for three years.

Not everyone hailed Remolino as a great victory. One who had not been let in on the secret was General William T. Sherman. "Mackenzie will of course be sustained," Sherman wrote to Sheridan, "but for the sake of history, I would like to have him report clearly the facts that induced him to know that the Indians he attacked and captured were the identical Indians that engaged in raiding Texas. Had he followed a fresh trail there would be law to back him." Less cerebral than the general-in-chief, Sheridan replied: "I am fully satisfied that Mackenzie struck the right Indians for there is none of them guiltless."[21]

At the same time, Augur's northern frontier boiled toward an eruption. On the Kiowa and Comanche reservation surrounding Fort Sill and the Cheyenne and Arapaho reservation farther north, inadequate rations, encroaching cattle ranchers, whiskey sellers, and horse thieves made reservation life miserable, while to the west white buffalo hunters decimated the herds that had so long supported tribal life. In spring 1874 the pace of Kiowa and Comanche raiding in Texas picked up, and Cheyennes raided north into Kansas. Sheridan demanded permission to unleash his regiments on the reservation Indians. In July 1874 the Interior Department finally agreed, on condition that the so-called friendlies be separated from the so-called hostiles. When the agents began compiling lists of the friendlies, the majority (certain to be classified as hostile) fled to the west. The Red River War of 1874–75 ensued.[22]

The Red River War lapped over two military departments: John Pope's Department of the Missouri and C. C. Augur's Department of Texas. Sheridan's strategy called for columns converging on the Texas Panhandle.

Pope would launch two, one under Colonel Nelson A. Miles south from Fort Dodge, Kansas, and the other under Major William R. Price east from Fort Bascom, New Mexico. Augur would field three: one under Colonel Ranald S. Mackenzie north from Fort Concho, one under Lieutenant Colonel George P. Buell northwest from Fort Griffin, and a third under Lieutenant Colonel John W. Davidson west from Fort Sill.

Largely without oversight from higher headquarters, the several columns made their own way in their own time into the area of hostilities. Both Miles and Mackenzie scored major victories. Mackenzie surprised a combined Comanche, Kiowa, and Cheyenne camp in Palo Duro Canyon. The campaign stretched into the winter, when freezing storms drove the columns back to their bases, Mackenzie by Christmas. Miles stayed out, and by spring all the fugitives had been driven into their agencies.

As early as October 1874 the warriors and their families had begun drifting into Fort Sill and returning to normal life—except that Sheridan contemplated punishment rather than normal life. In October he arrived at Fort Sill and conferred with both Augur and Pope. His solutions, however, came to nothing. By the spring of 1875, after all the Indians had returned to the agencies, those judged to be the worst offenders were sent east for imprisonment.

In 1875, as the Red River War was ending in the conquest of the southern plains tribes, both General Sheridan and General Augur were diverted from Indian affairs. Reconstruction Louisiana had boiled with violence since the end of the Civil War, with factions of both parties and white supremacists contending with one another. President Grant sent Sheridan as his representative. After a complicated and controversial series of moves, Sheridan succeeded in having the Department of the Gulf added to the Division of the Missouri and placing General Augur in command on March 27, 1875.[23]

A letter of March 12, 1875, signed by 138 residents of San Antonio and West Texas was testimony to the esteem in which Texans held General Augur, expressing regret that he was leaving for another station. The letter heaped fulsome praise on Augur's "justice, force, and judgment" in commanding the Department of Texas and noted that he and his family would be missed from the city's social scene. Moreover, they would warmly welcome him back to the Texas command.[24]

Augur did not return to the western frontier for six years. His command of the Department of the Gulf lasted from July 1, 1878, when he took over the

Department of the South, until December 26, 1880. On January 2, 1881, he found himself again in San Antonio in charge of the Department of Texas.

Under Augur's predecessor Brigadier General Edward O. C. Ord, the department had struggled through a tumultuous five years, involving Indians, Mexicans, and the army chain of command. Now, however, Augur faced a much quieter department. He rightly attributed this largely to the rapid expansion of the railroads across Texas. The Southern Pacific and the Texas and Pacific sliced through traditional Indian raiding trails. The Red River War had quelled the raiders from the Indian Territory. The Mexican Indians had been largely pacified by more U.S. crossings of the international boundary. By the end of 1881 Augur reported that only one serious incursion in the vicinity of Fort Clark had disturbed the calm, and the offenders had been caught and punished. Apaches created minor problems in far West Texas, but in most of Texas Indian hostilities had subsided.[25] By late 1883 Augur could optimistically report: "There is no reason to believe that a hostile Indian has been within the limits of this department during the past year."[26]

Across the West, except in Arizona, the Indian Wars were winding down. As Augur surely understood, his own career was winding down too. He was sixty-two years of age and had spent forty years in the army. Nevertheless, he put in another two years commanding the Department of the Missouri, with headquarters at Fort Leavenworth, Kansas. On July 10, 1885, he retired from the army, settling in Georgetown, D.C., near the nation's capital. He died on January 16, 1898, at the age of seventy-seven and was buried in Arlington National Cemetery.

Christopher C. Augur had an exemplary military career. He distinguished himself in the Civil War and even more so as a department commander in the West during the height of the Indian Wars. His low-key manner of command, combined with his preference for commanding from his headquarters rather than striving for a conspicuous presence leading troops in the field, kept him from achieving the public notoriety that crowned others such as George Crook and Nelson Miles. But as Augur presided quietly over the Departments of the Platte and of Texas, he achieved a significance ranking above most of his counterparts. Moreover, his success strengthened his already firm friendship with Lieutenant General Sheridan.

Despite his low profile in history, Christopher C. Augur must be counted one of the most significant officers in the West after the Civil War.

Brigadier General George Crook, commanding
Department of the Columbia, 1868–1870;
Department of Arizona, 1871–1875, 1882–1886;
Department of the Platte, 1875–1882, 1886–1888.
U.S. Army Military History Institute.

CHAPTER THREE

GEORGE CROOK

To the postwar army and to the public at large, George Crook bore the reputation of being the foremost authority on Indians. He sustained that reputation during nearly a quarter of a century of service in three regions of the West. He was an officer not content to sit at a frontier post or a department headquarters, letting other officers bear the hardships of active field operations. He aggressively took the field himself, which kept his name before the public. Crook the Indian-fighter eclipsed Crook the Civil War general.[1]

Yet, both professionally and personally, Crook the Indian-fighter had traits that he kept carefully concealed from the public, his superiors, and even himself. He took such pride in his exploits that he often exaggerated their importance in his official reports, glossed over or made excuses for what were plainly shortcomings, blamed others for his own failures, or took refuge in obstacles of topography or climate and even the bad faith of the enemy. He stubbornly clung to his own opinions despite arguments from authoritative sources. Without changing his opinions, even when conclusively demonstrated to be wrong, he dutifully carried out contrary orders from above.

What may have been a natural disposition to reticence and introspection may also have been a deliberately cultivated persona. Acquaintances all noted his quiet, almost wordless demeanor. He rarely shared his opinions with anyone, even his adoring aides. To set himself apart from other ranking officers, he fashioned his beard in two long spikes, sometimes tied at the ends with ribbons. He shunned the uniform and in the field clothed himself in a canvas suit topped by a cork sun helmet, rode a mule and carried a shotgun, and in camp usually messed with his mule-packers rather than his fellow officers. In his office he wore civilian clothes and made sure his staff did too.

Some of Crook's eccentricities evolved before and during the Civil War. Others suddenly took root after the war, which leads to the suspicion that they were deliberately conceived as a way to enhance his public visibility.[2]

SERVICE IN THE PACIFIC NORTHWEST

George Crook was a seasoned Indian-fighter even before the Civil War broke out. Born on a western Ohio farm on September 8, 1828, he entered the U.S. Military Academy at West Point in June 1848. Throughout his four-year tenure, he proved an undistinguished cadet, always in the bottom half of his class. For a time his roommate was fellow Ohioan Philip H. Sheridan, with whom he would have a longtime relationship, both friendly and hostile. Cadet Sheridan, however, assaulted another cadet and was suspended for a year. Crook graduated in 1852, a year before Sheridan, ranking thirty-eighth out of forty-three.

As was customary, Crook was commissioned a brevet second lieutenant to serve until a vacancy opened the way to full second lieutenant. Posted to the Fourth Infantry, he traveled the Isthmus of Panama route to the Pacific Coast to join his company and begin his career as an Indian-fighter.

It began inauspiciously. In October 1853, now a full second lieutenant, Crook and his company, together with another company, took station at newly constructed Fort Jones, in mountainous northern California. They arrived at the conclusion of the first Rogue River War, a conflict pitting a group of tribes against the Indian-hating white settlers and miners flocking to Oregon and California. The whites brutalized the Indians, who in return stole livestock and menaced the settlements.

The post commander at Fort Jones was Captain Henry M. Judah, an officer who quickly drew Crook's enmity. Judah tended toward tyranny, indecisiveness, mood swings, and selfishness. His overriding flaw, however, was severe alcoholism. He made this disability plain to Crook. In January 1854 Judah led the two companies of the Fourth Infantry and a contingent of volunteers up the Klamath River to avenge the reported killing of a citizen. The command, mounted on mules, made its way through a swirling mountain blizzard and deep drifts of snow. The first day out, Judah got almost helplessly drunk and

GEORGE CROOK   37

suffered through four days of delirium tremens. Trapping some Indians in a cave, he pondered how to kill or capture them without exposing his men to a murderous fire from above. Finally, he sent Crook to Fort Lane, across the boundary in Oregon, to obtain a mountain howitzer. Crook returned with the howitzer and also Captain Andrew J. Smith and a party of dragoons. Smith ranked Judah, still suffering from his bout with whiskey, and took command. Howitzer shells did no damage to the corralled Indians because the tubes could not be elevated sufficiently, but the noise and smoke disconcerted them. They offered to surrender to Captain Smith. Parleying with the their leader, Smith discovered that they were the innocent victims of the miners' vindictiveness and called off the expedition. Crook and his fellow infantrymen returned to Fort Jones, concluding what he termed a "grand farce."[3]

At Fort Jones Crook began what would be a lifelong obsession: hunting and fishing. In company with Brevet Second Lieutenant John Bell Hood, he took to the mountains seeking any animal or fowl or fish worth carrying back for supper. All of Crook's spare time, then and later, was devoted to hunting and fishing.[4]

Not all of Crook's service in the Pacific Northwest amounted to a "grand farce." In 1855 he rode as part of an escort to the expedition of Lieutenant R. S. Williamson exploring the Cascade Mountains, which afforded Crook ample opportunity to acquaint himself with the country and indulge his passion for hunting. He also renewed his friendship with his old friend Lieutenant Philip H. Sheridan, also assigned to the Fourth Infantry as a replacement for Lieutenant Hood.

The Williamson expedition ended as the second Rogue River War broke out. Crook took the field in the spring of 1856, shortly after his promotion to first lieutenant on March 11. On this expedition he did much marching and hunting and on occasion collided with Indians. In fact, during one skirmish, he killed his first Indian with a pistol shot.

Crook's principal action in the Rogue River War took place in 1857. During the Pitt River expedition, Captain Judah, drunk most of the time, led his troops in one futile operation after another. At length he turned the command over to Crook and returned to Fort Jones. Crook proved a more aggressive commander, skirmishing with Indians in close combat on three occasions during the summer. In one engagement a shower of arrows rained down on his group, and one arrow struck him in the right hip. He grabbed the shaft and yanked it out, but the arrowhead remained embedded in his hip. A relief party headed by a drunken Captain Judah hurried toward the scene, but Judah fell by the wayside. After examining Crook, the post surgeon decided to let the wound heal, which it did, allowing Crook to continue his leadership throughout subsequent combat operations. The arrowhead remained in his hip for the rest of his life.[5]

Captain Judah's example probably reinforced Crook's aversion to excessive use of intoxicants, the bane of the frontier army. Although he occasionally took a drink, he never overindulged and also never used tobacco.

Crook's final active service in the Pacific Northwest occurred during spring and summer of 1858, in the area of Washington Territory drained by the Columbia River. Crook commanded his company of the Fourth Infantry as part of an expedition under Major Robert Garnett. Much marching through scenic country took the troops almost to the Canadian border. Their mission was to seek the killers of some gold miners the previous April, who had taken refuge with friendly Indians west of the Columbia. The expedition succeeded, and Crook himself had five of the culprits executed by firing squad.[6]

Such were the highlights of Crook's introduction to Indian warfare. They exemplify the constant pursuit of and combat with a host of separate Indian tribal groups that fell to his lot. All of the tribes had been subdued by 1859. Crook had played a prominent part in these operations and acquired combat skills vital to his role in later Indian hostilities. He had also concluded that most Indian hostilities arose from mistreatment of the Indians by white people, which forced the army to make war on people with whom its officers and men often sympathized. From his experience in the Pacific Northwest, Crook shaped a personal philosophy on how to treat Indians: teach them the power of the government by thoroughly whipping them in combat, then deal with them in peace authoritatively but considerately. Also, never make promises that could not be kept and always keep truth in the forefront. As Crook would discover, such idealistic goals often foundered in the face of the contrary actions and attitudes of other officers and civilian government officials and unsympathetic public opinion.

Crook passed his final three years in the Pacific Northwest at Fort Terwah, California, engaged in routine garrison duties. On May 14, 1861, he was promoted to captain in his regiment.

In September 1860 Crook took his first leave of absence and returned to Ohio for a visit with family and friends. He took little interest in the great national issue then sweeping the country. Even the election of 1860, carrying Abraham Lincoln into the presidency and sparking a cascade of Southern states to rebel against the Union, seems to have aroused no more than passing interest in him. By Christmas 1860 Crook was back in California, settled at Fort Terwah. In spring 1861, with civil war gathering in the East, the two infantry regiments on the Pacific Coast were ordered to travel to the scene of the war.

By September 1861 Captain Crook was in Washington, D.C., scouting opportunities for wartime service.

CIVIL WAR

Crook swiftly perceived that the war would be fought almost entirely by the Volunteer Army being mobilized by the Lincoln administration and not by the Regular Army. At first the War Department tried to keep the Regular Army intact, and Crook employed Ohio political influence to gain permission to seek a Volunteer commission. The governor of Ohio granted him the colonelcy of the Thirty-Sixth Ohio Infantry, which launched Crook's wartime career. As a recently mustered unit, posted to Summersville, in western Virginia, the Thirty-Sixth lacked any trace of discipline, organization, order, or even uniforms and arms. Taking command on September 12, 1861, Crook rose to the occasion and, by drill, discipline, and field training, transformed the unit into an effective regiment by the end of the year.

As a West Pointer with almost a decade of professional service in the field, Colonel Crook easily outclassed his amateur officers, only recently drawn from civilian life and holding their commissions by election of the enlisted men (a custom that he abolished). On May 1, 1862, the Thirty-Sixth was combined with two other regiments to form a provisional brigade under Crook's command. The brigade participated on the fringes of a campaign in the Shenandoah Valley to the east. On May 23, 1862, Crook achieved victory over a Confederate force in a battle at Lewisburg, during which a bullet struck him in the foot, inflicting a painful wound. For "gallant and meritorious service" at Lewisburg, Crook received a brevet of major in the Regular Army.[7]

After Lewisburg, Crook's brigade shifted to the Army of the Potomac. From a ridge-line, the brigade observed General John Pope's crushing defeat at Second Manassas, then in September 1862 marched north to join General George B. McClellan's effort to head off Robert E. Lee's invasion of Maryland.

In the Antietam campaign Crook's brigade fought valiantly in the Battle of South Mountain on September 14 and in the horrendous bloodletting of Antietam on September 17. In the first of these encounters Crook distinguished himself leading a bayonet charge; in the second he failed to reach a bridge over Antietam Creek that he had been ordered to seize. He spent the rest of his life trying to justify his failure to attack the bridge and cast the blame elsewhere. Even so, on October 1 Crook received word of his promotion on September 7 to brigadier general of Volunteers. Orders also directed him to rise from brigade level to division level and take command of the Kanawha Division, named for the river where it was deployed.

Throughout 1863, commanding two other divisions in sequence, Crook participated in the Tennessee campaigns that centered on Chattanooga. In September he led one of his divisions in the Battle of Chickamauga, fighting tenaciously with the rest of the Union army to stave off defeat by the Confederate forces led by General Braxton Bragg. With the rest of the federal units, his division was driven back in disorder. After Chickamauga, he kept busy fighting Confederate outfits both in Tennessee and Alabama. None of the conflicts achieved much significance, but they revealed Crook as a competent division commander. In the spring of 1864 he returned to his West Virginia base and resumed command of the Kanawha Division.

One of the brigades of the Kanawha Division was commanded by Colonel Rutherford B. Hayes, an Ohio politician who had secured a military posting. In contrast to most political generals, Hayes proved an able commander. He greatly admired Crook, and the two established a personal friendship that ripened over the years and involved Hayes's full family. It proved useful to Crook when Hayes won the presidency in 1876.

Since the beginning of the war, both sides had struggled to dominate the Shenandoah Valley, which helped feed the Confederate Army and harbored strategic railway junctions.

Because ineffective generals on both sides had failed to achieve decisive results, this "breadbasket of the Confederacy" remained contested. When Ulysses S. Grant came east in spring 1864 and donned three stars as general-in-chief, the valley took a place high on the Union priority list. Crook had campaigned in the valley enough to become thoroughly acquainted with it, so Grant summoned him to his headquarters to confer on future operations. For a year, as the Shenandoah took high rank as a Union theater of war, Crook's service lay in the Shenandoah Valley. At times he distinguished himself, at times he turned in an undistinguished performance, but throughout he functioned as one of the second tier of generals. Reinforcing his new stature, on July 18, 1864, he was breveted major general of volunteers, which permitted him to don shoulder straps bearing two stars.

Union fortunes in the Shenandoah Valley revived on August 8, 1864, when Major General Philip H. Sheridan arrived to assume command of the Army of the Shenandoah. His long-range objective was to drive the Confederate army of Lieutenant General Jubal Early from the valley and then to lay waste to the area so that it would cease to supply Southern armies with provender. To accomplish his mission, Sheridan had three infantry corps, of which Crook's Eighth was one, and three brigades of cavalry from the Army of the Potomac. The Army of the Shenandoah numbered about thirty thousand men. In Crook, Sheridan found a congenial old friend from West Point and the Pacific Northwest. The two got along personally, and Sheridan frequently sought Crook's professional advice.

After a month of marching and countermarching, on September 19 Sheridan committed the Army of the Shenandoah to a major battle with General Early outside Winchester. All three corps took part as well as some of the cavalry. In a decisive move, Crook saw an opportunity to turn the enemy's left flank. He wheeled his corps in such a fashion that he was able to launch a charge against the Confederate line. The line collapsed, and the Confederates fled south.

The Battle of Opequon Creek represented Sheridan's first triumph in the Shenandoah Valley, and he received warm accolades from Washington. Crook's role had been critical. What should have been cause for jubilation, however, turned to a rancorous memory that haunted him to the end of his days. In his report Sheridan failed to give Crook proper credit and made the move on the Southern left flank seem like part of his own plan. Crook never forgave his superior.[8]

Next General Early posted his army in a long defensive line on Fisher's Hill. Sheridan scouted the position and, so he wrote, determined that the Confederate right and center were too strong to assault but that the left might be turned, as had occurred at Opequon Creek. Crook examined the position on his own and conceived a scheme for marching his corps stealthily through the forests of North Mountain, which abutted the Confederate left, and surprising the defenders' left flank. Sheridan and his two other corps commanders doubted that such a move could be carried out without being discovered. Crook brought in Hayes, now brigadier general, to back the proposal with his lawyer's eloquence. Sheridan and the other generals reluctantly consented. Crook successfully led his corps through the mountain forests and on September 22 fell on the Confederate left in a surprise attack. Early's line doubled up and collapsed. The enemy fled south, with Crook and his men in pursuit.

Again Sheridan received warm praise in Washington while failing to give Crook or any of his other subordinates much credit. In his account he implied that Crook's success was part of his own plan. Even so, a month later Crook was appointed major general of volunteers. The following spring, on March 13, 1865, he was breveted major general in the regular army for his role in the Battle of Fisher's Hill.

Assuming that Early had decided to withdraw from the valley, Sheridan in mid-October accepted the invitation of Grant and Secretary of War Edwin Stanton to travel to Washington and confer on future operations. In his absence, the Army of the Shenandoah lay in a north-south axis on the eastern bank of Cedar Creek. Crook's corps held the left flank, extending to the south. At dawn on October 19 Early's army emerged from the morning fog and fell on Crook's corps. Taken by surprise, the troops fled north, spreading the panic into the other corps. In one of the Civil War's most dramatic moments, usually exaggerated, Sheridan galloped into the fray on his black horse Reinzi. The troops rallied, turned, and regained their original positions. Later in the afternoon Sheridan thrust his army into Early's defenses at Fisher's Hill and won a stunning victory.

The collapse of the Eighth Corps at Cedar Creek opened Crook to the charge of negligence, and in fact several of his decisions merited the charge. Fortunately for him, all the other generals could also be accused of exposing their troops to Early's surprise, so Crook escaped condemnation. Nevertheless, as the years went by, he increasingly resented the glory showered on Sheridan for the battles of Opequon, Fisher's Hill, and Cedar Creek. A year before his death, Crook returned to the battlefields. Exposing his darker side in his diary, he concluded that Sheridan's actions in allowing the public to believe what he knew to be fiction were "contemptible." "The adulation heaped on him by a grateful nation for his supposed genius turned his head, which, added to his natural disposition, caused him to bloat his little carcass with debauchery and dissipation, which carried him off prematurely."[9]

Crook's next major episode caused him acute embarrassment. After the valley campaign, he resumed command of the Department of West Virginia, with headquarters in Cumberland, Maryland. He bunked in the Revere Hotel, near another hotel that housed Major General Benjamin Kelley, whose division guarded the Baltimore and Ohio Railroad. Cumberland lay in the midst of a population of largely Southern sympathizers and teemed with Confederate guerrilla bands. Never known to be especially interested in women, Crook fell for the daughter of the hotel's owner, Mary Dailey. It seems not to have daunted Crook that her family embraced the secessionist cause and her brother rode with one of the partisan bands (which he probably did not know). At 3:00 A.M. on February 20, 1865, however, Crook was awakened in his bedroom by a squad of Confederate rangers. They took him and General Kelley captive and hurried out of town, having tricked and overpowered the guards.

After a 150-mile ride on horseback through bitter winter weather, the two generals and their escort faced General Jubal Early. Delighted with the prize, Early forwarded them to Richmond for confinement in Libby Prison. General Lee, however, promptly contacted Union headquarters and arranged an exchange. By mid-March the two embarrassed Union generals were back home. Secretary Stanton had proposed making an example of them by mustering them out of the service and letting them remain in Libby Prison, but General Grant wanted them back and prevailed.

Crook expected to be returned to command his Eighth Corps in Maryland, but General Grant assigned him to command the remaining cavalry division in the Army of the Potomac, the others having been withdrawn and placed under Sheridan. Crook rightly viewed this as a lesser command than he had held for two years and suspected that it was form of rebuke for allowing himself to be captured, which it may have been. His new assignment, however, ensured that he would participate in the campaign that led to Lee's surrender of the Army of Northern Virginia at Appomattox Courthouse on April 9, 1865.

On April 1 the Battle of Five Forks opened the campaign, as Grant sought to force Lee's army from its defenses south of Petersburg. Crook's division played a significant role in the preliminaries to the battle when it bore the brunt of a Confederate assault on March 31, held its ground until ammunition ran short, and then fell back. The day's fighting cost one-third of the division's strength. In the main battle the next day Crook's battered division acted on the defensive. On April 2 and 3 they trailed the rest of the army, guarding wagon trains. Thereafter, however, they joined with other infantry and cavalry units to contend with the retreating Confederates. On April 6, at the Battle of Saylor's Creek, Crook's division played a conspicuous part in crushing major elements of the Confederate army. For the three days remaining until the climax at Appomattox, Crook's cavalry fought as bravely as the rest of the Union force. At least once Crook found himself fighting in the center of the battlefield. Surrounded and facing capture, he fought his way to safety.

Unlike other top commanders, however, when Lee surrendered to Grant, Crook remained with his own command and was not present at Appomattox Courthouse.

In the Appomattox campaign Crook had acted, led, and fought with bravery and distinction. He could be proud of his role in the final scenes of the conflict with Lee's army. In the larger sense, Crook had performed well, sometimes brilliantly, in the entire war. He emerged as one of the second tier of Union generals to merit distinction. Only his embarrassing capture by Confederate partisans stained his record.

On August 22, 1865, awaiting assignment in Baltimore, Crook and Mary Dailey were married. He hardly mentioned the nuptials in his memoir and rarely wrote of her in later years. Even so, the little available evidence indicates that it was a stable marriage, marred only by Crook's long absences in the field.

In his autobiography Crook sourly lamented: "I regret to say that I learned too late that it was not what a person did, but it was what he got the credit of doing that gave him a reputation and at the close of the war gave him position."[10] As if to validate his conviction, as the postwar Regular Army took shape in 1866, the War Department offered him the post of major of the Third Infantry, a plunge of five grades from major general. He complained bitterly that officers of less rank were receiving higher appointments and called for reconsideration. As a result, he was appointed lieutenant colonel of the Twenty-Third Infantry. Importantly, however, he retained his brevet of major general in the Regular Army.

THE PACIFIC NORTHWEST—AGAIN

Unlike other Civil War generals, Lieutenant Colonel Crook insisted on being addressed by his regular rank. He reached his new posting, Fort Boise, Idaho, headquarters of the Military District of Boise, in December 1866. As commander of the district, Crook reported to Major General Frederick Steele, who headed the Department of the Columbia, a unit of the Division of the Pacific. Crook brought to his first postwar assignment ample experience as an Indian fighter in this very area. The enemies were Paiutes, Shoshones, Bannocks, Pitt Rivers, and others who had made life tough for immigrants and miners in northern California, Oregon, and Washington as well as Idaho.

Crook had no sooner assumed command than Indians struck only twenty miles from Fort Boise. He seized the occasion to organize and lead a winter campaign. The stormy, freezing winter, combined with rough topography, made operations agonizingly difficult for officers and enlisted men alike. Crook intended to put into effect what would be standard operating procedure: get on the trail and don't relinquish it until the enemy is found and defeated. Also, in addition to forty troopers of the First Cavalry under Captain David Perry, he took along ten Indian scouts; employing Indians against Indians would become another Crook hallmark.

Crook's command overtook the Paiute raiders in their home ranchería on the Owyhee River. Creeping into position on Christmas night 1866, he led his men in surprise dawn attack that overwhelmed the quarry, killed thirty men, and took nine women and children captive. Rather than return to Fort Boise, Crook continued the campaign, although he sent back for additional Indian scouts. In fact, as he boasted in his autobiography, he continued the campaign for two years without returning to Fort Boise.

Backtracking up the Owyhee River to the Snake River, Crook paused to await resupply. He then worked west into Oregon up the Malheur River, where he took thirty prisoners at an Indian village on January 3, 1867, and attacked another on January 28, downing sixty defenders and taking another twenty-seven prisoners.[11]

Archie McIntosh, a Scottish half-blood scout with vast experience in the wilds, was the last of Crook's scouts during these operations and would remain in Crook's entourage as he moved on to higher positions. That September McIntosh led Crook to a gathering of more than one hundred Achumawis, Modocs, and Paiutes on the south fork of the Pitt River in northeastern California. The tribesmen were ensconced in caves, fissures, and fortified ledges high on a 700-foot lava cliff. Although it was a virtually unassailable position, Crook resolved to storm it. In a two-day battle, on September 16 and 17, the troops scaled the heights while exchanging fire with the hidden warriors. By evening on the second day the Indians had made their way to safety through underground passages. The attack took the lives of at least twenty defenders, while others left enough blood on the rocks to indicate a higher casualty rate. Crook's command lost an officer and two enlisted men killed and nine others wounded. Graphically, the affair became known as the Battle of Infernal Caverns.[12]

In July 1868, when Crook again took the field with a large command, he had in person led a dozen scouts and participated in six fights. The Paiutes had been allowed no rest for a year and a half and forced to fight forty times. Aside from their exhaustion and inability to procure their usual food supplies, they had lost, according to army reports, 329 killed, 20 wounded, and 225 captured.[13] After a month-long operation, culminating in negotiations with the principal chief, Weawea, Crook could report that the Indian war was over.[14]

George Crook merited the accolade of his division commander, Major General Henry W. Halleck: "Too much praise cannot be given General Crook for his energy and skill with which he has conducted the war. He has endured many hardships, privations and dangers."[15]

Crook had made enough of a name for himself that he was selected to head the command of the Department of the Columbia when it fell vacant until a successor had been named. For two years he enjoyed a quiet routine life in Portland, Oregon, until Brigadier General Edward R. S. Canby arrived to take command in August 1870.

While he engaged in temporary staff assignments, two division commanders urged him to take charge of the Department of Arizona, scourged for years by Apache hostilities. He steadfastly refused, in part because he was tired of Indian work and in part because his elevation would cause resentment among the many officers of higher grade. In May 1871, however, the adjutant general informed Crook that President Grant wanted him assigned to Arizona in his brevet rank of major general, a move that incurred the enmity of all the colonels of the line, as he had feared. On June 4, at headquarters in Wilmington, California, he formally relieved his predecessor, Colonel George Stoneman, and took command of the Department of Arizona.

Crook's record in the Indian wars of 1866–68 in Idaho, Oregon, and California rose in distinction above any other army officer's accomplishments in the first years after the Civil War. It drew on his prewar success with these same Indians, the advantage of his wartime mastery of the art of command, and his determination to do his duty in whatever role his superiors assigned him. No other postwar officer, regardless of rank, could make such a claim. The only officer to warrant such distinction was George Crook. As he left the Department of the Columbia, Crook had taken his second step toward a reputation as the army's foremost authority on Indians.

APACHES

Arriving in Tucson, Crook went to work with characteristic vigor. He summoned the department's principal officers to learn all he could about the country, the Apaches, and his troops. Then he formed a command of five troops of the Third Cavalry, supported by a pack train of sturdy mules, and set forth to explore his desert and mountain domain for himself. As always in his operations, Crook formed a contingent of scouts, partly Mexicans and partly local Indians; he regarded these as temporary until he could replace them with Apaches. Archie McIntosh, the invaluable veteran of Crook's campaigns in the north country, led the scout detachment. McIntosh was ignorant of Arizona, but Crook trusted his instinct. Another capable professional who accompanied him from Idaho was Tom Moore, an expert mule-skinner. Crook made him chief packer for the department. McIntosh and Moore signaled Crook's intent to rely heavily on Indian scouts and pack mules.

Heading east from Tucson on July 11, the command camped for three days beginning July 14 at Fort Bowie, guardian of strategic Apache Pass through the Chiricahua Mountains and center of the domain of the indomitable Chiricahua Apache chieftain Cochise. From Fort Bowie the column turned north into the White Mountains and Camp Apache. Here Crook counseled with the White Mountain Apaches, who proved friendly and so responsive to Crook's talk that seventy-five of them stepped forward to enlist in Crook's scout unit. Paid the same as enlisted white troops, these became the nucleus of units that Crook would employ as combat troops in his projected offensive against the Apaches in the Tonto Basin. The Mexicans in the scout unit were discharged and sent home.

Leaving Captain Guy V. Henry to organize a compact striking force of cavalry and scouts to penetrate the Tonto Basin, Crook took the rest of the command into the Mogollon Mountains and proceeded west along the narrow Mogollon Rim, blazing a 216-mile route through the wilderness that came to be known as the Crook Trail. It ended in the Verde River Valley at Camp Verde. From here Crook climbed to the town of Prescott and made Fort Whipple the headquarters of the Department of Arizona.[16]

Crook learned at Camp Verde that his planned campaign in the Tonto Basin had been interrupted. President Grant had inaugurated his so-called Peace Policy, which aimed at conquering the western Indians by kindness. A peace commissioner, Vincent Colyer, had arrived in Arizona and cavalierly began to travel from agency to agency making peace with the various Apache tribes. Immensely frustrated by "Vincent the Good," Crook had no choice but to suspend all military operations.

By October 1871 Colyer had completed his mission, having created reservations for Chiricahuas, Tontos, and Yavapais. Those who wished to remain at peace would assemble on the reservations, while those who refused would be labeled hostile. Ultimately Colyer's work failed, but in the meantime Crook planned his offensive. At the top of his list of objectives was achieving peace with the Chiricahuas, Cochise, and his people. This now proved impossible because another Washington emissary had concluded a peace agreement with the chief. Brigadier General Oliver O. Howard, the one-armed "Christian General," had accomplished this feat, although Crook could find no document that set the terms to paper. In his autobiography Crook recounted his first meeting with Howard, who had recently resigned as head of the postwar Freedmen's Bureau: "I was very much amused at the General's opinion of himself. He told me that he thought the Creator had placed him on earth to be the Moses to the Negro. Having accomplished that mission [at the Freedmen's Bureau], he felt satisfied that his next mission was with the Indian."[17]

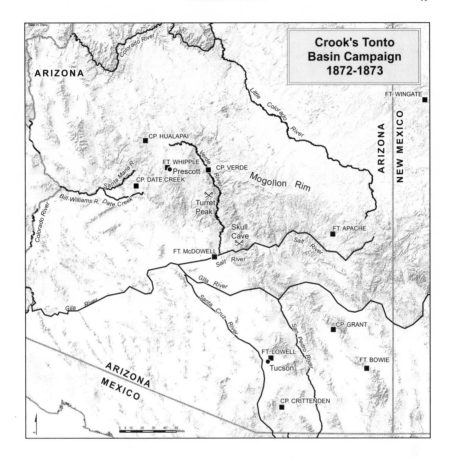

Delayed by Colyer and thwarted with the Chiricahuas by Howard, Crook late in 1872 proceeded with his Tonto Basin campaign. He formed nine compact striking columns, each consisting of a troop of cavalry, a contingent of Indian scouts, and a mule pack train. The scouts were led by Archie McIntosh and Al Sieber, a Civil War veteran who had come west and made himself an experienced match for McIntosh. The columns were to range independently seeking the quarry, their captains being the sole judge of their operations. The scouts would spread out as much as a day or two in advance. Crook himself would ride the periphery of the Tonto Basin, supporting and counseling his captains.

All the commands behaved outstandingly, keeping the Apaches on the run, unable to feed themselves. In twenty conflicts during winter 1872–73 the troops and their Indian scouts killed nearly two hundred Yavapais and Tontos. Highlights of the campaign were the battles of Skull Cave on December 28, 1872, and Turret Peak on March 27, 1873. At Skull Cave Captain William H. Brown trapped one hundred Yavapais in a cave high on the cliffs of Salt River Canyon. As in Crook's fight at Infernal Caverns in California, fire against the roof of the cave swept the occupants, killing seventy-five. In the second engagement, the denouement of the offensive, Captain George M. Randall launched a surprise attack on a sleeping ranchería atop Turret Peak. Twenty-three died in the assault.

After Turret Peak, Tontos and Yavapais flocked into their reservations and surrendered. The offensive gained Crook high praise in all quarters. He deserved it, because it was the most brilliant operation of his career. In October 1873, at Fort Whipple, the telegraph brought word of Crook's promotion from lieutenant colonel to brigadier general. Over the protest of General Sherman and amid the outcry of all the colonels of the line, President Grant insisted on rewarding Crook.[18]

NORTHERN PLAINS TRIBES

On April 27, 1875, two days after reaching Omaha, Nebraska, General Crook assumed command of the Department of the Platte. He had been summoned to his new position by Lieutenant General Philip H. Sheridan, his superior as commander of the Military Division of the Missouri. From his offices in Chicago, Sheridan presided over the Department of Dakota, Department of the Missouri, and Department of Texas—in short all the country east of the continental divide. Crook's primary focus while he commanded the Department of the Platte would be the northern plains and their Sioux and Cheyenne occupants.

The center of Crook's immediate interest was the Black Hills. They sprawled along the western edge of the Great Sioux Reservation, which encompassed all the land west of the Missouri River within what would become the state of South Dakota. The reservation had been set aside by the Treaty of 1868 to provide a home for the five tribes of Teton Sioux. Some of them settled there and drew government rations. Others continued to roam the Powder River country west of the reservation. Called the "Northern Roamers," these tribes owed fealty to Sitting Bull and Crazy Horse. They pursued the old nomadic life, subsisting on the bison herds. The Black Hills held special value for all the Sioux as a cool, well-watered oasis amid the hot, dry plains below, a source of lodgepole pines for tipi poles, and, some said, an area of spiritual significance.

The issue that confronted Crook in 1875 originated with a military expedition in the summer of 1874 that discovered gold in the Black Hills. It was commanded by the flamboyant lieutenant colonel of the Seventh Cavalry, George Armstrong Custer, based at Fort Abraham Lincoln on the Missouri River in General Alfred H. Terry's Department of Dakota. Now the hills swarmed with gold-seekers, violating the Treaty of 1868. The army's mission was to enforce the terms of the treaty by expelling the non-Indian invaders.

A force of infantry and cavalry under Lieutenant Colonel Richard I. Dodge had entered the hills in May 1875, escorting a civilian expedition charged with confirming the presence of gold. Dodge confirmed modest payloads but did not disturb the miners at their diggings. Sheridan ordered Crook to travel to the hills and oust the miners. In July Crook rendezvoused with Dodge and set about talking with the diggers. He openly sympathized with them and condemned the Sioux, pointing out that they had repeatedly violated the treaty by carrying off stock belonging to settlers along the Platte River. Crook and Colonel Dodge persuaded the miners to record their claims so that they could return and exploit them once the government had acquired the hills from the Sioux.[19]

The miners' return, of course, depended on the government obtaining the Black Hills. A commission chaired by Senator William B. Allison swiftly discovered that the Sioux had no intention of selling. Barring miners from the hills, however, was not politically acceptable. In Washington top officials contrived a deceitful scheme that would force the Indians into hostility and lead to the Great Sioux War of 1876. Crook, still essentially a field general, would play a key role in the hostilities.[20]

General Sheridan had planned a three-pronged offensive against the Sioux in the Powder River country—the same strategy employed in Kansas and Texas in General John Pope's Red River campaign of 1874–75. Crook would lead the southern prong advancing north from Fort Fetterman, Wyoming. The other two prongs would originate in General Terry's Department of Dakota. From the east Terry would thrust west from Fort Abraham Lincoln to the Yellowstone River, while from the west Colonel John Gibbon would move down the Yellowstone from Fort Ellis. Inexperienced in Indian warfare, Terry intended to unleash his cavalry commander, Lieutenant Colonel George A. Custer.

Sheridan's scheme collapsed under the weight of a northern plains winter. Terry could not get underway until the spring thaw, and Gibbon had to delay until Terry could reach the Yellowstone. The opening phase of the campaign of 1876 therefore fell to George Crook.

The expedition filed out of Fort Fetterman on March 1, 1876. It consisted of nearly a thousand infantry and cavalry supplied by a mule pack train. On March 7–10 a fierce snowstorm driven by high winds sank the temperature below zero and pummeled the straggling command to frigid exhaustion. In his report Crook stressed, unconvincingly, that he accompanied the expedition merely as an observer, not as the commander. He wrote that he wanted to test the notion that troops could not campaign in a northern plains winter. Actual command would rest with the colonel of the Third Cavalry, Joseph J. Reynolds. Thus, when scouts sighted two Indians working east through the snow, Reynolds commanded the force sent to follow (three cavalry squadrons of two troops each). On March 16 they discovered a village strung along the banks of the Powder River. At dawn on March 17 they attacked.

The Battle of Powder River opened with a surprise assault from two directions by two of the squadrons, while the third aimed for the pony herd. Only one of the two assault squadrons managed to penetrate the village. The third squadron rounded up six hundred animals and herded them to safety. Driven from their lodges by the troopers who charged into their village, warriors assembled in the hills overlooking the valley, then roared into the village in a successful counterattack. The surprised cavalrymen were busy destroying the tipis and the winter store of food when hit and swept out of the village—so hastily that they left two dead soldiers behind. Far worse, in the absence of security that night, the Indians dashed in and recovered their pony herd. As Crook correctly concluded, two squadron commanders and Reynolds himself failed to exercise adequate leadership. To continue the campaign, according to Crook, the expedition needed the provisions that had been burned and abandoned in the village and the ponies and horses with which he had intended to remount the command. Therefore he led the column back to Fort Fetterman. On the day of arrival, he preferred charges against Colonel Reynolds.[21]

Crook accurately assessed the causes of the failure of the Battle of Powder River. He erred only in believing that Reynolds had struck the village of Crazy Horse and in attributing the abandonment of the campaign to Reynolds's failure to secure the Indian provisions and pony herd. In truth, the winter hardships that he hoped to show could be overcome had proved the expedition's undoing. As Colonel Reynolds complained to General Sherman, "these winter campaigns in these latitudes should be prohibited. [Illegible] is no name for them—the month of March has told on me more than any five years of my life."[22]

The central objective of Sheridan's three-pronged campaign was to surprise the Indians in their winter encampments, before the spring grasses freed them to roam and opened the way for reservation Indians to ride out to join them for a summer's frolic. Winter shattered that concept, but the three-pronged movement resumed anyway. Again Crook would march from the south as Terry and Gibbon marched from east and west farther north.

On May 29, 1876, Crook once more led his column out of Fort Fetterman. It consisted of fifteen troops of cavalry and two companies of infantry to guard the supply wagons and pack mules, in all slightly more than a thousand officers and enlisted men. Far to the north, close to the Montana border, he established a base camp on Goose Creek, an affluent of Tongue River. There 176 Crow and 86 Shoshone warriors joined him on June 14. Hereditary enemies of the Sioux, the Crows and Shoshones came to fight as auxiliaries rather than to scout for the army.

The Crows believed that the Sioux were camped on Tongue River to the north, in Montana. On June 16, therefore, Crook cut loose from his supply base and took up the march again, carrying only four days' rations. After crossing from the Tongue to the Rosebud River, early in the morning of June 17 the troops lolled on the banks of the Rosebud, brewing coffee and in some cases, including Crook, playing whist. Suddenly the Indian allies came pouring over the ridge line, followed by hundreds of whooping Sioux warriors. Taken by surprise, the soldiers scrambled to organize for battle while the Crow and Shoshone warriors turned and held the Sioux at bay for twenty minutes, while the cavalry formed a battle line.

The Battle of the Rosebud was a vicious six-hour combat, in which both sides sustained casualties. Both cavalry and auxiliaries fought valiantly against equally valiant charging Sioux. Crook sought to control the action but exerted little influence. His main contribution was to attempt to draw some of the men from the line to charge down a box canyon toward where he believed the Sioux village to be. His belief was erroneous, and his fear that his men would be ambushed from the canyon rims caused a withdrawal of the units creeping tentatively into the gorge. By this time, late in the afternoon, the attackers had broken off the fight and turned back to their village.[23]

Badly battered, the command limped back to the base camp on Goose Creek. Crook withdrew, he explained to Sheridan, because he carried only four days' rations and had to care for his wounded. Moreover, he stoutly boasted, he had won the battle, because the enemy had left him in possession of the battlefield. In fact, the Sioux had won the battle. Crook had forced his own withdrawal by taking only four days' rations, and his wounded could have been cared for without falling back to Goose Creek. To compound the flaws in his generalship, Crook dawdled at Goose Creek, awaiting rein-forcements from June 20 to August 5 before again taking the field. In the meantime the Sioux village lay across a mountainous divide to the west, on a tributary of the Little Bighorn River. By June 25 it was sprawled down the valley of the Little Bighorn. On that day, as Crook relaxed hunting in the Bighorn Mountains, Custer and his cavalry attacked, with the catastrophic result that has resonated in history. Had Crook continued his northward march down the Rosebud after the battle of June 17, he would have met Custer and changed the course of history.

The hesitant, plodding general of the Sioux campaign stood in marked contrast to the aggressive, innovative general of the Apache campaign.

Reinforced by a regiment of cavalry, on August 5 Crook's expedition broke camp and headed north, down the Rosebud. The command now numbered 2,000: 25 troops of cavalry, 10 companies of infantry, and 213 Shoshone auxiliaries under Chief Washakie. Crook's mission was to unite with Terry and follow the trail of the Sioux who had overwhelmed Custer on the Little Bighorn. Marching down the Rosebud, on August 10 Crook met Terry en route upstream. Terry led 12 troops of cavalry and 12 companies of infantry, 1,700 strong. Now nearly 4,000 in number, the combined force was so ponderous as to be unlikely to overtake the mobile aggregation of approximately 2,500 warriors (albeit encumbered with their families) even in ideal weather. Instead rain and mud bogged down the troops, making any movement at all extremely difficult. To compound the problem, the huge expedition consumed more supplies than could readily be brought up the Missouri River by steamboat. Early in September, camped in cold rain on the Yellowstone, Crook and Terry differed on what to do next. Terry favored operating from a Yellowstone depot. Crook favored a direct probe east, following the Indian trail. The two generals parted, each to follow his own plan. Crook had not gone far before mud swallowed the trail. He continued to struggle east until discovering a faint trail headed south. Although within marching distance of Fort Lincoln—in Terry's department, where the more senior Terry would command—Crook resolved to turn south on the trail. Sending couriers to Lincoln to wire Sheridan to send provisions to the Black Hills, he began what came to be known as the "Mud March" and the "Horsemeat March." Rain and mud continued to break down the troops, whose rations soon became so diminished that horsemeat furnished the only food. On September 7 Crook sent a detachment mounted on the strongest horses to hasten to the Black Hills and hurry rations to the column. En route, the detachment discovered a small Sioux village and attacked. The Battle of Slim Buttes proved a victory but also caused a delay, especially when a force of warriors under Crazy Horse opened fire from surrounding bluffs. Gaining a slight measure of strength from dried meat in the captured village, the troops struggled on south in the mud, weakened by hunger and exhaustion.[24] On September 13 they finally reached the Belle Fourche River and were greeted by a herd of beef cattle advancing on their front.

Thus, ingloriously, ended the Sioux campaign of 1876. Terry had already called a halt and returned to his St. Paul headquarters. Slim Buttes had proved the only victory of the entire operation. As Sheridan summarized for Sherman, "The fact of the case is, the operations of Genls. Terry and Crook will not bear criticism, and my only thought has been to let them sleep. I approved what was done, for the sake of the troops, but in doing so, I was not approving much, as you know."[25]

During the spring and summer of 1876, both Crook and Terry had proved poor field generals. It remained to Colonel Nelson A. Miles and his Fifth Infantry, about five hundred strong, to reverse the loss of the two field generals. Terry had left Miles and his regiment on the Yellowstone River to erect two forts. In early October Sitting Bull and his followers crossed the Yellowstone from the south side and confronted Miles and his "walk-a-heaps" (as the

Indians called the infantry). The colonel first negotiated with Sitting Bull for surrender, then engaged him in a two-day running battle that drove him back across the Yellowstone on October 24. The chief did not remain, however, but hurried back north as far as the Missouri River. Miles followed and throughout December skirmished with the elusive Sioux on the Missouri. He vowed to stay out all winter if necessary to trounce the enemy, which included Crazy Horse in the Powder River country south of the Yellowstone. Miles would validate Crook's hope that military campaigns could be waged in winter.

In the meantime, far to the south at Fort Fetterman, Wyoming, Crook prepared to launch his own winter campaign. Again, the expedition was huge: 2,200 men in 11 troops of cavalry and 15 companies of infantry, 400 Arapaho, Bannock, Shoshone, and Pawnee allies, 300 civilians manning 168 supply wagons and 400 pack mules. Still haunted by the ghosts of the Rosebud and Little Bighorn, Crook could not shed his fear of not having enough strength to confront the enemy. Colonel Miles had demonstrated what could be accomplished with less than one-fourth Crook's strength.

Among Crook's fresh reinforcements was Ranald S. Mackenzie, hard-bitten colonel of the Fourth Cavalry. A veteran Indian fighter and Civil War hero, Mackenzie could be expected to confront the Indians with the same zeal as Colonel Miles did. Crook's expedition shoved off on November 14, pushing north toward Crazy Horse country. A blizzard immobilized the column for three days. Diverting attention from Crazy Horse, scouts brought word of a large camp of Cheyennes nestled in a canyon of the Bighorn Mountains to the west. Crook sent Mackenzie with ten troops of cavalry and all the Indian auxiliaries to find and attack the village. Mackenzie succeeded, and at dawn of November 25 he fell on about two hundred lodges of the Cheyenne chiefs Dull Knife and Little Wolf. Surprised, the Indians ran from their lodges with only the clothes on their backs and took refuge in the surrounding bluffs. Mackenzie scored about thirty dead but inflicted a disaster far beyond casualties. Thrown into bitter cold without food, clothing, or shelter, many of the Cheyennes froze or starved to death before the others found relief with Crazy Horse to the north.

Crook had his own struggle with weather. In a reprise of the storm-battered advance toward the Battle of Powder River in March 1876, his force suffered repeated blizzards and freezing temperatures, aggravated by the near impossibility of keeping his expansive force supplied. Late in December he surrendered to adversity and called off the campaign. Units returned to their home stations.

In his annual report Crook dealt with the so-called Big Horn and Yellowstone Expedition in one brief, uninformative paragraph and relegated Mackenzie's victory to two bland sentences.[26] He no doubt failed to appreciate the irony of those two sentences in light of his years-long bitterness toward Sheridan for slighting him in his reports of the Shenandoah battles.

After disbanding the Powder River expedition, Crook lingered at Camps Robinson and Sheridan, Nebraska, near the Red Cloud and Spotted Tail Agencies. The government had resolved to move these two chiefs and their people to the Missouri River, where they would be more readily supplied. The Indians did not want to go and sought Crook's support to stave off the move.

Crook's objective now was to secure the surrender of Crazy Horse and his people. To the north, Colonel Miles had campaigned all winter and fought one major battle in a raging blizzard. The ambitious Miles worked to gain the surrender of Crazy Horse and thus earn the laurels of ending the war. Crook as badly wanted the surrender to be to him. Miles and Crook waged a long-distance competition for the prize.

Seeking to use Chief Spotted Tail as a peace emissary, Crook promised to help Spotted Tail and Red Cloud avoid the move to the Missouri River. As Spotted Tail knew, Crook held influence with the Great Father, President Rutherford B. Hayes. Crook knew it too and hoped to persuade the president to intervene. Thus he violated one of his basic precepts: make no promises that you are not certain can be kept.

Preceding Spotted Tail, George Sword, a nephew of Red Cloud, rode north as a peace emissary. Spotted Tail and a large contingent bearing gifts followed. Much to Miles's anger, they prevailed. Throughout early spring of 1877 contingents of Crazy Horse's followers drifted into the Red Cloud and Spotted Tail Agencies. At last, on May 6, Crazy Horse and his immediate followers rode into Red Cloud Agency and threw their rifles on the ground. With Sitting Bull beyond reach in Canada, the Great Sioux War had sputtered to a conclusion.

For Crazy Horse, the war ended with a mortal finality. Some reservation chiefs considered him a threat, and rumors circulated that he intended to break away. While soldiers were attempting to confine Crazy Horse to the guardhouse, a soldier's bayonet ended his life.

Crook's problems had not ended. The Sioux chiefs insisted that his promise to fend off the dreaded move to the Missouri be honored. The months following the surrender of Crazy Horse were packed with much maneuvering, including an unrewarding visit to Washington by Red Cloud and Spotted Tail. But not even Crook's friendship with the president could overpower the entrenched Washington bureaucracy. He won some concessions, including a commitment that the move would be temporary, but had to acquiesce in an immediate move. Oppressed in addition by the killing of Crazy Horse, the Sioux plodded dejectedly to their new homes to the east. Crook reported the events, but so briefly and guardedly that no onus fell on him.[27]

To Spotted Tail and Red Cloud, Crook had at least implied a promise that he only partly kept, although President Hayes had granted one major concession. After a year on the Missouri, where rations were already stockpiled, the Sioux could move west again. In 1878 Red Cloud and his people settled on the Pine Ridge Reservation and Spotted Tail and his people on the Rosebud Reservation.

Not so fortunate were the Northern Cheyennes. Smashed by Ranald Mackenzie in their Bighorn Mountain canyon in November 1876, they had fled to Crazy Horse's camp farther north, then surrendered with the Sioux at Camp Robinson in April 1877. Their new homes were in the south, in the Indian Territory, where the Southern Cheyennes occupied reservations. Mountain dwellers, the Northern Cheyennes failed to adapt to the lower, humid environment. Plagued by disease, fevers, and hunger, many died. In September 1878 Little Wolf and Dull Knife led their people in a desperate breakout. Traveling in two separate bodies (one led by Dull Knife and the other by Little Wolf), they fought off army attempts to stop them until Dull Knife was forced to surrender near Camp Robinson. Little Wolf continued the flight northward. With winter advancing, Dull Knife's people were confined to unheated empty barracks in the fort.

Uncharacteristically, Crook did not confront this crisis in the field but remained in his Omaha office. He clearly sympathized with the Cheyennes, but he had orders, dictated largely by the Indian Bureau, to return them to the Indian Territory. He passed down the orders but left the issue largely to the local commander, Captain Henry W. Wessells. Confronted with 150 defiant men, women, and children who vowed to die fighting rather than return to gradual death in the south, Wessells concluded that he had but one choice. Temperatures ranged between zero and forty below, and snow drifts piled up around the barracks. Early in January 1879, after failing to persuade the women and children to emerge, he cut off rations. On January 9, after a week of hunger, thirst, and deadly temperatures, the Cheyennes surged from broken windows, shot their guards with a few firearms hidden at the time of surrender, and raced from the fort. The garrison gave chase and ultimately shot down nearly half the fugitives, including women and children.

The tragedy gained Dull Knife's people a reprieve. They settled with the Sioux on the Pine Ridge Reservation. Dull Knife and his people had surrendered farther north. They too gained a reservation near the Yellowstone River.

How Crook might have handled Little Wolf's Cheyennes had he gone to Camp Robinson is unknown. Orders were to move the Indians, and negotiation had proved futile, as did being placed in a freezing barracks and withdrawal of water and rations. All he could have done was try to talk the Cheyennes into moving south peaceably. What he did instead was to lay out his sentiments bluntly and unequivocally in his annual report. Even that got sharply undercut by General Sheridan's ruthless characterization of the Cheyennes as deserving their fate.[28]

A similar issue struck Crook at nearly the same time. A mistake in the Treaty of 1868 had included the Ponca Indian homeland within the Great Sioux Reservation. The Sioux wanted the Poncas out and frequently roughed them up. The government decided to solve the problem by moving the Poncas to the Indian Territory. In 1877 they went, inconsolably, suffering disease and death en route and after they settled in their new homes. Chief Standing Bear lost five members of his family, including his only son. Determined that his son should be buried in his homeland, Standing Bear, accompanied by thirty tribesmen, returned to Nebraska in early 1879. Crook received orders to return them to Indian Territory. An Omaha newsman, Thomas H. Tibbles, intervened, however, and publicized the story. Standing Bear made his case in Crook's office, but Crook replied that he had no choice but to send the Poncas back. At the same time, he let Tibbles know that he sided with the Poncas. Tibbles's agitated report gained nationwide sympathy for the Poncas and in April 1879 led to a suit in U.S. District Court, *Standing Bear v. Crook*. After Standing Bear's eloquent and moving testimony, the judge ruled that Crook had to free the Poncas.

The litigation failed to end the controversy. On the contrary, it set off a groundswell of contention over the condition of the Indian people. A decade of advocacy by Indian rights organizations and prominent humanitarians led to court decisions and legislation that redefined the status of American Indians.[29]

On July 14, 1882, War Department orders ended George Crook's tenure as commanding general of the Department of the Platte. Apache turmoil again wracked Arizona, and Crook again assumed command of the department.

Crook's Arizona exploits in the 1870s had been exemplary. They were brief but brilliant, the height of his long career. His command of the Department of the Platte from 1875 to 1882 represented the depth of his career. He did almost nothing right. In 1879 Sheridan wrote to Sherman: "*Writing confidentially,* I am sorry to say, that very few things have been well done in that Department since Crook came in command of it." It was a fair judgment.[30]

ARIZONA AGAIN

In all their dealings with the Indians officers must be careful not only to observe the strictest fidelity, but to make no promises not in their power to carry out; all grievances arising within their jurisdiction should be redressed, so that an accumulation of them may not cause an outbreak. Grievances, however petty, if permitted to accumulate, will be like embers that smolder and eventually break into flame.[31]

Thus General Crook in 1882 expressed a philosophy for dealing with Indians that took root when he was a second lieutenant before the Civil War. No other frontier general articulated such a thoughtful and humane approach to his mission. Crook had applied this doctrine during his first tour in Arizona. It tended to fade during his field service in the Department of the Platte. He would try to give it full force in his final Arizona service.

Crook began his mission in Arizona as he had before: a council with the White Mountain Apaches, not at Camp Apache but at San Carlos, the central agency at that time for most Apaches. He told them that they had made no progress since he had been there eight years before. Now he wanted them to scatter over the White Mountain Reservation to the north in bands beholden to their headmen. They should adopt farming and so far as possible livestock raising. Apache scouts would be enlisted and placed among the bands to keep order. The brewing of *tizwin*, the potent native intoxicant that lay deep in Apache culture, had to cease. "When I was here before I tried to break up this tizwin business, and told you to put all your money in cattle and brood mares; you paid no attention to me, and let all your brains run down in your stomachs."[32] Crook's effort to eradicating *tizwin* would fail.

Crook's most vexing problem lay not with the White Mountain Apaches but with the Chiricahuas. In the early 1870s General O. O. Howard had made peace with Cochise and established him on his own reservation. That forced Crook to abort his plans to campaign against the Chiricahuas. Circumstances had now changed. Cochise was dead, and in 1876 the Chiricahuas had been moved to the San Carlos Reservation. Some of them lost no time in breaking free and following a fierce warrior named Geronimo, ensconcing themselves in Mexico's towering Sierra Madre. From Mexico they could raid with impunity across the border into New Mexico and Arizona, then return to Mexico, with the international boundary shielding them from pursuit.

Crook had to dig the Chiricahuas out of the Sierra Madre, so he once again assumed the role of a field general.[33] When the governors and military authorities of Sonora and Chihuahua proved receptive to American troops crossing into Mexico, Crook assembled a formidable expedition reflecting his mode of Indian campaigning: one troop of cavalry 40 strong, 193 Apache scouts, and 350 pack mules managed by 76 packers. The march, begun on May 1, 1883, lasted a month and a half and involved incredible hardships in ascending the rugged ridges and peaks of the Sierra Madre. The Apache scouts proved their worth daily and finally forced Geronimo into a conference with Crook, where Geronimo and other Apache leaders agreed to return to San Carlos.

Even before the Chiricahuas reached the reservation—indeed, Geronimo did not arrive for another eight months—Crook confronted a major crisis: the civilian authorities did not want the Chiricahuas back at San Carlos, fearing that they would cause trouble with the other Apaches. Secretary of the Interior Henry M. Teller backed the local agent, Philip P. Wilcox. Crook journeyed to Washington for an interagency meeting that produced a

Memorandum of Agreement in July 1883. The Chiricahuas would be subject to War Department control on the White Mountain Reservation. Likewise, Crook would exercise "police control" over San Carlos and White Mountain, while the civilian agent would manage the Indians. Captain Emmet Crawford would be Crook's policeman at San Carlos. The memorandum was intended as a civilian-military compromise but instead ensured conflict.[34]

Rancorous feuding between Crawford and the San Carlos agent continued month after month. Crook tried to resign but was denied. Crawford at length requested to be relieved, which Crook granted. Less trouble prevailed in the north, because the Chiricahuas were under the exclusive control of the military, overseen by Lieutenant Britton Davis. Here, however, Geronimo proved a festering sore. On May 15, 1885, he tricked the other chiefs into joining him in a major break for Mexico. Once more Crook took the field to round up the Apaches.

Apache scouts once again were a mainstay of Crook's operation. He stoutly believed that the only Apaches could conquer other Apaches. Crook therefore fielded two expeditions consisting of a troop of cavalry and a large number of Apache scouts. As in 1872–73 and 1883, they performed superbly. Although they did not contest Crook's reputation as the preeminent authority on Indian warfare, a number of highly placed officials regarded the scouts as unreliable, remembering a time in 1881 when they had mutinied rather than attack an Apache medicine man. None distrusted scouts more than the commanding general of the army, Lieutenant General Philip H. Sheridan, who had inherited the post when Sherman retired in 1883. As Sheridan declared, "it became a belief in mind that the Indian scouts could not be wholly depended upon to fight and kill their own people. I think they were faithful so far as to try to capture or to induce the surrender of the hostiles, but they had no wish to kill their own kindred."[35] Crook had seen what scouts could do: "Apache scouts, for this class of warfare, are as worthy of trust as any soldiers in the world, and in all the experience I have had with them they have proved themselves energetic, reliable, truthful, and honest."[36] The dispute had greater consequences. Apart from military operations, the conflicting opinions about Apache scouts strained Sheridan and Crook's relationship.

Month after month Crook's columns ranged the peaks and canyons of Mexico, breaking down men, horses, and mules. Many of the mules slipped off canyon trails and fell to their deaths. Although inconclusive, the few skirmishes that occurred demonstrated to the fugitives that they had to keep on the run or be discovered and attacked. Finally, worn out, they allowed themselves to be coaxed into a meeting with General Crook. It took place on March 25, 1886, in a wooded glen named Cañon de los Embudos, twenty-five miles south of the border. Crook confronted Geronimo with harsh words that offended the Apache leader. He ended the conference by fixing Geronimo with a scowl and declaring: "If you stay out I'll keep after you and kill the last one, if it takes fifty years."[37] The Apaches did not agree to give up for two days, at the price of exile in the East for two years.

Leaving Lieutenant Marion P. Maus to escort the Indians back to Fort Bowie, Crook hastened to the fort to wire Sheridan about the agreement with the chiefs. En route with Maus, however, the Apaches obtained whiskey from an itinerant trader, got uproariously drunk, and bolted for the mountains. Before learning of this event Crook received a wire from Sheridan declaring that the president had ruled the surrender terms unacceptable. Crook was to reopen negotiations and demand unconditional surrender, only sparing the Indians' lives. In Crook's mind this would not only involve breaking faith with the Apaches but also stampede them back to the mountains.

When he learned they had already gone to the mountains, Crook considered heading for the mountains himself, with his ever-reliable Apache scouts. Instead he addressed another wire to Sheridan on April 1, 1886: "I believe that the plan upon which I have conducted operations is the one most likely to prove successful in the end. It may be, however, that I am too wedded to my own views in this matter, and as I have spent nearly eight years of the hardest work of my life in this Department, I respectfully request that I may be now relieved from its command." On the very same day, orders reached Fort Leavenworth, Kansas, directing Brigadier General Nelson A. Miles to assume command of the Department of Arizona.[38]

Nelson Miles campaigned strenuously for four months, hiding the role of Apache scouts and highlighting the operations of regular troops. Geronimo finally surrendered on August 26, 1886, but only through the effort of Apache scouts, which he carefully obscured. Miles had the prisoners escorted to confinement in Florida. Even the Apache scouts who had engineered the surrender went as prisoners. He directed all the glory to his unit commanders.

Except for the Civil War years, Crook had passed his entire service in the U.S. Army preoccupied with Indians, whether Paiutes, Apaches, Sioux, or

Poncas. Now his relief by General Miles freed him from such responsibilities but not from concern. Tucked away once more in the now-quiet Department of the Platte, he pursued the routine duties of department command. He also worried about the fate of the Chiricahua Apaches exiled to Florida and then to Alabama, with no hope of return to Arizona.

When Major General Alfred Terry retired in spring 1889, Crook, now the senior brigadier general in the army, was promoted to major general and assigned to Terry's former command, the Military Division of the Missouri in Chicago. Almost immediately Crook was asked to join a commission to persuade the Sioux to accept a land deal that would drastically reduce the Great Sioux Reservation. He was the only member conversant with Indians and readily maneuvered the chiefs into leading their people to sign. Ever since the Sioux wars of 1876–77, the Sioux leaders had harbored a trust for General Crook that aided him in achieving this result.

In Chicago George and Mary Crook enjoyed the attractions and the social attentions of the city's prominent citizens. They traveled for pleasure and otherwise enjoyed life, but his pace slowed as his health began to decline.

The condition of the Apaches in Alabama, however, motivated Crook to work in their behalf. Allied with the Indian Rights Association and other reformers, as well as General Oliver O. Howard, he worked with members of Congress and others of influence. General Miles opposed these efforts as a negative reflection on his stature. Returning the Apaches to their beloved Arizona homeland proved politically impossible, but in 1894 they were moved to a more congenial environment at Fort Sill, Oklahoma.

George Crook did not live to see this culmination of the long battle concerning justice for the Chiricahuas. On March 21, 1890, in his suite at the Grand Pacific Hotel in Chicago, heart failure struck him dead at the age at sixty-one. He was buried first in Maryland, but his body was ultimately moved to Arlington National Cemetery.

General Crook emerges from his last conflict as a martyr, defeated by three top officials who possessed no understanding of the Apaches: President Grover Cleveland, Secretary of War William C. Endicott, and Lieutenant General Philip H. Sheridan. Crook doubtless valued that image. It bolstered an ego long kept hidden from the public and kept intact his reputation, both before the public and to himself, as the ultimate authority on Apaches.

A closer look at the last decisive week, however, suggests that Crook failed to handle the issue with his usual acumen. First, he left the surrender site immediately and was therefore absent when the Apaches went on the spree that fueled their breakaway. Lieutenant Maus was a fine officer, but Crook's presence could well have headed off the binge. Second, the key to the final capitulation of Geronimo and the other headmen was an Apache named Kayatena. He had made trouble on the reservation and been sent to Alcatraz Prison. The experience led him to embrace the white man's way, and Crook believed that he might help persuade the Chiricahuas to surrender. He did, but Crook waited too long to summon him from San Francisco, which delayed Crook's departure for the final surrender talks. Meanwhile the Apaches launched their drunken party. Finally, and most critical, Crook had been unequivocally ordered not to promise the Apaches that they could return to Arizona. He explained that this was the only way he could get them to surrender—true, but hardly sufficient to override a bedrock principle of policy.[39]

If Crook did not merit martyrdom, he did merit the distinguished image that he left to history. He knew Indians, whatever the tribe, and understood their minds. He was one of the few so-called humanitarian generals who sympathized with the plight of the Indians and exerted every effort to lighten their ordeal. He was also a field general, always leading troops in the field rather than directing subordinates from his department headquarters. He was a fighter as well as a peacemaker, pursuing his strategy of first whipping enemies, then treating them with kindness as well as firm authority. In an era when most army officers, and even the curriculum at West Point, embraced the tenets of orthodox warfare, Crook was an innovative thinker. Mules, rather than wagons, moved supplies rapidly into terrain unsuited to wagons. Recruiting Indians to fight other Indians set him apart from most other Indian Wars officers. Small mobile units, composed of regular cavalry and Indian scouts and supplied by pack mules, adhered to his dictum to get on the trail and never stop until overtaking the enemy. This tactic stood in vivid contrast to the usual offensive of large columns of regulars bound to slow-moving wagon trains.

In short, only one other Indian-fighting general, Nelson A. Miles, could match Crook's record as a frontier army leader. Personal idiosyncrasies set him apart from other generals and offended some while amusing others. His reticence and unwillingness to share opinions or even plans frustrated aides and others with whom he had to cooperate. His unconventional attire, usually supplanting a uniform, combined with his messing and sleeping with his mule packers, irritated many colleagues. Whether these idiosyncrasies were deliberately cultivated or were simply features of his persona, Crook failed to recognize the damage that they did to his relations with officers whom he needed to cultivate.

General George Crook does not deserve the exalted view that history accords him. But he does deserve to be remembered as one of the great generals of the frontier army.

CHAPTER FOUR

OLIVER O. HOWARD

=== ★★ ===

T he army knew Oliver Otis Howard as the "Christian General," and so history remembers him. Howard was much more, but his abiding piety tended to obscure other qualities. He deeply believed that God oversaw his every thought and move and ordained the result of every action. To maintain his purity, fight off ambition, and beseech the Lord for guidance, he constantly buried himself in prayer. In the presence of others, even his fellow generals, he wore his sobriquet "Christian General" as conspicuously as the empty right sleeve tied to his belt or a brass button on the front of his uniform. He eschewed profanity, strong drink, and tobacco, a rarity in a military society. Howard did nothing to suppress his feelings when among his peers—so much so that they made fun of him, sometimes in his presence. When offended, he simply walked away.

Although it was obscured by the Christian image, Howard displayed qualities of military leadership, developed by experience in the Civil War. He learned from his mistakes and rarely repeated them and was personally courageous in battle. He was loyal to superiors and considerate of subordinates. Howard cared for his men and did all he could, consistent with military imperatives, to ease their burden, avoid casualties, and keep them well fed and well clothed. Despite his Christian principles, he sometimes engaged in the intrigue that roiled the top command and was highly sensitive to the prerogatives of rank. Howard cultivated political friends who worked for his promotion. Even so, he learned how to command brigades, divisions, corps, and finally an army in combat. Two controversial combat actions, however, stigmatized his reputation. He lessened the stigma in his

Brigadier General Oliver O. Howard, commanding
Department of the Columbia, 1874–1878;
Department of the Platte, 1882–1886.
Oregon Historical Society.

last operations of the war, when he demonstrated his competence. Howard emerged from the war among the second tier of Union generals, a brevet major general and brigadier general in the Regular Army.[1]

Born on November 8, 1830, in Leeds, Maine, Howard attended Bowdoin College for four years, leaving in 1850 to enter West Point Military Academy. Graduating fourth in his class of forty-six in 1854, he was commissioned in the Ordnance Corps, testimony to his class standing and guarantee of an easier life than in one of the combat arms. Such were his tours at Watervliet and Kennebeck arsenals in New York and as chief ordnance officer during hostilities with the Seminole Indians of Florida in 1857. From 1857 to 1861 he taught mathematics at the military academy at West Point. When the Civil War broke out, therefore, First Lieutenant Howard could point only to seven years of staff duty. Nevertheless, he gained the support of Maine politicians and in May 1861 took command of the Third Maine Infantry with the rank of Colonel of Volunteers.

CIVIL WAR

At First Bull Run (or Manassas) the former ordnance officer commanded a brigade of four regiments, three from Maine and one from Vermont. Together with most of the rest of the Union Army, his brigade fled the field in disorder. Even so, in September he was appointed brigadier general of Volunteers. Commanding a brigade, Howard participated in General George B. McClellan's Peninsular Campaign. On June 1, 1862, the second day of the Battle of Fair Oaks, Howard led his brigade in a charge against Confederate lines. A bullet hit his right elbow, another felled his horse, and a third penetrated his forearm near the first. In a field hospital, the attending surgeon concluded that the arm had to be amputated and did so late in the afternoon. Howard returned to Maine to recuperate.

After convalescing, Howard returned to the Army of the Potomac at the end of August 1862, in time to lead his brigade in the Battle of Antietam on September 16–17, 1862. During a disastrous assault on the Confederate left, Howard's division commander, John Sedgwick, was wounded. By virtue of rank, Howard assumed command of the division and presided over its repulse and retreat.

Because General Robert E. Lee surrendered the battlefield to McClellan, Antietam was considered a Union victory, but McClellan's pursued the retreating Confederate army half-heartedly, prompting President Lincoln to relieve him from command. At the same time, on November 29, 1862, Howard gained promotion to major general of Volunteers, thanks largely to the Maine political leadership's lobbying in his behalf.

On December 13, 1862, Howard led his division in General Ambrose Burnside's suicidal attack on the heights above Fredericksburg, Virginia. Together with all the other units of the army, Howard's division was thrown back with heavy casualties.

When spring 1863 thawed the Virginia countryside, the Army of the Potomac sprang to life. General Burnside had given way to General Joseph Hooker, who reorganized the army, naming Major General Daniel Sickles to command the Third Corps, which included Howard's division. Howard ranked Sickles and at once protested to Hooker, who made amends by turning over the Eleventh Corps to Howard. This was largely a German-American corps, recently commanded by the German Franz Sigel. The troops received their new leader with a touch of resentment and generally behaved unresponsively. The mix was not good, as became painfully apparent at the Battle of Chancellorsville on May 2–4, 1863.

Howard's corps held the extreme right flank of the Union army facing Lee's army. His own right extended to the edge of heavy timber. He ensured that defenses were erected to protect the flank in case of an attack. But Hooker was convinced that Lee's army was retreating, and Howard accepted his view. Although evidence accumulated during the day that Lee was maneuvering in front of the Union line instead of withdrawing, Hooker still failed to take alarm. After nightfall the maneuvering became apparent when Stonewall Jackson's corps of 26,000 men burst from the timber and stormed the Eleventh Corps defenses. Hearing the firing, Howard rushed to the scene. Some units stood and fought but had to give way as Howard tried in vain to stem the panicked flight. During the assault, Jackson was accidentally shot and mortally wounded by his own men. Even though Hooker badly mismanaged the battle, Howard and his Germans bore the brunt of the criticism and were widely regarded as pariahs in the Army of the Potomac.

While Howard traveled to Washington to defend his role in the Battle of Chancellorsville to Lincoln, Secretary Stanton, and General-in-Chief Henry Halleck, Lee prepared to march again into Maryland and on to

Pennsylvania. Departing from Washington uncensured, Howard resumed command of Eleventh Corps, which with two other corps formed the left wing of the Army of the Potomac, now under General George G. Meade. When Howard reached Gettysburg on July 1, the battle was already raging. General John F. Reynolds, commanding the left wing, was conducting the Union forces in the fight. When word reached Howard that Reynolds had been killed, he became the senior officer on the field.

When the leading divisions of Eleventh corps reached Howard on Cemetery Hill, he sent two through Gettysburg to engage the Confederates and held the third to prepare defenses on Cemetery Hill. Reinforced, the Confederates drove Howard's two divisions back through town to the Cemetery Hill, where Howard arranged his own units and others arriving as reinforcements in defensive positions.

At this juncture Major General Winfield Scott Hancock arrived on the hill bearing an order from General Meade to take command. Howard pointed out that he ranked Hancock and suggested that Hancock take charge of the left of the line while Howard directed the right. Hancock acquiesced. In this way the first day's battle played out on Cemetery Hill until General John Slocum, senior to both, rode up and took command.

Howard, believing he had performed admirably, resented Meade's implied criticism and seeming partiality toward Hancock, his junior in rank. After all, Howard had selected and held the hill at the center of the Union line that would prove crucial in the remaining two days of the battle. And for this he later received congressional thanks, although Hancock and his friends took offense at the omission of Hancock's name from the congressional resolution. Thus the Battle of Gettysburg placed a second stain on Howard's reputation.

Howard found escape from ill feeling in the Army of the Potomac by transferring to the western theater of the war. The Confederate victory in the Battle of Chickamauga on September 19–20, 1863, bottled up the Union forces in Chattanooga, Tennessee, choking the supply lines running to the city. A new team of generals—Ulysses S. Grant, William T. Sherman, and George H. Thomas—sought to reverse the tide at Chattanooga when reinforcements from the East arrived to help in the form of General Joseph Hooker and his Eleventh and Twelfth Corps.

On the night of October 28, scarcely two weeks after arriving, Howard's corps played a prominent part in a confused battle at Wauhatchie. His Germans drove attacking Confederates down a slope and won victory. In his first fight in the West Howard had the opportunity to leave the misfortunes of the East behind him and get a fresh start. "God has been good and sparing," he wrote.[2]

The Eleventh Corps played a supporting role in the Union assault on Missionary Ridge and a major role in the dash to relieve the beleaguered command of General Ambrose Burnside at Knoxville, Tennessee. With the Confederate army withdrawing south into Georgia, the Union troops settled into winter quarters at Chattanooga. Spring 1864, however, brought preparations for General Sherman's advance on Atlanta. During the Chattanooga fighting, Sherman had come to admire Howard and mentioned him favorably in his official reports, penning a personal note that characterized him as "one who mingled so gracefully and perfectly the polished Christian gentleman and the prompt, zealous, and gallant soldier."[3] In reorganizing the army, Sherman gave Howard command of the Fourth Corps, a much larger and more important unit than the Eleventh Corps.

From May through August 1864 Sherman's force—George H. Thomas's Army of the Cumberland and James B. McPherson's Army of the Tennessee—pushed south toward Atlanta. General Joseph E. Johnston tried to stop the Union advance, but Sherman succeeded in flanking some Confederate defenses and launched an attack where flanking proved impossible. General McPherson was killed in a hard-fought action on July 21. General John A. Logan, a highly competent and popular political general, inherited the army by virtue of seniority. He and Hooker contended for the permanent command, but Sherman instead named Howard to head the Army of the Tennessee, at 27,000 men the largest unit that he had yet led. In the remaining fighting around Atlanta Howard demonstrated the soundness of Sherman's judgment. He especially distinguished himself in the Battle of Ezra Church, on July 28, 1864, when Lieutenant General John B. Hood, his West Point classmate, assaulted his position. Hood threw more than 18,000 Confederates against Howard's 13,000 but was decisively routed with a loss of 3,000 men. Howard's casualties numbered 642. Ezra Church was Howard's battle; he conceived it and shared it with no other general. For this action he was breveted major general in the Regular Army. Howard had not wiped Chancellorsville and Gettysburg from his record but had redeemed his name as a competent Union general.

Sherman's legendary "March to the Sea" began in Atlanta on November 15, 1864, and reached Savannah, Georgia, on December 21. From Atlanta Sherman divided his army and left Generals Thomas and Schofield to contend with General Hood's Confederates. Sherman then took with him 60,000 men, divided into two wings, each consisting of two corps, with Howard commanding the right wing and Henry W. Slocum the left wing. The march was an expedition of foraging, destruction, and terrifying civilians, with occasional skirmishes but no important engagements until the seizure of Fort McAllister on the outskirts of Savannah.

After resting a month in Savannah, Sherman turned north. His units marched out of the city late in January 1865. His aim was to unite with General Grant's army at Petersburg, Virginia. Sherman divided his 60,000 men into three wings: Howard with the Army of the Tennessee on the right, a wing consisting of the Army of the Ohio, which had been brought east under General John M. Schofield, and a wing of two corps under Slocum. Sherman's army marched 425 miles and fought six actions with the Confederate army of General Joseph E. Johnston, which on April 26 surrendered to Sherman near Hillsboro, North Carolina. Lee had already surrendered to Grant. The war had essentially ended.

During the northward march, Howard learned that on December 21, the same day that Savannah fell, he had been promoted to brigadier general in the Regular Army. His political friends in Maine had worked toward this result, but his record also played a part.

Although he did not engage in any significant battles after the fall of Atlanta, Howard had demonstrated skill in managing two corps, 27,000 men, in the march to Savannah and then into North Carolina.

On the second day of the Grand Review of the victorious armies up Pennsylvania Avenue in Washington, D.C, on May 24, 1865, General Howard expected to ride in front of the Army of the Tennessee. With General Logan still smarting over failure to get that command, Sherman asked Howard to yield him the honor of leading it in the parade. Howard readily consented and at Sherman's invitation rode next to him at the head of the entire western army.

THE FREEDMEN'S BUREAU

Even before Lee and Johnston's surrender in April 1865, Congress and President Lincoln confronted the issue of what to do with the liberated slaves of the South. On March 3 Congress passed and the president signed the first of a sequence of so-called Freedmen's Bureau bills, creating a sprawling bureaucracy within the War Department charged with aiding former slaves through food and housing, oversight, education, health care, and employment contracts with private landowners. Both Lincoln and Secretary Stanton wanted General Howard to head the bureau, as did President Andrew Johnson after Lincoln's assassination. Almost certainly, this was due to Howard's reputation as the Christian General rather than his war record.

On May 10, probably flattered that Lincoln, Stanton, and Johnson desired him to take on this assignment, Howard accepted. It would be more than daunting, as General Sherman recognized at the time. Pledging his support for Howard in gracious terms, Sherman nonetheless declared (May 15, 1865): "God has limited the power of man, and though in the kindness of your heart you would alleviate all the ills of humanity it is not in your power. Nor is it in your power to fulfill one-tenth part of the expectations of those who framed the bureau of freedmen, refugees, and abandoned estates. It is simply impracticable."

And so it proved. Until Congress shut down the bureau in 1872, Howard struggled to supervise a huge bureaucracy, care for 4 million former slaves, fight off the open and sometimes violent opposition of unreconciled Southerners, and deal with the growing rift between Congress and President Johnson. More immediately, Johnson grew increasingly hostile toward the bureau. His benign Southern policy, which emboldened Southerners hostile to the bureau, to congressional Reconstruction, and to the civil rights acts, greatly complicated the task of Howard's subordinates on the scene. The bureau—and Howard—became increasingly controversial, battered on one side by political enemies and on the other by elements convinced that the bureau should do more for the former black slaves. One notable success of the bureau, however, was in establishing black educational institutions. Howard University in Washington, D.C., is the enduring monument.

Predictably, unscrupulous enemies made Howard a target. They publicized a "Freedmen's Bureau ring" that financially profited from various fraudulent schemes.[4] Howard himself was alleged to have grown rich, in part through illegal use of government funds in support of Howard University. In spring 1870 a select committee of the House of Representatives began hearings into the charges against Howard and his bureau. The committee took testimony for four months before submitting a report that essentially exonerated Howard. In fact, the affair had been a Democratic vendetta. Howard had profited by having a Republican majority on the committee. Even so, the hearings generated publicity that cast a shadow over the bureau and its director for decades.

In February 1872, five months before Congress terminated the Freedmen's Bureau, the secretary of the interior asked for Howard's services to journey to Arizona and try to make peace with the warring Apaches. Once again, his reputation as Christian General probably lay behind the selection. Howard gracefully accepted the assignment and by May was in the Department of Arizona. After visiting the various agencies and conferring with the chiefs, he met with the department commander, General George Crook. Although Howard found the Apaches and some other tribes actively hostile to the encroaching white settlers, his arrival, combined with the junket of a previous peace commissioner, Vincent Colyer, forced Crook to suspend a long-planned offensive. Angry at such interference and quietly contemptuous of Howard, Crook greeted him politely and made a good impression.

Late in June Howard recruited a delegation of chiefs and escorted them to Washington, D.C., to impress them with white society's civilization. His mission in Arizona had accomplished little and in one major respect had failed. He had been unable to arrange a meeting with the Chiricahua Apache chief Cochise, the most difficult of all. Howard returned to Arizona and tried for a month to gain a meeting with Cochise. He finally succeeded and on October 10, 1872, negotiated an agreement creating a reservation for Cochise and his people. Even though Crook resented the invulnerability that Howard conferred on Cochise, peace with Cochise would remain one of General Howard's proudest memories.[5]

Back in Washington, Howard's affairs progressed unfavorably. Congress was attempting to wrap up the affairs of the Freedmen's Bureau, but the clerks in the War Department had lost and mixed up the bureau's records. The confusion prompted some of Howard's enemies to charge him with malfeasance, and Secretary of War William W. Belknap proved hostile.

Howard's old opponents in Congress intervened to make matters worse. After Howard's testimony before the House Committee on Military Affairs, the House debated a resolution calling for the army to court-martial him, but in the final version it settled for a court of inquiry.

President Grant named General Sherman to preside over the court of inquiry, and the other members proved generally favorable or neutral. The court sat from March 10 to May 9, 1873. Many who took the stand, including some within the War Department, ravaged Howard for all manner of frauds while commissioner of the bureau, but Howard called a formidable array of defenders. Reaching a verdict on May 9, the court found "that General Oliver O. Howard did his whole duty, and believes that he deserves well of the country"—hardly an enthusiastic acquittal.[6]

As he struggled through his ordeals with the Freedmen's Bureau, Howard increasingly considered retiring from the army. Arizona changed his mind. On November 11, 1872, as soon as he returned to Washington, he queried Sherman about a command assignment. Sherman replied at once with words that offered little encouragement:

> I have always endeavored to befriend you all I could, and hope to continue; but I must preserve like relations to others, who have been constant on duty, at remote places where they had no means to plead their own cause. I know you regarded your duties here as of infinite importance to the Government, but they were non-military; and for your own sake I wish you had taken command of a department two years ago, when according to the notions of the army generally your promotion would have met universal favor. Now they would impute it to personal presence, and personal influence with the president.[7]

In essence, Howard would have to wait his turn. When death or retirement of officers who had served in a military rather than civilian capacity opened the way, Sherman would see what he could do.

The business of phasing out the Freedmen's Bureau occupied Howard into 1873, and he still had to suffer through a congressional investigation and a court of inquiry. When no command was forthcoming, he again addressed Sherman on November 29, 1873, who replied the same day. Sherman reminded Howard that he had warned him when he accepted the

Freedmen's Bureau position in 1865 of the result that seemed inevitable, as it turned out to be. Again in 1869, when Grant's election to the presidency brought Sherman to Washington, he had advised Howard to accept a departmental command, but Howard had refused. "I am glad therefore that you have come to the manly conclusion to assume your appropriate place among the officers of our army." When occasion arose, Sherman would assign Howard to a command appropriate to his rank.[8]

DEPARTMENT OF THE COLUMBIA

Howard had less than a year to wait. On September 1, 1874, he assumed command of the Department of Columbia, with headquarters at Portland, Oregon. The department consisted of Washington, Oregon, Idaho, and Alaska and formed part of the Division of the Pacific, commanded by Major General Irvin McDowell from San Francisco.

For his first two years, Howard confronted no major problems. He toured his department, including Alaska, and undertook religious work in Portland. He attended church regularly, taught a Bible class, presided over the local Young Men's Christian Association, and strove to get his eldest son, Guy (a recent Yale graduate), a direct commission in the Regular Army. He succeeded.

In 1875 a long-brewing problem with the Nez Perce Indians drew Howard into affairs that belonged to the Indian Bureau. His humanitarian instincts prevailed, however, as he recognized the wrongs inflicted on the Indians by an influx of miners and settlers. Like most Indian tribes, the Nez Perces grappled with factionalism: progressive versus nonprogressive, Christian versus adherents of traditional spiritual beliefs and customs, and treaty versus nontreaty, derived from an 1855 treaty followed by an 1863 treaty paring the Nez Perce country into an ever-shrinking reservation in Idaho to make way for white gold-seekers. The signatories were mostly Christian and progressive; the nontreaty Nez Perces were those who refused to surrender their homeland.

The people who attracted Howard's special sympathy were the nontreaty adherents of Chief Joseph, who occupied Oregon's Wallowa Valley. Although the valley was their traditional homeland, the fertile, mountain-girt expanse attracted white farmers and ranchers, who began to take land there in the early 1870s. Howard's solution was not to evict the intruders but to pay Joseph to yield his land and take his people to the reservation in Idaho and to use force and if they refused. In June 1876 two white men killed a Wallowa Valley tribesman. This led Howard to recommend a commission to settle the issue of Joseph's claim to the valley as well as the murder of the Wallowa Indian. The secretary of the interior responded by appointing a commission, including Howard as a member but not as chairman, charged with the entire issue of roaming nontreaty Indians.

The commission met on November 13–14, 1876, in a church at the Lapwai Agency, with the meeting centering mainly on a dialogue between General Howard and Chief Joseph. Dignified, thoughtful, and articulate, Chief Joseph made his case, dwelling on his people's claim to the land and their spiritual ties to it. Joseph emphasized that the earth was his mother and that his father, Old Joseph, had enjoined him never to sell the bones of their ancestors. The commissioners were greatly impressed with Joseph's demeanor and sincerity, even to his point of forgiving the white men who killed his tribesman. But they confronted the reality that Joseph would not budge: the Wallowa Valley was his land and he would not give it up.

Because of his own spiritual beliefs, General Howard was uniquely unqualified to understand Joseph's mind. In particular, Joseph's talk of the earth as his mother struck Howard as nonsense. Deeply meaningful to Joseph, it was completely alien to Howard's Christian principles. He willingly signed the commission's recommendation that the Wallowa band, and indeed all roving nontreaty Indians, move within the boundaries of the Idaho reservation established by the Treaty of 1863. If they failed to go voluntarily, force should be used.

On March 7, 1877, the interior secretary again requested military help in making the nontreaty Indians move to the reservation. Spooked by the prospect of the army being blamed for starting another Indian war, Secretary Belknap, General Sherman, and General McDowell all cautioned Howard to act strictly in support of the Indian Bureau. Any blame attached must fall on the Indian Bureau, not the army.

On May 3–7, 1877, Howard and agent J. B. Montieth met with Joseph, this time in a tent on the parade ground of Fort Lapwaiand not only with Joseph but with three powerful religious leaders. In three days of rancorous debate, the Nez Perces argued with Howard. For two days, Toohoolhoolzote stood up to the general. In brusque language, he explained Indian concepts of land and faulted the whites for their own antithetical concepts. Howard

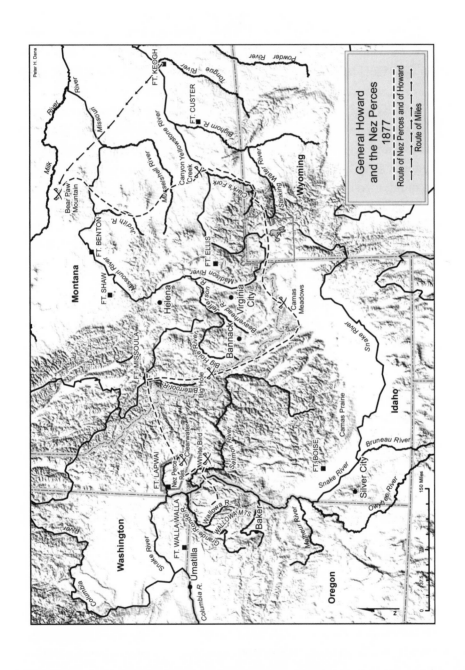

General Howard
and the Nez Perces
1877

- - - Route of Nez Perces and of Howard
← ↑ → Route of Miles

Peter H. Dana

Washington

Montana

Idaho

Wyoming

Oregon

Columbia River
Snake River
FT. WALLA WALLA
Umatilla
Columbia R.
Grande Ronde R.
Wallowa R.
WALLOWA MTS
Baker
Malheur River
Owyhee River
Bruneau River
Silver City
Snake River
FT. BOISE
Camas Prairie
Salmon River
White Bird
Nez Perces Res.
Clearwater
FT. LAPWAI
FT. MISSOULA
Bitterroot R.
Big Hole River
Big Hole
FT. SHAW
Missouri River
Helena
FT. BENTON
Judith R.
Bear Paw Mountain
Milk River
Missouri River
River
Marias River
Teton River
FT. ELLIS
Madison River
Jefferson R.
Beaverhead R.
Bannack
Virginia City
Camas Meadows
Snake River
Stinking Water River
Clark's Fork
Canyon Yellowstone Creek
Musselshell River
Bighorn R.
FT. CUSTER
Tongue River
Powder River
FT. KEOGH

N

0   75   150 Miles

37.5

took offense at what Toohoolhoolzote said and how he said it. He lectured Toohoolhoolzote just as bluntly, declaring that he wanted to hear no more about the earth as their mother, that they had to do what the Great Father commanded: go to the reservation. Toohoolhoolzote refused to back down, so Howard had him removed from the tent and placed in the guardhouse. The Nez Perce chiefs yielded and agreed to move. Howard gave them thirty days.[9]

When the chiefs made ready to move, Joseph lost stock in the arduous crossing of the swollen Snake River. The rest of the people, almost all non-treaty Indians, gathered at a lake on the Camas Prairie to talk over Howard's order. A spirit of resistance began to rise. They were in a receptive frame of mind, therefore, when three young men, full of whiskey, embarked on a revenge expedition on June 13, 1877. Strengthened by other warriors, the raiders left in their trail through June 14 and 15 more than a score of dead farmers and raped women as well as great destruction.

General Howard had returned to Fort Lapwai from his Portland head-quarters to witness the gathering of the Nez Perces. Alerted to the killings, he dispersed what few units he had to protect the settlers, but he now faced the major Indian war against which his superiors had warned him. He himself was partly to blame for bringing it on.

Howard dispatched two troops of cavalry under Captain David Perry to ride to the relief of settlers on the Salmon River and Camas Prairie. At dawn on June 17, strengthened by eleven volunteers, Perry led his one hundred troopers down White Bird Canyon in an effort to cut off Joseph and his people before they could cross the Salmon River. The Nez Perces waited at the foot of the canyon. Springing the trap, they drove the troops back up the canyon with the loss of one officer and thirty-three men killed.

A triumph for the Nez Perces, the Battle of White Bird Canyon was a disaster for the army and for General Howard, who now called for more troops from his department and from other departments. When he had his pursuing force assembled, it numbered more than four hundred infantry and cavalry, together with large units of civilian volunteers. He intended to take the field himself.

For the first week of July Howard's column maneuvered through the tortuous mountains trying to run down the agile Nez Perces, who easily eluded him. Detachments fanned out in Howard's front, encountering stiff resistance from the Nez Perces who were shielding the northward movement of their village. In one clash a lieutenant and ten men were wiped out by the Nez Perce rearguard. Finally, on July 11, Howard freed the pursuing column from the mountains and overtook the Nez Perces. Solidly established on a plateau overlooking the Clearwater River and the Nez Perce village, the troops fended off assault parties working their way up the ravines draining the plateau. The battle continued for two days, with both sides fighting hard and valorously. At length a strong military advance forced the Nez Perces from their refuges and won the Battle of the Clearwater. Howard tarried for a day, however, which allowed his Indian quarry to escape.

The Battle of the Clearwater came at an opportune time for Howard. Alarmed at the murderous excesses of the Nez Perces, President Rutherford B. Hayes questioned Howard's military competence and discussed with his cabinet whether to replace him with his own protégé, General George Crook. But for the signal victory at the Clearwater, Howard undoubtedly would have been relieved.

Howard confronted a formidable array of Nez Perces: about three hundred warriors with five hundred women and children. A bloc of strong chiefs led the people, including Looking Glass, White Bird, Toohoolhoolzote, Joseph, and Ollokot. Looking Glass was deemed the most experienced war leader and functioned in that role. In issues of war Joseph remained in the background.

On July 13, 1877, Howard took up the march and caught up with the Nez Perces as they were crossing the Clearwater River. An exchange of fire followed, but the troops did not press the issue. In fact, the larger issue was already apparent. The chiefs had decided to lead their people across the rugged Bitterroot Mountains by way of the Lolo Trail. The Nez Perces had used this route for generations to reach the buffalo plains of Montana and their friends the Crow Indians. They hoped now to seek refuge with the Crows or even go on to Canada and join with Sitting Bull's exiled Lakotas.

As the Nez Perces began their trek up the Lolo Trail, Howard tended to think that they were about to become someone else's problem, for they would leave the Department of the Columbia and enter the Department of Dakota. But General Sherman made it clear that Howard was to ignore department boundaries and continue the pursuit. Thus Howard started his march on July 30, his command now consisting of more than 700 troops and 74 civilian volunteers with 70 mule packers. Another force of nearly 500 men under

Colonel Frank Wheaton, en route from Georgia, would strike in a circular route to the north and join Howard in Montana. A third force of nearly 300 men would remain behind to protect the settlers. Howard's delay afforded the Nez Perces a two-week start. His own formidable command, including artillery, faced stiff logistical challenges in surmounting the Lolo Trail, which was narrow, obstructed by heavy timber, sliced by numerous deep ravines, and covered with slippery mud.

When the Nez Perces approached the eastern end of the trail, a small command of soldiers and volunteers from Montana confronted them. A parley with the Nez Perce chiefs on July 27 ended indecisively. That night, as the blocking riflemen dug in to defend themselves, the entire body of Nez Perces slipped around the position and left it behind.

As the Nez Perces turned south up the Bitterroot Valley, Howard and the main force were just starting up the Lolo Trail a hundred miles to the west. The effort had indeed fallen to the Department of the Dakota, specifically to Colonel John Gibbon and his infantrymen at Fort Shaw, Montana.

With 15 officers and 146 enlisted men, Colonel Gibbon got on the Indian trail in the Bitterroot Valley. He dispatched a courier to General Howard asking that cavalry be rushed up the Lolo Trail to his aid. Ahead, Looking Glass had determined that the women and children needed rest and decreed that camp be made on Big Hole Prairie. At dawn on August 9, 1877, Gibbon's infantry burst from hiding, splashed across the Big Hole River, and swept the lodges at the edge of the Nez Perce village with rifle fire. The Nez Perce men gathered their families and fled into the hills. Gibbon's men took possession of the village and began to burn the lodges and their contents. In the meantime the Nez Perce warriors rallied and counterattacked with such vigor that they drove the infantrymen out of the village and laid siege to them beyond it. All day and night the warriors kept the troops pinned down under incessant fire. By morning they were withdrawing and packing up their village to move on south.

Rifle fire killed nearly 100 Nez Perces, many women and children, but the warriors had won the battle, driving off the soldiers, capturing and drawing off their howitzer, and inflicting severe casualties. Gibbon lost 2 officers, 21 enlisted men, and 6 civilians killed and 5 officers, 31 enlisted men, and 4 citizens wounded. Rarely in the Indian Wars did a military contingent sustain such casualties.

On August 11, as Gibbon's men buried their dead, General Howard rode up with an advance guard of his command. The remainder arrived two days later. The Nez Perce War again reverted to Howard's responsibility, and he reluctantly took up the pursuit.

Howard, his troops, and his animals were all exhausted after the Lolo Trail and the Bitterroot Valley. Moreover, the general's heart was not in a further exhausting pursuit, especially since the Nez Perces appeared to be headed into either General Alfred Terry's Department of Dakota or General Crook's Department of the Platte. But Howard continued on the trail, which shifted back and forth across the continental divide between Montana and Idaho. Growing evidence indicated that the Indians were killing settlers, stealing horses, and burning buildings.

Alerted by his guide that the Nez Perces would turn east toward Yellowstone Park, Howard took a shortcut to try to catch up. He managed to reach a Nez Perce campsite on Camas Meadow, south of Henry's Lake, abandoned only that morning. On the night of August 19 the troops bivouacked on the Indian campsite, intending to follow the next morning. Before dawn, however, rifle fire roused the sleeping soldiers and volunteers from their tents. During the night 200 Nez Perce warriors had doubled back on their trail and dashed in among the mule herd. They tried to run off both horses and mules, but the horses had been hobbled. The Nez Perces got away with 150 mules.

At daybreak Major George B. Sanford and four cavalry troops rode out to try to overtake the Nez Perces and regain the stolen stock. They succeeded but encountered a line of well-posted warriors directing a heavy fire against them. The cavalry dismounted, with every fourth man holding the horses, and fired back. The two sides maneuvered and fought for about an hour until Sanford ordered a withdrawal. On the way back the cavalry met Howard with a relief column. The battle had cost Sanford one enlisted man killed and one officer and six enlisted men wounded.

Howard had almost been relieved of his command before the Battle of the Clearwater. He had endured constant newspaper criticism, and he and his men were so fatigued that he thought it pointless to go on. As he paused at Camas Meadows to refit, he rode to Virginia City, Montana, for provisions. From there on August 24 he telegraphed General Sherman, who was not in Washington but had been touring Yellowstone National Park and was now in Helena. If troops from either of the departments that he was approaching could head off the Nez Perces, Howard wired: "I think I may stop where I am, and in a few days work my way back to Fort Boise slowly." Sherman fired back at once: "That force of yours should pursue the Nez Perces to the death," he commanded. "If you are tired, give the command to some young energetic officer." Stung by Sherman's words as well as similar scolding from General McDowell, Howard protested: "I never flag. Neither you nor General McDowell can doubt my pluck or energy."[10]

Of course, doubting Howard's pluck and energy was exactly what both generals had done and in fact what Howard himself had confessed. He was tired, and his command was broken down. But he summoned the will to resume the march on August 28. At that very time, unknown to Howard, Sherman had already ordered another commander into the field to supplant Howard and free him to return to Oregon. The two officers never made contact, however, and Howard continued the pursuit.

As Howard led his column on the Nez Perce trail through Yellowstone National Park, he came on four haggard men who had escaped from a party of tourists captured by the Nez Perces, the first of several indications that tourist groups were being attacked. Later he discovered a place where the Nez Perces had seized an entire tourist group and ended by having a fatal gun battle with them.

Troops hastened from the east to block the passages from Yellowstone National Park. Colonel Nelson A. Miles dispatched six troops of cavalry from Fort Keogh, on the Yellowstone River in the Department of Dakota, and Colonel Wesley Merritt led a cavalry force northwest from the Department of the Platte. The Nez Perces, however, outwitted the blocking units and emerged from the park onto the plains by way of Clark's Fork of the Yellowstone. Embarrassed, Colonel Samuel D. Sturgis, now under Miles's command, raced to overtake the quarry. He caught up on the north side of the Yellowstone, where on September 13 the Nez Perces defeated him in the Battle of Canyon Creek. The Nez Perces had now discovered that the Crows could provide no refuge because they were allied with the white soldiers in fighting the Sioux. The only alternative seemed to be Sitting Bull in Canada. They moved northward.

Howard and his men labored behind, and at the Yellowstone River the general dispatched a courier to Fort Keogh explaining to Colonel Miles how the Nez Perces had eluded Sturgis and asking him to try to intercept them before they could reach Canada. By the next morning Miles had moved his command of infantry and cavalry across the Yellowstone and headed northwest. Augmented by other units en route, Miles's command numbered about 450 men.

On October 4 General Howard and an escort arrived at the battlefield of Bear Paw Mountains, forty miles short of the international boundary. Colonel Miles had struck the Nez Perce camp five days earlier, on September 30, and encountered a firestorm of opposition. In the day's sharp fighting, he sustained losses of 2 officers killed and 4 wounded and 22 enlisted men killed and 38 wounded. He decided on a siege, which was the situation when Howard reached the field four days later. The intensely ambitious Miles feared that Howard would take command and rob him of his rightful credit. But Howard assured Miles that until after the surrender the field was his. On October 5 Chief Joseph came out to make the memorable statement that he would fight no more forever.

As each chief emerged to hand over his rifle, Howard pointed to Miles, who received the surrender. Typically, Miles's dispatch to Terry boasted of his victory at Bear Paw Mountains while mentioning Howard almost as an afterthought. The newspapers, which had faulted Howard throughout the pursuit, omitted his name altogether. Nelson A. Miles emerged as the hero of Bear Paw Mountain and by inference of the Nez Perce War. Deeply offended by his friend's betrayal, Howard fired back, setting off a public feud that lasted until June 1878, despite reprimands from Sherman and Sheridan. The quarrel led to a complete break in relations. Miles had been an aide to Howard for a time during the Civil War and had even held up his arm while the surgeon sawed it off. Ever since they had been close friends. No more.

Nor were the Nez Perces treated humanely. Exiled to the Indian Territory for several years, they were eventually allowed to return to the Pacific Northwest but not to their homeland. Joseph died on the Colville Reservation in eastern Washington in 1904.

To the army and to the public at large, Howard's conduct during the Nez Perce War was the most conspicuous episode of his service in the Pacific Northwest. It dimmed his image both with the public and in the officer corps. The exchange of telegrams between Howard and his superiors became part of the public record, so all knew that he had wanted to call off the chase and leave the Nez Perces to other officers. In fact, despite several serious errors, he had done as well as almost any other general could have done, perhaps better. Yet the Nez Perce stigma clung to his record, like Chancellorsville and Gettysburg.

The more difficult Indian war that General Howard oversaw in the summer of 1878 was a different situation. The same congeries of tribes that General George Crook had conquered in 1866–68 once more rose against encroaching white settlers: Bannocks, Paiutes, Shoshones, Umatillas, and Sheepeaters. Throughout the summer of 1878, the campaign ranged across southern Idaho and eastern Oregon and Washington, featuring three decisive battles. The country was even more difficult than in the Nez Perce operation and the various enemy bands harder to separate and pin down. But Howard skillfully maneuvered his subordinate units to overcome the adversaries and compel their surrender. As he concluded: "The campaign has been a hard, long, and expensive one. Many of the troops have marched greater distances than during the Nez Perce war, and in all the services I have been called upon to render the government I have never known officers and soldiers to encounter and overcome greater obstacles."[11]

DEPARTMENT OF WEST POINT

Once again General Howard's pious, humanitarian reputation played a part in his next assignment. As he contended with the Nez Perces in the summer of 1877, the army experimented with further integration of black soldiers into the ranks. Two cavalry and two infantry regiments already consisted of black enlisted men and white officers. In 1870 West Point Military Academy admitted its first black cadet. Not until 1877, however, did one graduate. Henry Flipper had been ostracized and discriminated against by white cadets for four years. Earlier black cadets had encountered the same environment. All failed.

In April 1880 a scandal erupted that gained national attention and confronted authorities with a dilemma. Cadet Johnson C. Whittaker was found tied to his bed, cut up, bruised, and unconscious. He claimed that white cadets had been guilty of the attack. No one believed him, and he was accused of mutilating himself. The academy's superintendent, Major General John M. Schofield, claimed a sterling war record but badly mishandled the Whittaker case. He immediately judged Whittaker guilty and declared his belief that West Point should be closed to black cadets. Whittaker requested a court of inquiry, which made headlines throughout the country. The court upheld Schofield's decision. Adverse publicity, however, prompted him to ask for another command, which was hastily granted. In December 1880 President Rutherford B. Hayes summoned General Howard to Washington. Without even consulting General Sherman, he named Howard to the West Point superintendency.

As the motive for the change of command, the Whittaker case received no publicity. As General Sherman wrote to Howard, however, "I believe if you go to West Point, the inference will be that it has reference to this case, and to the race question, but I do not believe that West Point is the place to try the experiment of social equality."[12]

Howard took command on January 21, 1881, and quickly ordered a court-martial to determine the truth of Whittaker's claim. Brigadier General Nelson A. Miles sat as president when the court opened in June 1881. Again the verdict was guilty, but Secretary of War Robert T. Lincoln declared the proceedings invalid on a technicality, a decision ratified by President Chester Arthur. Nonetheless, on March 22, 1882, Lincoln ordered Whittaker dismissed for failing an examination.

Throughout the Whittaker ordeal, General Howard seems to have concerned himself with academy matters rather than with the court-martial. His tenure was limited to two years, the same period during which the Whittaker issue played out. On September 1, 1882, he turned over the superintendency of West Point to Colonel Wesley Merritt.[13]

Generals Schofield and Howard both served as superintendents of the military academy and as commanders of the Department of West Point. This afforded a billet for generals, but it proved unsatisfactory. The appointment of Colonel Merritt at West Point marked the close of this system, the academy's return to field-grade officers, and the abolition of the Department of West Point.

DEPARTMENT OF THE PLATTE

Howard's next assignment was to replace General George Crook in command of the Department of the Platte when Crook returned once again to the Department of Arizona to contend with the Apaches. In September 1882 Howard moved his family to Omaha, Nebraska, to take command of the

Department of the Platte, a part of the Military Division of the Missouri. For the first time, he fell under the command of Lieutenant General Philip H. Sheridan.

Crook's service in this department, beginning in 1875, was marked by almost continuous Indian difficulties, including active field operations, difficult negotiations, and oversight of contentious issues. By contrast, Howard inherited a benign department. The Sioux had been conquered and the Northern Cheyenne troubles suppressed. Indian hostilities no longer seemed probable, but Howard held training exercises to ensure that his troops were ready in the event of problems. Mainly he simply administered the department. He began writing and publishing articles and then books and as always immersed himself in church work. He lectured and traveled, once to Europe and once with his family to Yellowstone National Park. Howard University continued to require his attention and financial support.

MAJOR GENERAL

In late 1885 the approaching retirement of Major General John Pope set off the usual scramble among brigadiers for presidential appointment to the major general's vacancy. Howard was the senior brigadier, but Alfred Terry sought the promotion as well. When the death of General Winfield S. Hancock early in February 1886 created a second vacancy, Terry won the first opening and Howard the second, to rank from March 19, 1886.

As a major general, Howard now rated a division command. He received the Military Division of the Pacific, with headquarters at San Francisco. Howard's new assignment was as routine as the Department of the Platte, although General Nelson Miles often ignored him in conducting the Geronimo campaign in Arizona and dealt directly with General Sheridan in Washington. The assignment in San Francisco lasted only two years, when Sheridan's death and Terry's retirement opened the way for Howard's final transfer. Howard was ranked only by General Schofield, who took command of the army, leaving the most prestigious post to Howard. On December 12, 1888, Howard assumed command of the Division of the Atlantic, with headquarters on Governor's Island in New York Harbor. A pleasant six years passed before his retirement on November 8, 1894.

Settling in Burlington, Vermont, Howard continued to write and publish, including a book setting forth his version of the Nez Perce War. He also lectured extensively throughout the country and involved himself in the Spanish-American War with the Christian Commission.

Howard died in Burlington on October 26, 1909, at the age of seventy-six and was buried there.

Both in the Civil War and in the Indian Wars, Oliver Otis Howard had a checkered career. Despite mitigating circumstances, Chancellorsville and Gettysburg represented low points of his Civil War service, while Atlanta and the March to the Sea represented high points. The Nez Perce War, representing the high point of his postwar career, was only a qualified success. He made military mistakes and erroneous judgment calls. Another officer rightly claimed the victory, but Howard's sometime tenacity made that victory possible. The following year he conducted a near-flawless operation against Bannocks, Paiutes, and Shoshones.

When Howard stepped out of a purely military role, as in the long ordeal of the Freedmen's Bureau, he fell victim to forces beyond his control and even somewhat beyond his understanding. General Sherman plainly saw the traps that Howard set for himself and bluntly advised, then reproached him. His career would have been more successful had he heeded Sherman's sage advice to adhere strictly to the military profession.

Throughout his long career Howard's major drawback lay in his devout Christianity, aggravated by a conspicuous public display. It governed at least three of his appointments (the Freedmen's Bureau, Apache peace-making, and West Point) and held him up to the ridicule of less pious senior officers. It did not interfere with his military duties, but it did influence his relations with fellow officers.

By the standards of his time in the East and the West, Oliver Otis Howard's army service may be judged slightly above mediocre.

Brigadier General Nelson A. Miles, commanding
Department of the Columbia, 1881–1885;
Department of the Missouri, 1885–1886;
Department of Arizona, 1886–1888.
U.S. Army Military History Institute.

CHAPTER FIVE

NELSON A. MILES

$$=\!\!=\!\!\bigstar\!\bigstar\!=\!\!=$$

Vain, arrogant, ambitious, egotistical, dogmatic, obstinate, duplicitous, abrasive, petulant, quarrelsome, scheming: Nelson A. Miles was perhaps the frontier army's most detestable officer. As he verged on retirement, President Theodore Roosevelt labeled him "brave peacock," an apt description.[1] Yet Miles was the frontier army's most successful field officer. He triumphed not as a general but as a colonel of infantry. These successes entitle him to being recognized as superior to all other Indian fighters.

Miles's other major distinction, both in the Civil War and on the frontier, lay in his civilian origins. He did not attend West Point. He and Alfred Terry were the only two western department commanders who could not claim a West Point education. It seems not to have marred their careers, although the army contained officers who believed that West Point was essential to the military profession. In forty-three years Nelson A. Miles rose from first lieutenant to lieutenant general, the last commanding general in the history of the U.S. Army.

Born on August 6, 1839, on a farm near Westminster, Massachusetts, fifty-five miles west of Boston, Nelson Appleton Miles grew into a robust country lad with a scattering of formal education. As an adult occupation, however, farming did not appeal to him. He yearned for a more satisfying and prosperous life. For a farm youth of eighteen, Boston seemed to offer a path to prosperity. In 1857 Miles was working in a Boston fruit market and a year later in a crockery store. At the same time, recognizing his educational limitations, he enrolled in a commercial college.

CIVIL WAR

But commerce did not lie in Miles's future. He and a group of patriotic friends formed a drill club and persuaded a former French army colonel to instruct them. Their fervor intensified as the secession crisis split the nation in 1860 and 1861. After the Union's disastrous defeat at Bull Run in July 1861, Miles used family loans to recruit and equip a company of volunteers. By September seventy men had responded and elected him as their captain. Captain Miles offered his company's service to Governor John A. Andrew. The unit became Company E of the Twenty-Second Massachusetts Infantry, but not with Miles its captain. The governor judged him not mature enough at twenty-two and commissioned him a first lieutenant, to date from October 7, 1861.

The regiment camped across the Potomac from Washington and took its place as part of General George B. McClellan's Army of the Potomac. Dull routine prompted Lieutenant Miles to scout the army for more promising opportunities. He attracted the attention of brigade commander Brigadier General Oliver O. Howard and early in November won appointment as aide on the general's staff. Howard, called the "Christian General" because of his deep piety, grew fond of the young officer and granted him the flexibility to observe the workings of the army.

When General McClellan moved the Army of the Potomac by ship to the Virginia peninsula with the objective of seizing Richmond from the southeast, the ensuing Seven Days Battle gave Miles his first exposure to combat. At the Battle of Fair Oaks, on May 31, 1862, Howard dispatched his aide to try to rally a crumbling regiment that had lost its field officers. Although wounded in the foot, Miles zealously and courageously carried out his assignment. Howard and other ranking officers praised his conduct. Fair Oaks also brought Miles close to General Howard, who sustained a wound that required the amputation of his right arm. In the field hospital Miles held up his general's arm while a surgeon sawed it off.

Such was the untrained youth's baptism of fire. With Howard out of action, Miles fought in the remaining battles of the peninsular campaign as an aide to Brigadier General John C. Caldwell. He made up for his lack of formal training by demonstrating that he could excel in combat. In each battle he earned commendations for bravery and leadership. A newfound friend, Lieutenant Colonel (and future general) Francis Barlow, had observed Miles's battlefield conduct and urged the governor of New York to commission him in a New York regiment. With rank backdated to May 31, 1862, Lieutenant Miles became Lieutenant Colonel Miles of the Sixty-First New York. Boasting a brief but sterling combat record and acutely aware of the importance of influential friends, Nelson Miles began his climb up the chain of command.

On September 17, 1862, the Sixty-First New York, combined with another New York regiment, entered the Battle of Antietam, Maryland, under the command of General Francis Barlow. In an assault on Confederate lines, Barlow was wounded. Command of the two regiments fell to Lieutenant Colonel Miles. Once again he acquitted himself so handsomely that superiors showered him with praise. He emerged a full colonel one year after he had been commissioned first lieutenant.

At Fredericksburg on December 10, 1862, Colonel Miles and his New Yorkers were in the thick of the fight when storming Mayre's Heights proved a futile, bloody catastrophe. A bullet struck him in the throat but did not disable him. Miles pleaded for authority to continue the advance, but his superiors wisely ordered withdrawal. Fulsome acclaim followed the colonel into convalescence with his family in Massachusetts.

Back with the army in time for the Battle of Chancellorsville, on May 2, 1863, Miles led his regiment in combat with his accustomed competence. Astride his horse, he presented a good target for a Georgia sharpshooter, who put a round in Miles's stomach. The bullet buried itself in his hip. Miles fell from his horse paralyzed from the waist down. Once more he convalesced at his Massachusetts home.

Miles remained away from the front for almost a year, largely to accommodate the slow healing process. He accepted other assignments to pass the time but early in 1864 took command of a five-regiment brigade in General Barlow's First Division of General Winfield Scott Hancock's Second Corps. The Battle of the Wilderness in May 1864, leading to the deadly conflict at Spotsylvania Courthouse, left the division and brigade with heavy casualties but afforded Miles further opportunity to distinguish himself. Impressed, Generals Barlow, Hancock, and George G. Meade all urged that Miles be promoted to brigadier general of Volunteers. The Senate agreed, again with a backdated rank of May 12, 1864.

On June 3 General Miles's brigade advanced in the forefront of the assault on Lee's entrenched lines at Cold Harbor. The terrible casualties of Cold

Harbor prompted General Grant to abandon frontal attacks and instead lead his army in a circling movement east around Richmond to the rail junction of Petersburg. Siege lines wrapped around Petersburg on the south. With the rest of the Army of the Potomac, Miles and his men fortified positions for a long siege.

In July Pennsylvania coal miners in General Burnside's Ninth Corps conceived a plan of tunneling under the Confederate lines and blowing them up. While the digging progressed, Hancock joined his corps with others to stage a diversion north of the James River. At Deep Bottom on July 27 the Union forces attacked Confederate entrenchments. As had become customary, Miles's brigade took the lead. The assault failed but achieved the intended diversionary effect.

On July 30, from their positions on the Petersburg line, Miles and his men observed the huge explosion that blew up part of the Confederate defenses and created a deep crater. Union troops rushed into the crater and became disorganized. Confederates rallied on the rim and swept the bottom with heavy rifle fire, turning the Battle of the Crater into a deadly fiasco. Miles's brigade played no part in this battle, but the general sat on a board to fix blame for the disaster.

On August 14 Hancock launched another effort at Deep Bottom. It failed, and Miles's brigade suffered 274 casualties in the fruitless attack.

On August 17 General Barlow, suffering from exhaustion and wounds received at Antietam and Gettysburg, relinquished command of his division to Brigadier General Miles and returned to his New York home for recuperation. Burdened by a large infusion of inexperienced recruits, Miles's division did little to distinguish itself in occasional skirmishes that followed second Deep Bottom. Nonetheless, his division participated in the Battle of Reim's Station on August 25, part of an operation to tear up a railroad link essential to the Confederates in Petersburg. When a furious Southern attack on Miles's position punctured his lines, only the vigorous efforts of Hancock and Miles rallied enough troops to plug the gap. Despite the poor performance of the Second Corps, Miles was brevetted major general of volunteers for Reim's Station.

The final campaign of the Army of the Potomac opened in spring 1865 with Grant's attempt to breech the Petersburg defenses. Hancock had departed the Second Corps, which was now commanded by Major General Andrew J. Humphreys. Miles's First Division fought in the Battle of Five

Forks, on April 1–2, which led to General Lee's evacuation of Petersburg. On the second day Miles threw his division at the critical rail junction of Sutherland's Station. Twice the division was repulsed, but the third attack overwhelmed the defenders and earned Miles further distinction and commendation from both Generals Meade and Grant.

The First Division played a prominent part in the series of battles that traced the flight of Lee's Army of Northern Virginia up the Appomattox River to the denouement at Appomattox Courthouse.

The young Boston crockery clerk emerged from the Civil War as an outstanding professional soldier. Miles quickly acquired the skills and insights that made him a military success. Brave and prudent under fire, bold in executing battlefield maneuvers, solicitous for the welfare of his men, he evolved into an ideal combat commander. His exploits gained the acclamation of superiors from Generals Barlow through Hancock, Meade, Humphreys, and finally Grant. The army recognized his merit the following October with appointment as major general of volunteers. By then he had resolved to make the army his career.[2]

General Miles led his division in the march back to Washington but was not permitted to lead it in the grand parade up Pennsylvania Avenue on May 24. Five days earlier he had been called to report at once to General Grant's headquarters. The general-in-chief informed him that he had been selected to command the Military District of Fort Monroe, Virginia, and that he should depart at once. The assignment, however, was far more than a district command. Miles was also to serve as Jefferson Davis's jailer. The Confederate president had been seized on May 10 and now was aboard a steamer anchored off the fort awaiting transfer to his imprisonment. Miles conducted him and a former Southern senator to their cell, one of the fort's gun casements.

The task was difficult and controversial. Davis and later his wife hated Miles and stirred up as much opposition as possible. The War Department, fearing an escape attempt but concerned for Davis's health, bombarded Miles with contradictory instructions. Newspapers ran any condemnations they could find. For fifteen months Miles endured the demands and disputes of the position. He also worried about his future, imploring Secretary Stanton to find him a place suitable for his rank.

The Army Act of July 28, 1866, brought Miles appointment to the Regular Army. With testimonials from Generals Howard, Hancock, Sheridan, and

Meade, he received the colonelcy of the Fortieth Infantry. It was a black regiment, yet to be recruited, and represented a lower rank than Miles believed he deserved.

Miles and his new regiment drew assignment to Reconstruction duty in North Carolina. It proved as contentious as his watch over Jefferson Davis and lasted longer, nearly three years. As a subordinate in General Howard's Freedmen's Bureau, Miles had to deal with North Carolina politicians, the Ku Klux Klan, irate white Southerners, and the bureaucracy of the Freedmen's Bureau. He survived an angry clash with General Meade and otherwise performed his duty satisfactorily. He also found time to indulge what would become a lifetime habit—seeking support from influential politicians and army officers. Frequent trips to Washington abetted this effort. During one such stay in 1867, he fell in love with Mary Sherman, daughter of a federal judge and niece of Senator John Sherman and General William T. Sherman. Married on June 30, 1868, Miles and his wife exploited the family relationship in an effort to advance his military ambitions throughout his career. Sherman abhorred influence peddling, but that failed to deter his niece's husband. Mile's thirst for preferment sustained years of labor, most of which succeeded only in exasperating the general.

DEPARTMENT OF THE PLATTE

On March 4, 1869, Ulysses S. Grant took the oath of president. The day before, Congress had cut the size of the Regular Army from 54,000 to 37,313. The Fortieth Infantry was one of the casualties. The army reduction doomed Miles's efforts to win a brigadier's star, but he managed to be transferred to Kansas as colonel of the Fifth Infantry. Most of the balance of his career would center on the West and its Indians. Nothing in his eastern background prepared him for the West, but he adapted quickly and soon amassed a record in Indian warfare overshadowing his Civil War record.

Miles and his regiment were assigned to the Department of the Platte. His superior at Fort Leavenworth, Kansas, was Brigadier General John Pope. Miles rarely enjoyed amicable relations with any superior, and Pope proved no exception.

Like other regiments posted to the West, the Fifth's companies were scattered among several posts in Kansas to guard the overland emigrant trails and the railroads. Miles established regimental headquarters at Fort

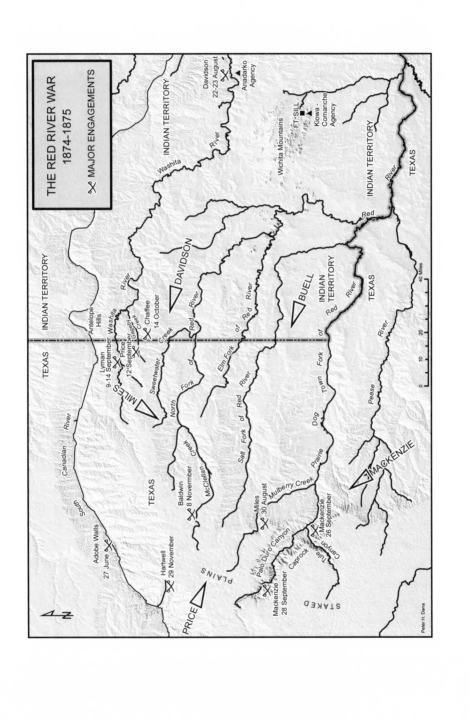

THE RED RIVER WAR
1874-1875

⚔ MAJOR ENGAGEMENTS

INDIAN TERRITORY

Davidson
22-23 August

Anadarko
Agency

Ft. SILL
Kiowa -
Comanche
Agency

Wichita Mountains

INDIAN TERRITORY

TEXAS

Red

River

Washita

River

INDIAN TERRITORY

TEXAS

Antelope
Hills

Washita

River

DAVIDSON

Chaffee
14 October

Sweetwater Creek

Price
12 September
(Gageby) Creek

Red River

Lyman
9-14 September

MILES

North Fork of Red River

Elm Fork of Red River

BUELL

INDIAN
TERRITORY

Red River

TEXAS

McClellan Creek

Baldwin
8 November

Salt Fork of Red River

Dog Town Fork of Red River

Prairie

Pease River

MACKENZIE

Canadian River

South

Adobe Walls
27 June

Hartwell
29 November

TEXAS

Mulberry Creek

Miles
30 August

Mackenzie
26 September

Palo Duro Canyon

Caprock

Tule
Canyon

PLAINS

Mackenzie
28 September

STAKED

0   10   20   40 Miles

Peter H. Dana

N

Hays, where he became close friends with another Civil War general, Lieutenant Colonel George A. Custer of the Seventh Cavalry. They remained
friends for the years remaining to the cavalryman. However, Miles moved
his headquarters to the more comfortable Fort Harker and then in 1871 to
the even more comfortable Fort Leavenworth. Mary quickly adapted to
role of the regimental commander's wife and continued to use her family
connections to further her husband's career.

For the next three years routine assignments, combined with incessant
politicking, occupied Miles. General Sherman in particular felt the brunt
of his quests for higher or more active commands. At length, the Red River
War of 1874–75 afforded Miles his first opportunity for an Indian campaign.

The Kiowas and Comanches occupied the Fort Sill Reservation, the
Cheyennes and Arapahos the Darlington Reservation on the north. The
Kiowas and Comanches continued their long tradition of raiding south into
Texas, while the Cheyennes and Arapahos less frequently, but under strong
provocation, raided into Kansas. Under President Grant's "Peace Policy,"
the reservations were sacrosanct. The army was barred from pursuing
raiders into them.

Aggravating the tradition of raids was the widespread slaughter of the
bison herds by professional hunters. When a group of hunters built a trading
post called Adobe Walls in the Texas Panhandle, Cheyennes and Comanches
attacked it on June 27, 1874. The warriors could not match high-powered
rifles in the hands of skilled marksmen and were beaten off with severe
losses. Angry, they stepped up the pace of raiding.

The secretary of the interior yielded to the imprecations of the army and
dropped the ban excluding the military from the reservations. On July 20,
1874, General Sherman alerted Lieutenant General Sheridan, commanding
the Division of the Missouri, to declare war. Registration of the "friendlies"
at the agencies led to the flight of "hostiles" west to the Staked Plains of the
Texas Panhandle and the intervening country drained by the Washita and
Red Rivers. Sheridan directed three columns to converge on this country.

The campaign involved two departments: General John Pope's Department of the Missouri and General Christopher Augur's Department of
Texas. Augur launched three commands: Lieutenant Colonel John W.
Davidson west from Fort Sill, Lieutenant Colonel George P. Buell northwest from Fort Griffin, and Colonel Ranald S. Mackenzie north from Fort

Concho. Pope oversaw two commands: Major William R. Price east from
Fort Union, New Mexico, and Colonel Nelson A. Miles south from Fort
Dodge, Kansas.

Miles's command consisted of four companies of his Fifth Infantry
and eight troops of the Sixth Cavalry: 744 officers and men, together with
a howitzer and a Gatling gun. Of special value was the unit of scouts,
commanded by First Lieutenant Frank D. Baldwin: 29 Delaware Indians,
17 white frontiersmen, and a detachment of 18 Sixth Cavalrymen. Baldwin
was a distinguished Civil War veteran, noted for bravery at the Battle of
Peachtree Creek, Georgia. Miles came to rely heavily on him, especially
because the Fifth Infantry contained many laggard officers unfriendly to
their colonel and others verging on disability because of alcoholism.[3]

Miles's command confronted a more deadly enemy than Indians late
that summer: weather and terrain. Drought of unusual length, searing
heat, dry riverbeds, and alkaline waterholes plagued the men, who grew
so desperate that some opened their veins for blood.

As Miles's column approached the base of the Staked Plains on August 30,
his advance guard, consisting of Baldwin's scouts, came under fire from
about 200 Cheyennes. The Delaware Indians and the white scouts repulsed
the charging Cheyennes, and Miles quickly brought the main force into
action. With the infantry in the center and a cavalry squadron on each
flank, he advanced from one ridge to another. At each ridge the Indians,
now numbering about 600 with the addition of Kiowas and Comanches,
spread out to make a stand. As he reached each ridge, Miles unlimbered
his artillery and swept the defensive lines, while the infantry and cavalry
charged. Abandoning their villages, the Indians retreated up Tule Canyon
to the top of the Staked Plains. Lack of supplies stalled Miles's pursuit, so
his command fell back to await supplies after destroying the Indian villages.
Even so, Miles had won his first Indian fight.[4]

On September 7 the weather abruptly changed. Unrelenting storms
pounded the plains, rivers overflowed, and the thinly grassed prairies turned
to mud. Immobilized by the drenching rains and deep mud, Miles seethed
at the quartermasters' slow forwarding of supplies, the incompetence of
some of his officers, and the criticism of department commander General
Pope. Meanwhile, on September 9 about 250 Kiowa and Comanche warriors
attacked Miles's supply train. Captain Wyllys Lyman corralled his thirty-six

wagons, and his infantry and cavalry escort threw back repeated warrior charges. The siege lasted three days under cold, drenching rains. Only the approach of Major Price's cavalry from New Mexico, skirmishing with Indians as they advanced, caused the besiegers to withdraw.

With Indians harassing his supply line and the weather preventing active operations, Miles settled his command in camps along the Washita and South Canadian Rivers and Sweetwater Creek. From the beginning of the campaign, Miles's major concern had been that another officer would strike the first blow and deprive him of the honor. He especially feared the aggressive Colonel Mackenzie, then advancing north from General Augur's department. Miles's battle of August 30 at Tule Canyon had given him the honor of the first victory, but Mackenzie's surprise attack on a large village of Kiowas, Comanches, and Cheyennes in Palo Duro Canyon on September 28 robbed Miles of much of the glory. Mackenzie inflicted few casualties but destroyed several hundred lodges and large quantities of stores.

Miles's complaints to Pope about the sluggish quartermaster system brought no reform and irritated the department commander. In October, even though the other commands were returning to their bases, Miles resolved to continue the campaign with a winter offensive on the Staked Plains. A routine assignment, however, intervened to reward him with a victory. On November 4, from the headquarters camp on the Red River at the foot of the Staked Plains, Miles dispatched the trustworthy and talented Lieutenant Baldwin to conduct twenty-three empty wagons drawn by six-mule teams to a supply camp on the Washita River. Baldwin commanded an escort of a troop of cavalry, a company of infantry, twelve scouts, and a howitzer, and Miles authorized him to attack any Indians he encountered.

Encounter them he did. On November 8, in the breaks of McClellan Creek, Baldwin discovered a Cheyenne village estimated to contain 600, including 200 warriors. When they came out to fight, Baldwin handled his men skillfully, attacking with cavalry on one flank and infantry on the other, using his howitzer charged with canister. For four and a half hours, charge and countercharge ranged back and forth on the level plain. Baldwin brought up the wagon train, loaded his infantry in wagons, and led an unorthodox assault that surprised and routed the Indians. In the abandoned village he found not only plunder to be destroyed but two little white girls, named Germain, taken captive in Kansas when the Cheyennes had ambushed their train and killed their parents. The girls reported two other sisters in captivity. The Battle of McClellan Creek gained more notoriety than Miles's Battle of Tule Canyon and also earned Baldwin a Medal of Honor.[5]

With the other columns back in their posts, on January 2, 1875, Miles undertook his final winter operation, a giant swing around the western edges of the Staked Plains. Winter storms pounded the area of operations. Although freezing weather tormented the troops, the infantrymen remained in high spirits, singing "Marching through Georgia" as they trudged across the frozen wastes. A month later, on February 3, the command marched into the Washita supply base. At Camp Supply Miles disbanded the expedition.

The operations of the five columns accomplished Sheridan's objective. The Indians began to surrender as early as October, and most of the balance had reported to their agencies by March 1875. Among the last to turn themselves in were Gray Beard and his Cheyennes, who also yielded the two older Germain sisters. Miles labored in behalf of the sisters and finally obtained congressional appropriations for their relief.

The Red River War ended hostilities on the southern plains and introduced Colonel Miles to Indian fighting and to the American West. He embraced both and profited from them, professionally and personally. The Battle of Tule Canyon and the winter sweep of the Staked Plains contributed to the surrender of the Indians. They also formed the first chapter in the evolution of Colonel Nelson A. Miles into the West's premier Indian fighter.

DEPARTMENT OF DAKOTA

Back at Fort Leavenworth after the Red River War, Miles and Mary settled into the comfortable life that the big fort afforded them. As 1876 opened with a brewing war against the Sioux and Cheyennes of the northern plains, Miles nevertheless restlessly eyed the possibility that he would be left out. The advance into the Powder River country of a column under General George Crook stoked a jealous animosity that would become chronic. Winter weather, however, had forced Crook to give up the expedition and join with two other columns in the same converging strategy that had won the Red River War. Early July 1876 brought news of the annihilation of part of the Seventh Cavalry and the death of the Miles's friend George A. Custer. Soon orders arrived for Miles to load six companies of the Fifth Infantry on vessels and steam up the Missouri and Yellowstone Rivers to General Alfred Terry's base camp. On August 2 the regiment debarked on the Yellowstone at the mouth of the Rosebud River, joining six companies of the Twenty-Second Infantry that had landed there the day before. The rest of the Fifth would arrive later.

Unlike the relative independence of command that Miles enjoyed in the Red River War, he found himself closely confined on the Yellowstone by a brigadier traumatized by the Little Bighorn. Lieutenant Baldwin recorded in his diary and letters the frustration felt by all of Miles's command over the slowness of General Terry to move out in search of the Indians' trail.[6]

Finally, the column broke camp on August 8 and marched up the Rosebud. On August 10 Terry's column moving south met General Crook's column moving north. The two generals decided to follow the Indian trail east toward the Tongue. Miles could predict how that would end: two cautious generals leading a ponderous army that would fail to close with the enemy. Anxious to distance himself from such a debacle, he persuaded Terry to send him and his six companies back to the Yellowstone. His mission would be to patrol the Yellowstone from the Tongue to the Powder and intercept any Indians seeking to cross to the north.[7] For Miles, the mission was not as important as an independent command. This mission was merely a step toward building his record further as an Indian fighter.

Adding to Miles's good fortune, General Sheridan decided to occupy the Yellowstone country during the winter. Miles would have the responsibility, with all ten companies of his Fifth Infantry and six companies of the Twenty-Second. He would build a cantonment at the mouth of Tongue River to shelter the troops during the winter. All other troops in the field, as well as General Terry, would return to their stations.[8] Still in the field, of course, were the Sioux and Cheyennes. Miles could anticipate that the cantonment would serve not only as a shelter but also as a base for active campaigning, which began even before winter descended.

Sitting Bull, the reigning chief at the Little Bighorn, had separated from the rest of the fleeing Sioux and on October 10 crossed to the north side of the Yellowstone, seeking bison. Five days later he fell on a wagon train, escorted by infantry, carrying winter supplies from a steamboat landing to Miles's cantonment. Alerted, Miles led his regiment down the Yellowstone River to rescue the train, which had succeeded in defending itself until Miles arrived. After ensuring the train's safety, he turned north to give chase to Sitting Bull, who had disengaged.

The regiment quickly overtook Sitting Bull's camp, which was halted for the men to take advantage of a large bison herd. Under a flag of truce, a Sioux delegation advanced on Miles. After some awkward contretemps, Miles sat facing his antagonist as a French mixed-blood scout in the Indian camp interpreted. Sitting Bull stated his terms: he would not shoot at the soldiers if they got out of his country. Miles stated his terms: surrender and go to the agencies. Another council convened the next day, with the same result. Neither would yield. On the third day, October 21, both sides prepared for battle. The Sioux drew up on a ridge line as Miles formed his regiment below and attacked, with his foot soldiers advancing and firing their long rifles. Abandoning one line after another, the Indians finally fled the scene. Heading south toward the Yellowstone, they also dropped most of their possessions along the way.

Miles followed, and for forty-two miles the two sides skirmished. The Indians crossed the Yellowstone and halted for a parley with the soldier chief. On October 26 five chiefs representing four hundred lodges talked with Miles and agreed to surrender. Sitting Bull was not among them. He and thirty lodges had broken off and turned north. The chiefs agreed to leave hostages with Miles to ensure that their people reported to their agencies. For Miles, Sitting Bull was now the quarry.[9]

On November 6 the Fifth Infantry turned north again, probing the broken terrain between the Yellowstone and the Missouri Rivers. Winter set in with a vengeance, blasting the country with "northers," dropping temperatures far below zero, and freezing the Missouri River. The troops suffered acutely in such winter clothing as the government provided. Miles draped himself in the furry hide of a bear, which led the Indians to name him "Bear Coat." Reaching the Missouri, he divided his regiment into three battalions and scoured the river bottoms east and west of the Fort Peck trading post, located where the Milk and Musselshell Rivers joined the Missouri. Strengthened by a hundred lodges led by other chiefs, Sitting Bull remained in the area, hoping that the soldiers would leave and he could trade at Fort Peck for ammunition. A runner had brought a message from Crazy Horse, south of the Yellowstone, asking Sitting Bull to obtain ammunition and bring his people to join him.

Three weeks of maneuvering in freezing, stormy weather failed to pin down Sitting Bull, now the head of about 120 lodges. Leaving the ever-reliable Lieutenant Baldwin on the Missouri, Miles marched the rest of the regiment into the Tongue River cantonment on December 14. Sitting Bull had obtained enough ammunition from traders and friendly Indians to move south for a union with Crazy Horse. On November 18, as Sitting Bull began breaking camp, Baldwin discovered him on Red Water Creek. Baldwin's three companies stormed into the Sioux village and quickly seized it. The occupants fled without casualties but with only what they wore on their backs. Baldwin burned the village and its contents and acquired enough bison robes to outfit the regiment in genuine cold-weather gear. He brought his command into the cantonment on December 23.[10]

Bear Coat's operations against Sitting Bull from October to December 1876 lifted him to high rank among the army's Indian fighters. No other field officer could have persisted so steadily against snow, ice, storms, and subzero weather and finally, thanks to Lieutenant Baldwin, claim to have routed Sitting Bull. This was a stellar achievement, and Miles knew it. Even in the midst of the campaign, in camp near Fort Peck, he could not help boasting of it to his wife's uncle. He could have captured Sitting Bull's whole outfit, he wrote to General Sherman on November 18 (bypassing both Terry and Sheridan), if he had one battalion of cavalry. "If you expect me to be successful," the colonel lectured the general-in-chief, "see that I am supported or give me command of the whole region and I will soon end this Sioux war." He went on to inform Sherman of his ambition to hold one of two positions: secretary of war or commander of a department. For the next eight years, until Sherman retired, Miles never perceived that such effrontery was unwelcome, unseemly, and unmilitary.[11]

Miles still had Sioux to contend with. Crazy Horse and his followers had established their winter camp on the upper Tongue River, near the Montana-Wyoming border. The chiefs were divided over whether to surrender or not. Miles had made contact with them and invited leaders into the cantonment to talk peace. On December 16, 1876, a delegation of chiefs accepted the invitation and approached the cantonment. Crow scouts camped nearby greeted five chiefs leading the group, surrounded them, and butchered them. The rest of the delegation fled back to their village. Aware of their offense and of Miles's furious reaction, the Crows quickly decamped, but the incident quelled the argument in Crazy Horse's camp.[12]

On December 27, 1876, undeterred by the winter weather, Miles marched up the Tongue to do battle with Crazy Horse. The command consisted of his entire regiment and two companies of the Twenty-Second Infantry, four hundred men strong, warmed by the buffalo robes Baldwin had captured at Red Water. The troops forced Crazy Horse to abandon his winter village of six hundred lodges and move up the Tongue into the canyons of the Wolf Mountains. On January 8, 1877, about six hundred warriors drew up to fight the foot soldiers there. Miles deployed his companies in line and for five hours contended with repeated attacks by forces of mounted warriors. Each assault was driven off, with the aid of a cannon hauled up in a wagon. The battle ended when a blizzard swept the battlefield, obscuring vision. Army casualties totaled three killed and eight wounded. Judging from bloodstains on the snow and ice, Miles believed that he had inflicted "severe" losses on the Sioux.[13]

The Battle of Wolf Mountain, once more in the teeth of a plains winter, added another well-deserved achievement to Miles's record. Even before dispatching his official report, he boasted of Wolf Mountain in another obnoxious missive to General Sherman, this time also heaping scorn on General Terry:

> I am satisfied that there is criminal neglect of duty at St. Paul or there is a determination that I shall not accomplish anything.... Now if I have not earned a command I never will, and if I have not given proof of my ability to bring my command into success-ful encounter with Indians every time I never will ... and unless you can give me a command and it should be no less than a department you can order my regiment out of this country as soon as you like for I have campaigned long enough for the benefit of thieves and contractors. If you will give me this com-mand and *one half the troops now in it, I will end this Sioux war once and forever in four months.*[14]

While Miles battled the Sioux north and south of the Yellowstone, Gen-eral Crook led another expedition north from the Platte. In equally harsh winter weather Crook's cavalry commander, Colonel Ranald S. Mackenzie, had stormed into a canyon of the Bighorn Mountains and struck a Cheyenne village. About forty Indians died, and the rest fled into the mountains with no clothing or stores. In freezing weather they staggered north to find succor with Crazy Horse. The weather proved too severe for Crook, who disbanded the expedition. The operations of both Miles and Crook fueled the peace sentiment in the Sioux villages, however, and both officers sought to entice the bands into surrender, to Miles at the cantonment or to Crook at Red Cloud Agency.

The success of his rival Crook, especially at the hands of his rival Mackenzie, motivated Miles to step up his effort to get the Sioux to surrender to him instead of to Crook. It also prompted him to heap his scorn for Crook on Sherman. Reacting to a fancied slight in the newspapers, and without naming Crook, he ridiculed the general's record from the beginning of the Sioux War to the latest operation. "These insinuations," he wrote, "come with very poor grace from a man who was a failure during the war and has been ever since."[15] Such antagonism defined the relationship between the two—and their acolytes—until Crook's death.

To Miles's chagrin, Crook won the contest for the largest number of Sioux and Cheyennes to give up. Responding to Miles's emissaries, three hundred people, mostly Cheyennes, came into the Tongue River cantonment on April 22. Crook, however, had persuaded Spotted Tail to go among the various camps and offer the possibility of better terms. On May 6 Crazy Horse himself led the final group to surrender at Red Cloud Agency. The number who gathered in the south amounted to more than three thousand. That left Sitting Bull and Lame Deer, who refused to yield. Two weeks after the Battle of Wolf Mountain, Sitting Bull had arrived in Crazy Horse's village with the requested ammunition. Sensing the growing sentiment for surrender, he turned his following to the north, ultimately to join other chiefs in the land of the "Great Mother" across the boundary. That left only Lame Deer, Miles's next objective.

Miles assembled a command consisting of four troops of the Second Cavalry from Fort Ellis, two companies of the Fifth Infantry and four of the Twenty-Second, 10 officers and 155 enlisted men. On May 1 they marched up the Tongue River, now free of snow. On May 5 they came on Lame Deer's trail, heading west to the Rosebud. The next day scouts located the Indian camp. A night march placed the command in position for a dawn attack. At 4:30 A.M. the advance guard stormed into the village of fifty-one lodges, seized the herd of 450 ponies, and drove the Indians into the steep, pine-covered bluffs to the west. With the full command on line, the soldiers pursued the Sioux in a running fight for six miles back to the Rosebud. Miles reported fourteen dead left on the field, including Lame Deer and the head warrior, Iron Star.

Miles's official report noted only that, in response to a demand to surrender, several Indians advanced as if to comply but then renewed firing. "This ended all pacific measures," he wrote, but he failed to tell the whole story. As described by a participant in a letter to the *Army and Navy Journal*, two Indians, Lame Deer and Iron Star, responding to the demand to surrender, warily approached Miles, with one hand extended and the other holding a carbine. Miles shook hands with Lame Deer, the adjutant with Iron Star. Miles motioned for them to lay down their arms. They did. Miles ordered a lieutenant to pick them up. As the officer bent to retrieve Iron Star's weapon, he suddenly seized the carbine, stepped back, and fired at Miles. At that instant, Miles shifted to bring up his rifle, which was laid over his saddle. His horse jerked slightly, causing the bullet to miss Miles and kill a cavalry trooper to his rear. Thus ended "pacific measures," as well as the lives of Lame Deer and Iron Star.[16]

The Battle of Muddy Creek cost Miles four enlisted men killed and one officer and seven enlisted men wounded, testimony to the tenacity of the Sioux resistance. Lame Deer's people had thirty killed, twenty wounded, and forty captured, testimony to the tenacity of Miles's veteran soldiers. The village contained thirty tons of dried meat, rifles, and ammunition as well as two hundred saddles.

Despite the casualties, Miles could rightly boast of an overwhelming victory against his adversaries at Muddy Creek, but Sitting Bull still worried him. Now in Canada with other bands of Sioux that had joined him, he might launch excursions across the border to hunt bison or commit depredations. Miles knew that Sitting Bull had met with the North-West Mounted Police but fretted that, whatever his agreement with the Canadian authorities, the chief could not control his young men. Miles wanted to take the field again to watch the border and if necessary cross it to punish errant Sioux.

The problem was more complicated than that. The Sioux had made friends with the chief of the redcoats, Major James M. Walsh. He and his superiors assured Sitting Bull that he and his people could live in the Great Mother's land so long as they obeyed her laws and did not venture back across the border. The issue, however, quickly became entangled in diplomacy between Canada (represented by London) and the United States. Canada wanted to shed responsibility for the Sioux altogether by persuading them to go home and surrender to the American authorities. The Sioux refused to leave a land of such freedom. For its part, the United States wanted the Canadians to take full responsibility for the Sioux or force them to surrender. Under such circumstances, it was risky to allow the volatile Nelson Miles near the border.

On July 16, 1877, a steamer docked at the Tongue River cantonment and landed Generals Sherman and Terry. Amid a round of inspections and ceremonies, Sherman found time to address Secretary of War George W. McCrary, about documents that he had received from the secretary of state setting forth the Canadian view of the Sitting Bull problem. In his usual blunt fashion, the general set forth the military position:

> The English authorities should *now* elect to adopt these refugee
> Indians as their own, or force them back to our side of the line
> before they recuperate their ponies and collect new supplies of
> ammunition. If these Indians numbering about fifteen hundred
> of the very worst class, be permitted to recuperate and to use
> British Territory as a base of operations against us, the act will
> surely be equivalent to an act of hostilities, which I am sure the
> English authorities do not intend.

Sherman added that "General Miles, commanding here, is very anxious to go to the border with a sufficient force to demand of the British agents that these Indians . . . be surrendered to him."[17]

Calmer minds prevailed, and a commission headed by General Terry journeyed to Fort Walsh, the police headquarters. On October 17, 1877, the commissioners met with Sitting Bull and other chiefs. Predictably, Sitting Bull flatly and rudely turned down General Terry's plea for the Sioux to return to the United States. The diplomatic stalemate continued.

Although still "very anxious" to march north to confront Sitting Bull once more, Miles remained at the cantonment overseeing construction of a permanent fort two miles to the west. It would be named Fort Keogh, after one of Custer's captains. Miles was also responsible for a second fort, Fort Custer, at the mouth of the Little Bighorn River. As General Terry made his way to Canada in the autumn of 1877, another issue distracted Miles. His old mentor and longtime friend Oliver O. Howard was pursing Nez Perce Indians from Idaho across the mountains to the plains. His mission had been to confine the Nez Perces to reservations marked out in Idaho, but they gathered with their chiefs, including Chief Joseph, and bolted to the east, hoping to find sanctuary with their friends the Crows or even Sitting Bull in Canada. General Howard exhausted his command and himself chasing the Nez Perces but could not overtake the quarry. A courier from Howard reached Fort Keogh on September 17, bringing a plea for Miles to try to head off the Nez Perces before they could reach Canada.

Miles reacted promptly, crossing the Yellowstone the next morning. As finally assembled, the expedition consisted of four companies of his own regiment mounted on Indian ponies seized at the Battle of Muddy Creek, three troops of the Seventh Cavalry, and three of the Second diverted from their mission of escorting General Terry to his Canadian rendezvous with Sitting Bull. Artillery, Indian scouts, and a long supply train of wagons and mules, guarded by another company of the Fifth Infantry, completed the column. The command numbered between 350 and 400 men.

The column marched rapidly to the Missouri River, where Miles learned that the Nez Perces had already crossed and were moving toward Canada. He commandeered a passing steamer and ferried his troops across for another march to the northwest. On September 30 he caught the Nez Perces in camp at Bear Paw Mountains. The attack proved costly, with twenty-two enlisted men killed and thirty-eight wounded. Nez Perce marksmen singled out officers and sergeants and hit six officers, two mortally. Seven sergeants were killed and three sergeants and two corporals wounded. Miles called off the battle and settled in for a siege. It lasted for five days; on the fourth day General Howard arrived on the scene. He generously permitted Miles to remain in command and, when the Nez Perces surrendered the next day, to receive the surrender.[18]

The Battle of Bear Paw Mountains added another star to Miles's record as an Indian fighter. He had sustained unusually heavy casualties but had prevented the bulk of the Nez Perces from reaching Canada, where Sitting Bull was indeed waiting. Marring the victory, however, he trumpeted his success without granting Howard much credit. Howard reacted, and the two waged war on each other for nearly a year before General Sherman ordered them to stop. The friendship that began at Fair Oaks in 1862, when Howard lost his arm, ended at Bear Paw Mountain in 1877.

By spring 1878 the threat posed by Sitting Bull that Miles and his superior had predicted began to materialize. Sitting Bull's original following of 800 lodges (including 45 lodges of Nez Perces that succeeded in reaching Canada) had been strengthened by 240 more lodges of Crazy Horse's people, who had fled the Red Cloud Agency after the chief's death in September 1877. That amounted to some 5,000 people, including about 1,500 warriors. Furthermore, the herds of bison, struck down by hide-hunters, had begun to decline precipitously. The tribes native to Canada that depended on the herds took offense at sharing them with the Sioux. As hunger stalked all the camps, parties inevitably crept across the boundary to bring meat home and also to commit depredations.

Eager to chastise the Sioux, Miles began to assemble a command at Fort Keogh as early as January 1878 to march to the boundary country. General Sherman read about these preparations in the newspapers and immediately made his views known to Sheridan and Terry. The government had no wish to provoke a war with "renegades" who wandered back and forth across the border, he declared. If any large body of Sioux came south toward the Yellowstone, Miles should attack them. If Terry was certain that a large confederation of tribes had moved south of the boundary intending to attack settlements or to interrupt traffic on the Missouri River, he should send three converging columns against them, from Forts Buford, Benton, and Keogh. Doubtless with the impulsive Miles in mind, Sherman wrote: "I am not willing that we should drift into a difficult and expensive war, which may be avoided by leaving time to work out a solution."[19]

Miles prepared to march, however, when reports from the north reached Fort Keogh in early February, indicating the presence of 410 lodges south of the boundary. He reported that he intended to aim for the country between the Milk River and the boundary, but a telegram from St. Paul on February 24 stopped him. When ordered to recall the column to Fort Keogh, Miles warned of dire consequences, which prompted Sherman's response of March 11: "I appreciate highly Genl Miles's zeal, but do not think we should be drawn into a costly war at this time."[20]

Stymied from operating along the border, Miles turned to other activities: social life at Fort Keogh, touring the scene of his friend Custer's death, serving on an equipment board in Washington, and imploring General Sherman for advancement, as always. He became so obnoxious that Sherman wrathfully turned on him. Finally, in 1879, Sitting Bull's people grew so bold south of the border (even as far south as the Yellowstone) that Miles got his chance.

In July 1879, with the apprehensive backing of Terry, Sheridan, and Sherman, Miles led a command north of the Missouri River to the Milk. It consisted of seven companies of the Fifth Infantry and seven troops of the Second Cavalry, 33 officers and 643 enlisted men, backed by 143 Indian scouts. On July 17, in a bend of the Milk River between Frenchman's Creek and Beaver Creek, the advance guard, a company of infantry and a troop of cavalry with 50 Indian scouts, encountered 400 Sioux. In a vigorous skirmish ranging over twelve miles, the warriors astutely withdrew, then suddenly turned and surrounded the small command. Miles hurried the main force forward and drove the Indians north in retreat. He followed as far as the Canadian boundary and bivouacked. Major James Walsh of the North-West Mounted Police came down from Fort Walsh for a consultation.[21]

On July 23, the day before Miles conferred with Major Walsh, President Hayes summoned Secretary McCrary and General Sherman to the Executive Mansion. He was concerned that an Indian war would erupt north of the Missouri River. He instructed McCrary and Sherman to prevent such an affair if at all possible. Miles was to confine his operations to country south of Milk River. The secretary of war reinforced the order in a telegram directly to General Sheridan, cautioning that it would be "exceedingly unfortunate if hostilities resulted from any over zeal on the part of Miles." Offended, Miles returned to Fort Keogh and disbanded the expedition.[22]

The Sitting Bull campaign of 1879 marked the end of Miles's years as a combat commander. It also marked the approaching end of Sitting Bull's freedom. Driven by hunger and pressed by the mounted police, Sitting Bull finally surrendered at Fort Buford in 1881, depriving Miles of credit for the surrender. For Miles, the challenge was to use all his influence and connections to secure one of the brigadier vacancies expected in 1880. Chief Signal Officer Albert J. Myer died in August, opening a vacancy that Miles vigorously sought. He failed. Major General Irvin McDowell and Brigadier General Edward O. C. Ord were approaching the age of sixty-two and would be eligible to retire. Neither wanted to, but President Hayes, under pressure to appoint a new brigadier before his term expired, forcibly retired Ord. The president gave Ord's star to Miles, to rank from December 15, 1880. Sherman considered Ord's compulsory retirement an outrage, especially because widespread sentiment held that Miles's political connections had prevailed.

The long-sought star on his shoulder straps did not remove Miles from Indian service, but it ended his career as a field commander directing troops on a battlefield. His exploits in the Red River War of 1874–75 and the Great Sioux War of 1876–79 established his reputation as an Indian fighter. The only officer who might have matched Miles was Colonel Ranald S. Mackenzie, whose reputation dimmed when he had to be confined to an insane asylum shortly after making brigadier. Despite many personal flaws, Nelson A. Miles ranks as the most successful Indian fighter of the post–Civil War West.

DEPARTMENT OF THE COLUMBIA

December 1880 also marked the time when the president summoned General Oliver O. Howard to Washington to place him in command of the Department of West Point, which proved unfeasible and was abandoned after only three years. Howard's transfer opened a department command for the new brigadier. Before Miles could even travel to the Department of the Columbia, however, he became entangled in the scandal that had brought Howard to West Point—the Johnson Whittaker case. Whittaker was a black cadet who accused white cadets of tying him to his bunk, beating him, and cutting him. No one believed him, but the case made nationwide news. Under Howard's auspices a court-martial was convened to try Johnson for lying to gain public sympathy. General Miles served as president of the court, which duly found Whittaker guilty, although President Chester Arthur voided the court's sentence. Even so, Whittaker was expelled for failing to pass a course.

Even before undertaking the court-martial assignment, Miles found himself appointed by President Hayes as a member of the Ponca Commission. This group, chaired by Miles's rival General Crook, was charged with determining whether Ponca Indians who had been confined to Indian

Territory but subsequently returned to their Nebraska homes should be allowed to stay. The commission ruled that they should.

On August 2, 1881, General Miles reached Vancouver Barracks, Washington Territory, and took command of the Department of the Columbia. No Indian hostilities disturbed the department; Generals Crook and Howard had taken care of that. Miles traveled extensively, visiting installations and garrisons in Oregon, Idaho, and Washington. He took special interest in Alaska, which fell under his command. After cruising the Inside Passage, he authorized exploring expeditions of the interior: one led by Lieutenant Frederick Schwatka in 1883, two in 1884, and one in 1885. He also joined with Senator John Sherman to speculate in Washington, D.C., real estate.

Vancouver Barracks, however, seemed too remote from the rest of the country for Miles's temperament. Mary Miles was unhappy too. While continuing to promote the virtues of the Pacific Northwest, and even hint at absorbing British Columbia into the United States, Miles quietly worked for another assignment. General Sherman retired in 1884, which deprived Miles of the source that he prized most highly for special favors, although he never grasped Sherman's abhorrence of nepotism. When General Augur retired in 1885, Miles worked to supersede him as commander of the Department of the Missouri, headquartered at Fort Leavenworth. General Sheridan, Sherman's successor as general-in-chief of the army, advanced his cause. and President Grover Cleveland made the appointment. Miles took command on July 28, 1885.

DEPARTMENT OF ARIZONA

From his comfortable billet at Fort Leavenworth, Miles kept an eye cocked on events transpiring in Arizona. His rival George Crook was trying to bring Geronimo and his Apaches to heel. Crook had commanded the Department of Arizona since 1882, actively campaigning against the Chiricahua Apaches, remote in sanctuaries high in Mexico's Sierra Madre. Crook believed that only an Apache could catch an Apache, as he had demonstrated in the Tonto Basin campaign of 1872–73. Two years after assuming command in Arizona, however, General Sherman's retirement elevated Philip Sheridan to the top position. Sheridan regarded Apache scouts as unreliable if not traitorous. He preferred regular troops. But Crook was universally acknowledged as the reigning expert on Apaches, so Sheridan did not interfere.

In March 1886 Crook's vigorous campaigning in Mexico finally succeeded, only to be dashed by the sudden drunken flight of Geronimo and
his immediate following. Other Apaches had surrendered, however, and
Sheridan demanded that Crook cancel the surrender and begin negotiations
again. Crook knew that would send all the Apaches back on the warpath.
When Sheridan refused to yield, he asked to be relieved.

Nelson Miles later claimed that he did not want the Arizona command,
yet he must have secretly welcomed a chance to succeed where Crook had
failed. The telegram that Miles received from Sheridan at Fort Leavenworth
on April 3, 1886, directed him to proceed at once to Arizona and supplant
Crook. It also "suggested" that he make "active and prominent use" of
regular troops: sideline the scouts and make the blue uniforms more visible.
Miles did that as soon as he took command, discharging some of the scouts
and keeping the others out of sight.[23]

Miles used the Southern Pacific Railroad to carry his headquarters from
one Arizona town to another. Before he could conceive a strategy, some of
his cavalry, acting on their own initiative, achieved three successes south
of the border. Miles's strategy then unfolded. Captain Henry W. Lawton
would lead a light column of infantry and cavalry with a contingent of
Apache scouts (none Chiricahua) into Mexico and try to bring the enemy
to bay. Lawton got under way from Fort Huachuca on May 4, 1886.[24]

Lawton's command marched 120 miles deep into Sonora. Hardships
pushed his troops to the limit of endurance. Rugged deserts, mountains,
canyons, and ridges combined with intense heat, humidity, and rain to
break down men and animals. On July 13 the troops descended a trail into
a canyon, where scouts had discovered Geronimo's camp. They charged
into the camp only to discover that their trail had been spotted, alerting
the Apaches in time for them to escape.[25]

While Lawton toiled for a month in Mexico, Miles conceived two other
strategies. One concerned the peaceful Chiricahuas tilling the soil at Fort
Apache. He wanted all the Chiricahuas, not just Geronimo's people, moved
out of Arizona altogether. On June 7 he proposed to Sheridan that the
Chiricahuas at Fort Apache be relocated in the Indian Territory. But that
could not be accomplished until Congress lifted a prohibition on Apaches
in the Indian Territory that it had already enacted. Sheridan vetoed the
plan, but Miles did not forget it.[26]

Miles had another strategy aimed at Geronimo and his followers. He had heard nothing from Lawton and worried that his regulars might not accomplish all that Sheridan desired. The solution was a return to Crook's methods, although not so conspicuously as to overshadow Lawton's troops. At Fort Apache Miles found two Chiricahuas, Kayitah and Martine, who had family with Geronimo's people and believed that they could approach them without being shot. Miles enlisted them as scouts and directed Lieutenant Charles B. Gatewood, the one officer that the Apaches trusted implicitly, to escort them into Mexico. Gatewood's mission was to find Lawton, then find Geronimo and try to persuade him to surrender.[27]

In July Miles revived his plan to move the reservation Chiricahuas to the Indian Territory but encountered the same obstacles. That did not stop him from arguing. Finally, on August 26, President Cleveland stopped the arguments. He directed that those Apaches be loaded on trains and moved to Fort Marion, Florida.

In Mexico Lieutenant Gatewood encountered a Captain Lawton who was hostile to the idea of any talk; he intended to attack Geronimo if he could be found. Gatewood was sick, Lawton and his command verged on breakdown, and the formidable mountains and canyons almost paralyzed operations. After many adventures (including one skirmish), however, Gatewood's party made contact with the elusive Chiricahua on August 25.

For two days the two sides camped near each other as Gatewood and Geronimo parleyed for hour after hour. Gatewood stated Miles's terms. Geronimo must surrender and go with his people to Florida, where the Chiricahuas who had surrendered to Crook had already been settled at old Fort Marion. Once there they would await the decision of President Grover Cleveland on their fate. Geronimo's only response was a demand to return him to the Fort Apache reservation or fight. Gatewood then informed Geronimo that all the Chiricahuas at Fort Apache had now been moved to Florida. The only Indians left there were enemies of the Chiricahuas.

Geronimo's only concession was to move north of the boundary and talk with General Miles. He and his people would travel separately and keep their arms. If Geronimo thought that the general could be trusted, perhaps they could work out a solution. The difficulty was that General Miles was distracted by transporting the reservation Chiricahuas to Florida and did not want to talk to Geronimo. He wanted Captain Lawton to handle the surrender.

Captain Lawton well knew that he could not handle the surrender. In Geronimo's state of mind, even Miles might fail. If they wanted surrender instead of fighting, Miles had to make it happen. Throughout the campaign Miles had kept his distance from his field commanders, leaving them to carry out his strategy. That was perhaps acceptable to this point, but now he failed to grasp the urgency of his personal intervention. Lawton pleaded but was rebuffed.[28]

On September 2 the Apaches and soldiers, traveling separately, reached Skeleton Canyon, opening west into Arizona's San Simon Valley. This was the appointed place for meeting General Miles, although whether he would come was still in doubt. Geronimo arranged his warriors on a plateau overlooking the canyon's mouth, prepared to fight if necessary. On September 3 the general at last arrived, and the meeting of the two war chiefs took place. Miles's terms were the same as those presented by Lieutenant Gatewood: go to Florida and await the decision of the president. Miles, however, went to elaborate lengths to demonstrate to Geronimo the terms of surrender, arranging rocks on the ground to represent Geronimo, the Fort Apache Chiricahuas, and Fort Marion, Florida. Geronimo liked what he saw in Miles: a general who did not "talk ugly" like General Crook. He surrendered.[29]

Miles shipped his prisoners by rail to Florida. The president had decreed that all Chiricahuas be settled in the East. Here they fell under War Department control, which meant that every Chiricahua was a prisoner of war, even all the Apache scouts who had served the U.S. Army, including Kayitah and Martine. Geronimo had believed that General Miles would take care of his people, but Miles was in the West, busy proclaiming the glory of his subjugation of Geronimo.

Controversy spoiled much of the glory, which was mostly local in any event. Miles had manipulated the surrender in such fashion as to anger President Cleveland, who wanted Geronimo's Chiricahuas tried in the civil courts, a dreadful idea. Instead Miles pursued his first priority: to get the Apaches out of Arizona. In that he succeeded, but he had a lot of explaining to do, which he prolonged by his skill in dissembling. Offsetting some of the official displeasure, however, the citizens of Tucson presented him a ceremonial sword in gratitude for ridding Arizona of the Apache menace.

Largely unnoticed outside the military hierarchy, contention afflicted the officers involved. Miles's superior, division commander Oliver O. Howard, complained that Miles had often ignored him and treated directly with General Sheridan. This was partly true and doubtless aggravated by the lingering dispute between them over the Nez Perce surrender. Also, Miles never admitted that he had succeeded by employing Crook's methods. Instead, relegating Lieutenant Gatewood to obscurity, he gave full credit to Captain Lawton and the regulars. His duplicity stoked the rivalry between the Crook and Miles factions, which continued as Crook interested himself in the fate of the Chiricahuas in Florida.

Nelson Miles's conduct of the Geronimo campaign was not his finest hour. His chain of victories as a colonel of infantry on the Yellowstone in 1876–79 shone more brightly. In Arizona he was eager to overshadow Crook and please Sheridan by making conspicuous use of regulars rather than Apache scouts. If the transport to Florida of the Fort Apache Chiricahuas was necessary for success, as it probably was despite its cruelty and injustice, Miles may be credited with making it happen. Beyond that, his turn to Apache scouts as the means to victory was a wise decision, even though he seems not to have recognized any incongruity in adopting Crook's method. Moreover, he was remarkably obtuse in failing to perceive the necessity of a personal meeting with Geronimo, ultimately the key to success. Finally, although it revealed some of his worst traits, his maneuvering to get the Chiricahuas out of Arizona was justified. Miles's Arizona command may therefore be judged a mixed success.

DIVISION OF THE PACIFIC

The death of General Sheridan in 1888 and the retirement of General Terry led to a shakeup in the top command. Major General Howard transferred to the prestigious Division of the Atlantic, which opened the Division of the Pacific. Although still a brigadier, Nelson Miles received the post in 1888. Both in Arizona and in San Francisco he kept himself in the public spotlight and cultivated influential friends. He lobbied intensely: for reviving the grade of lieutenant general, for gaining his second star, for reconfiguring military geography to support new major generals, and for other military reforms that he judged would advance his fortunes. But Geronimo's shadow continued to plague Miles.

The declining health of the Chiricahuas, now located in humid Alabama, animated the Indian reform movement and revived the festering issue of relocating them to a more healthful environment. Both Miles and Crook went east to promote their views. Crook favored moving them to Fort Sill in the Indian Territory. Miles opposed this vehemently. Although the Indian Territory had been Miles's idea, he now reversed his opinion. Both Crook and Miles (and their minions) brought the Crook-Miles feud to its highest point. The death of General Crook early in 1890 interrupted the feud and the outcome of the issue. Ironically, Miles won the major general's vacancy created by Crook's death and also Crook's command of the Division of the Missouri. Delighted, Miles moved his family from San Francisco to Chicago.

DIVISION OF THE MISSOURI

When Miles took command of the division in the spring of 1890, the Ghost Dance religion was already sweeping the western tribes. Through prescribed dances, participants could "die" and visit the other world, see their ancestors, and glimpse the idyllic life that awaited them. Essentially a peaceful religion, it began to edge toward violence on the Sioux reservations of North and South Dakota. The reservations lay within the Department of Dakota, commanded by Brigadier General Thomas H. Ruger from St. Paul, Minnesota. They were more accessible, however, from the railroad stretching west across Nebraska. That lay in the Department of the Platte, commanded by Brigadier General John R. Brooke from Omaha.

In late October 1890 Miles visited Pine Ridge Agency and talked with the Sioux chiefs. One defiantly told him that they would dance as long as they pleased. Even so, Miles concluded that the furor would die out. Indian agent Daniel F. Royer did not agree. A timid little political appointee, Royer was scared. He wanted troops to occupy the reservation.[30]

White ranchers and farmers surrounding the reservation also wanted that. As word of the temper of the Sioux spread rapidly, settlers abandoned their homes, newspapers stoked public interest, and Washington took alarm. When agent Royer made a breathless appeal for soldiers on November 15, Washington responded. Miles had his orders and conveyed his own orders to Brooke and Ruger.

General Brooke personally led a large column into Pine Ridge Agency on November 20. At the same time, another column arrived at the Rosebud Agency. Brooke's mission was not to fight but to protect government personnel and property and make every effort to avoid a fight. Miles remained in his Chicago headquarters, funneling fresh troops into Brooke's command and repeatedly sending cables instructing him never to let his soldiers get mixed up with Indians.

Miles's next move turned out to be a blunder, as he should have foreseen. He regarded Sitting Bull as the brightest spark fueling the Ghost Dance (which he was not) and believed that his arrest would help extinguish the fire. Standing Rock agent James McLaughlin, however, was a strong agent, closely allied with the post commander at Fort Yates, Lieutenant Colonel William F. Drum. They believed that Indian police should undertake the task of arresting Sitting Bull. Miles did not trust either McLaughlin or Drum.

At a banquet in Chicago on November 20, Miles ran into William F. "Buffalo Bill" Cody. They had campaigned against Sitting Bull in 1876, and for one season Cody had displayed Sitting Bull as a feature of his famous Wild West show. He and Sitting Bull were friends, the showman declared, and he could arrest the old Sioux chief if given official orders. Miles issued the orders and on the back of his calling card wrote instructions for all army officers to provide Cody with any assistance he needed. On November 27, still garbed in his tuxedo, Buffalo Bill and three of his publicists showed up at Fort Yates. Aware of the consequences if Cody attempted to extract Sitting Bull from his village of Ghost Dancers, McLaughlin and Drum conspired to prevent it. At the officers' club at Fort Yates, the officers staged an all-night drinking party, which they thought would send the old scout to bed. The next morning, however, none the worse for the alcohol-fueled night, Cody prepared to ride to Sitting Bull's home. With the aid of McLaughlin's schoolteacher at the Sitting Bull camp, Cody was tricked into believing that the chief had gone into the agency on another road. Returning to Standing Rock, Cody was shown a telegram withdrawing Miles's order. McLaughlin's protest had led through two cabinet secretaries to the Executive Mansion and a directive from President Benjamin Harrison canceling Miles's order. Buffalo Bill left Standing Rock and submitted his bill for expenses to General Miles.

Although unable to discover how Cody was deceived, Miles nonetheless conveyed to General Ruger his displeasure with Colonel Drum. He then turned to waging a loud campaign to place the Sioux entirely under military control. Journeying to Washington to promote this scheme, he gave the press declarations of alarm at the probability of an Indian war—at a time when General Brooke was striving to bring about a peaceful resolution of the crisis. Miles partially achieved his objective. The secretary of the interior decreed that the Sioux agents must cooperate with and obey the local post commander in all military operations.

On December 6, 1890, Brooke met with a delegation of chiefs from the remote camps to which they had fled when the soldiers came. The chiefs voiced their grievances at length, but Brooke encouraged them to return to their homes, after which grievances could be discussed. If they would come, Brooke would supply them with food. He wired Miles, predicting that the council would end the troubles. In return Miles reprimanded Brooke for even listening to grievances. Instead he should have demanded that the Indians obey his orders and put off grievances until later. Press dispatches reinforced Miles's dissatisfaction, and he again cabled Brooke that the newspaper accounts seemed to convey that the general was not in full control. Miles again repeated his admonition not to let troops get mixed up with Indians and said that applied to generals too.

With his officers now in control of the agencies, Miles expected Colonel Drum at Fort Yates to arrest Sitting Bull. Agent McLaughlin wanted to wait until winter weather became severe, then use his Indian police to make the arrest. Drum agreed. The police would arrest Sitting Bull while Drum's soldiers stood by in case of trouble. General Ruger also agreed, but on December 10 he received a telegram from Miles ordering him to direct Colonel Drum to arrest Sitting Bull and reminding him that the agent now fell under Drum's authority. Drum and McLaughlin made their move on December 15, pursuing their agreed-upon plan. Miles would not have approved; cavalry dashing into the camp would have held more appeal.

The Indian police took on more than they could handle. Sitting Bull's followers gathered around his cabin and blocked the exit of the police. One of the mob fired his Winchester and struck a policeman, who in falling shot and killed Sitting Bull. Drum's cavalry dashed into the camp and after a brief skirmish ended the conflict.

To oversee operations more closely, Miles boarded a train and transferred his headquarters to Rapid City, South Dakota, on the eastern fringe of the Black Hills, where he could watch General Brooke more closely. In fact, without relieving Brooke, Miles assumed command over the entire zone of turbulence.

Big Foot was another name on Miles's list of chiefs to be arrested. Miles had a squadron of cavalry watching Big Foot's camp. But the chief slipped away from his overseer, Lieutenant Colonel Edwin V. Sumner, and led his people south toward Pine Ridge Agency, where the chiefs had asked him to come help make peace. As troops fanned out over the reservation looking for Big Foot, Colonel Sumner endured Miles's fury, which featured the threat of a court of inquiry. A squadron of the Seventh Cavalry finally intercepted Big Foot and his people and led them to camp in the valley of Wounded Knee Creek. From his Pine Ridge headquarters General Brooke dispatched the rest of the Seventh Cavalry to Wounded Knee. Colonel James W. Forsyth bore instructions from Brooke, backed by Miles, to disarm the Indians and move them to the railroad for transport to Omaha.

On December 29, 1890, the disarmament process erupted into the terrible tragedy of Wounded Knee. Neither side expected a fight, but taking a warrior's rifle away from him had always been a delicate undertaking. A chanting medicine man precipitated the firing, and when it ended 25 soldiers and at least 153 Sioux men, women, and children lay dead; 44 wounded Indians and 39 wounded soldiers completed the tally. The army called Wounded Knee a battle, while the Indians called it a massacre. History has settled on the word "massacre."[31]

General Miles did not regard Wounded Knee as a victory. He did not use the word "massacre," but it came close to his opinion. More immediately, he regarded Wounded Knee as a blunder by Colonel Forsyth. On January 4, 1891, six days after Wounded Knee, "by direction of the President," he relieved Forsyth from command of the Seventh Cavalry and ordered a court of inquiry to examine whether the regiment had been so disposed as to fire into its own ranks and whether women and children had been killed.[32] The president had directed no such course. He had merely directed that Miles ascertain whether women and children had been killed.

Even so, Miles proceeded with his plan. His court consisted of three officers, one of whom was in the field and could not serve. The other two were members of Miles's staff, Major J. Ford Kent, and the ever-loyal Captain Frank D. Baldwin. They could be expected to reach a verdict pleasing to their commander. But they didn't. After exhaustive testimony by officers of the Seventh Cavalry, during which Miles tried to influence the minds of the two officers, they cleared Forsyth on both counts: his troop dispositions were not faulty, and every effort had been made during the fight to spare noncombatants. Miles refused to accept their conclusions. He ordered them to convene once more and reconsider their opinion. This time the officers bent to their chief's will and submitted a harsher assessment of Forsyth. Miles forwarded this document to Washington with his own lengthy indictment of Forsyth.

Neither commanding general John M. Schofield nor the secretary of war, Redfield Proctor, agreed. Miles had confused the whole issue with the same sort of dissimulation that he had displayed in the Geronimo surrender. Both officials probably also wished that the politically explosive issue would go away. Early in February, "by direction of the President," Miles had to restore Colonel Forsyth to command of the Seventh Cavalry.[33]

With 3,500 soldiers at his disposal, Miles could have launched the Indian war that he had predicted if he did not get his way in gaining military control of the reservations. Instead, in contrast to his generally maladroit conduct of the campaign, he put into effect a wise strategy for ending the affair peacefully. He used his troops to form a wide ring around the dispirited, factionalized refugees, then gradually tightened it while gently pushing them toward Pine Ridge Agency. At the same time, Miles sent conciliatory letters to the chiefs, encouraging them to surrender. Finally, on January 15, 1891, they did.

Miles alone deserves the honor of this outcome. Neither General Brooke nor General Ruger could likely have conceived and then executed the delicate maneuvers, military and diplomatic, that drew the Sioux into Pine Ridge. Neither possessed the understanding of the Indians that Miles's extensive Indian campaigning equipped him with. The peaceful conclusion of the Ghost Dance conflict represented a tribute to Miles's judgment. His command, nearly half the army's infantry and cavalry, could have overwhelmed the Sioux, even if they had scattered into small parties. The cost would have been still more dead women and children and much bloodshed, but victory would have ensued. War would have gained Miles more publicity, but peace gained him the approval of his Washington superiors and the large Indian reform movement.

On January 22, 1891, Miles savored his triumph with a grand review of his army at Pine Ridge. Bundled in an overcoat buttoned at the neck, he sat astride a big black horse on the crest of a knoll. A sandstorm obscured the scene. But as regiment after regiment passed in review, trumpets flourishing and bands playing, Miles swept off his hat and took the salute. When the Seventh Cavalry approached, its ranks depleted by Wounded Knee and its colonel yet to be restored, with the yellow linings of the troopers' capes flung over their shoulders, a band struck up Custer's battle song, "Garryowen." Miles hung his hat on the pommel of his saddle and let the wind whip his hair.

The grand review on January 22, 1891, provided General Miles with his final review as an Indian fighter. It was also the final review of the Indian-fighting army. The Ghost Dance was a spiritual uprising not an Indian war, but it brought about the last major military deployment of the Indian wars. Perhaps not coincidentally, in 1890 the Census Bureau found that a definable frontier of settlement no longer existed.

Freed from Indian concerns, Miles plunged into politics, making enemies in his efforts to reform the Indian service and to promote the presidential aspirations of his uncle, John Sherman. Miles's handling of the Wounded Knee aftermath still rankled many and stoked controversy in the army. A cruel blow struck in July 1891, when the War Department reorganized military topography by abolishing divisions. Miles lost the Departments of Dakota, the Platte, and Texas. From Chicago he now commanded only the Department of the Missouri.

As always, throughout the early 1890s Miles spent much time, thought, and effort in cultivating influential friends and using them to promote his own ends. Two causes in particular commanded his attention. First was an attempt to get Congress to revive the grade of lieutenant general. He saw himself as the next general-in-chief when Schofield retired. The second cause was to join with Civil War veterans in seeking Medals of Honor for wartime exploits. They succeeded to such a degree that the scores awarded cheapened the value. Even so, in 1892 Miles received a Medal of Honor for gallantry at Chancellorsville. At the same time, he busied himself securing medals for his favorite subordinates. Captain Baldwin received his medal through Miles's influence.

The Pullman Strike of 1894 in Chicago embroiled Miles in more con-troversy and earned him the enmity of General Schofield and President Cleveland. That same year, however, the retirement of General Howard opened the Department of the Atlantic. Miles moved to New York City to take command of this most prestigious of postings for general officers. In 1895 Congress restored the grade of lieutenant general. Schofield wore three stars until he retired in September 1895. A month later President Cleveland named Miles commanding general of the U.S. Army, but Schofield's three stars did not come with the position.

COMMANDING GENERAL

Major General Miles's U.S. Army was pathetically unready for the War with Spain, which Congress declared in April 1898. The army line, still 28,000 strong, had to expand to 220,000 regulars, volunteers, and National Guard. The War Department staff bureaus, products of the Indian wars, could not cope with the immense responsibilities of creating a fighting army. Russell Alger, the secretary of war, proved incompetent and, besides, could not get along with the abrasive Miles. Furthermore, President William McKinley had no confidence in the general-in-chief. Planning fell into disarray as Miles argued for an invasion of Puerto Rico and Alger and McKinley chose Cuba. General William R. Shafter, a hugely corpulent old Indian fighter, commanded in Cuba. Sent to Cuba by the president to observe Shafter's operations, Miles overstepped his authority and feuded with the field commander.

McKinley had already decided on an invasion of Puerto Rico as well as Cuba, and Miles returned to Washington to take command of the Puerto Rican campaign. On July 25, 1898, Miles landed the first of his army in Puerto Rico. With the beach head secured, the troops advanced inland, skirmishing with Spanish units. Other elements of Miles's invasion force, ultimately numbering 2,500 men, quickly routed the Spanish defenders. An armistice on August 12 brought the fighting to a close. Miles had conducted the operation efficiently, his only fault being an infuriating failure to keep Washington informed of events.

Distressed that Cuba had overshadowed Puerto Rico in the press, Miles made sure that the newspapers noticed him. In an interview with a reporter he blasted War Department incompetence and interference with his prerogatives. The interview caused an explosive reaction in the War Department and became a political issue between Democrats and Republicans. Secretary Alger eventually created an investigating commission to look into Miles's charges. On December 21 Miles took the stand to testify before the commission. He repeated his criticisms, fought back against the secretary and the staff, and got revenge on the staff by accusing it of providing canned "embalmed beef" in the soldiers' rations. As the beef controversy roiled the press, Miles continued to contribute to the furor. Even after the commission found the beef not contaminated, Miles added fuel to the fires by continuing to trumpet his opinion.

Even so, a bipartisan group worked for Miles's promotion to lieutenant general. That unleashed further controversy, scandalous accusations, and insults between partisans. But on June 6, 1900, Nelson Miles received his third star. But it proved useless against the new secretary of war, Elihu Root. The secretary entered office committed to a sweeping reform of the military establishment, creating a general staff and a chief of staff and abolishing the post of commanding general. Miles fought that, of course, and at the same time publicly criticized the new secretary. Far worse, he gave a speech in which he claimed that Colonel Theodore Roosevelt, the new vice president and soon-to-be president, did not lead the charge up San Juan Hill.

RETIREMENT

In February 1902, after bitter controversy, the Root reforms became law. On August 8, 1902, Miles turned sixty-four, the mandated retirement age. Both Root and President Roosevelt issued an order announcing the retirement of Lieutenant General Miles and directing that he return to his home, with no celebration, no commendation, no retirement ceremony. The last commanding general of the U.S. Army faded into retirement. But not quietly. He continued to emit his customary bombast. He also revived his long-dormant quest for the presidency, but the Democratic convention of 1904 gave him only a few votes. Probably to stoke that ambition, in 1896 he had published a massive volume entitled *Personal Recollections and Observations of General Nelson A. Miles*. He followed that in 1911 with *Serving the Republic: Memoirs of the Civil and Military Life of Nelson A. Miles, Lieutenant General, United States Army*.

Miles never quietly faded away. Based in his Washington apartment, he remained an active public figure for the rest of his life. In World War I he made every effort, each wilder than the last, to organize a command for himself. On May 16, 1925, he took his grandchildren to the circus. As he stood while the band played the "Star-Spangled Banner," a massive heart attack killed him. He was eighty-six. Only two Civil War major generals remained.

On May 19, 1925, the pageantry that had been denied Miles on his retirement ushered him across the Potomac River to Arlington National Cemetery: color guard, black horses, caisson, 2,500 marchers from the army, navy, and marines, a fifteen-gun salute, and taps. He would have judged the procession appropriate for the last commanding general of the U.S. Army.

Nelson A. Miles's claim to fame rested on far more than being the last army commanding general. It rested mainly on his service as colonel of the Fifth Infantry at a time when conventional wisdom held that only cavalry could prevail against Indians. He and his foot soldiers distinguished themselves primarily in the Great Sioux War of 1876–77 and secondarily in the Red River War of 1874–75. No other field officer, even Mackenzie, came close to matching his record. As a general officer commanding departments and a division, however, Miles's performance proved mediocre or worse. His many character flaws stained his stature in the frontier army. Still, he emerges as the most successful of the army's Indian fighters.

CHAPTER SIX

EDWARD O. C. ORD

E dward Ord was an individualist, his character and personality not entirely in harmony with military structure. An impulsive, restless nonconformist, he often ran afoul of the structure and as often sought to manipulate it. Within the structure, his quick mind and proficiency in mathematics won widespread admiration. Energetic, aggressive, imaginative, inventive, courageous to a fault, and possessed of uncommon endurance, he made a good soldier, though sometimes lacking judgment and inattentive to personal appearance.

Edward Otho Cresap Ord was born on October 18, 1818, in Cumberland, Maryland, his ancestry shrouded in mystery and said to involve English royalty. With political support from Maryland and nearby Washington, D.C., he entered the military academy at West Point in 1835 and graduated in 1839. As a second lieutenant in the Third Artillery, he immediately joined his regiment in Florida, where the Seminole Indian War was in progress. The hostilities lasted until 1842, and Lieutenant Ord distinguished himself scouting into the forbidding Everglades, skirmishing with Seminoles, and fighting in one vicious combat. In July 1841 he was promoted to first lieutenant.[1]

PACIFIC SERVICE

Recruiting service, the Coast Survey, and other routine duties kept Lieutenant Ord out of the Mexican War. After enduring the long voyage around Cape Horn to the Pacific, he arrived in Monterey, California, on January 27, 1847, three weeks after California had fallen to the Americans. A shipmate

Brigadier General Edward O. C. Ord, commanding
Department of California, 1868–1871;
Department of the Platte, 1871–1875;
Department of Texas, 1875–1880.
Brady Collection, U.S. Signal Corps (photo 111-B-4550),
National Archives and Records Administration, Washington, D.C.

was the other lieutenant of his company, William T. Sherman. Four months after arrival, the company's captain departed for the East, leaving Ord to take over the unit, with Lieutenant Sherman as his second in command. Based in Monterey, Ord and Sherman's artillery company and a company of dragoons formed the only regular army force in California. The two officers rode the countryside, sightseeing and getting acquainted with the people.

The discovery of gold in 1848 ignited a mad rush to the mines and swept dozens of deserters out of the little military command. Prices skyrocketed, overwhelming the low pay of the officers and soldiers, so both Ord and Sherman obtained leaves in an attempt to improve their finances. For Ord, a brief visit to the mines proved a failure, but he soon discovered that his experience in the Coast Survey equipped him to win contracts for surveying. Aside from Sacramento, site of pioneer John Sutter's fort, Ord's most significant contract led to the first survey of the burgeoning community of Los Angeles.

On January 1, 1850, Ord traveled to the East on a brief leave of absence. Back in California by autumn, he found himself promoted to captain of another company of the Third Artillery. It was stationed in Boston, so back east he went. After five years in the Coast Survey, he took his artillery company back to California. For the next three years he learned to be an Indian fighter.

Both the state of Oregon and the Territory of Washington were home to a variety of tribes, tormented by the Indian-hating white settlers. When they Indians resisted, the soldiers had to fight people with whom they sympathized. By 1855 the department commander, General John E. Wool, confronted two Indian wars, one in Oregon and another in Washington. In Oregon the Rogue River Indians, exasperated by the tyranny of white settlers, had fought one war and now brought on another. In Washington, gold discovered near Fort Colville, a Hudson's Bay Company trading post just south of the international boundary, brought a rush of prospectors across the homeland of the Yakima Indians. Chief Kamiakin rallied his and neighboring tribes to resist such encroachment.

Captain Ord took part in both wars.

In October 1855 Ord's company, based at Benecia Barracks near San Francisco, marched north to Fort Dalles, on the Columbia River, to form part of Major Gabriel J. Rains's expedition into the Yakima country. The command consisted of nearly four hundred Regulars and five hundred

Oregon Volunteers (operating independently of Rains). Ord took charge of three howitzers, but Rains proved so inept that the expedition returned to Fort Dalles after a month of blundering around the Yakima country, having accomplished nothing beyond marching 175 miles. Back in Benecia by late November, a disgusted Ord preferred charges of incompetence against Rains and expressed his outrage in letters to New York newspapers. These headstrong measures achieved no more than expressing his frustration and revealed a rashness that would cause him trouble in the future.[2]

The second Rogue River War had already broken out in Oregon, and Ord's artillery company was assigned to an expedition led by Major Robert C. Buchanan. (Throughout the hostilities in Oregon and Washington, artillery usually served as infantry.) Before setting out from California to the scene of hostilities early in January 1856, Ord informed the New York media of his opinion: the white settlers caused the war. Reaching Buchanan at the mouth of the Cheteco River in Oregon, Ord marched with the column to the mouth of Rogue River. On March 26 Buchanan assigned him to command an offensive expedition a short distance up the Rogue River against the Macanootenay village of Rogue River Indians. His command consisted of his own artillery company and a company of 112 infantrymen. The village proved to be recently abandoned, and the troops burned the thirteen lodges. At this point, about sixty warriors in canoes paddled across the river to attack the troops. Ord handled his command expertly, dispatching his two companies to different parts of the field to meet converging bands of Indians. After a vigorous contest, the warriors fell back to their canoes with ten killed and a few wounded. Ord's own loss amounted to one soldier wounded.

Assigned next to escort a supply train, Ord marched his company to the mouth of the Cheteco River, where he overtook a large party of Indians on April 28 and, although outnumbered, immediately attacked. Again he put the enemy to flight with enemy losses of half a dozen warriors killed, a few captured, and their stores seized. Ord lost one soldier killed and another wounded.

These actions demonstrated Ord's ability to command units in combat, and San Francisco newspapers praised him. He was among the officers commended by army headquarters for outstanding conduct in the Rogue River War.[3]

A Yakima War in 1858 again summoned Ord and his company from California to Washington. This Yakima War, which involved an alliance of several tribes, overshadowed the earlier one. Indian anger at white settlers and gold-seekers had smoldered since the first encounters and now became a full-scale uprising. The local commander was Colonel George Wright, with the newly formed Ninth Infantry, equipped with new long-range infantry rifles. A small command from Wright's regiment under Lieutenant Colonel Edward J. Steptoe ventured into the Yakima country to intimidate the Indians and reassure the Colville miners. On May 16 a thousand warriors from different tribes confronted Steptoe's 170 soldiers. The standoff culminated in the troops defending a hilltop for two days and nights. Ignominiously, under cover of night, Steptoe abandoned the position, his howitzers, and his six dead and slipped away.

Retaliating for the Steptoe disaster, Colonel Wright organized a major campaign. Ord's company joined Wright's command as part of a battalion of the Third Artillery under Captain Erasmus D. Keyes. With a command of six hundred infantry, dragoons, and artillery, Wright marched out of his supply base near Fort Walla Walla on August 27, headed north through rugged country. On August 30 his troops descended from a plain to a land of scattered lakes. On September 1 they encountered a force of about five hundred warriors drawn up on a hill to fight. With Ord's company in advance, the troops quickly drove the enemy off the hill, below which lay four lakes. Holding Ord's men as personal escort, Wright remained on the hill to watch his troops fight the Indians. The new long-range rifles proved decisive: they could be fired accurately at six hundred yards, while the Indian muskets had a range of three hundred yards. Suffering sixty casualties, the Indians fled the field. The Battle of Four Lakes gave Wright victory without a single casualty on his side.

On September 5, while advancing in sweltering heat across the broad Spokane Plain, Wright's troops fought a seven-hour battle with aggressive parties of mounted warriors. Ord's company joined with his own battalion as skirmishers in front of the main column, at one point dashing through flames where the Indians had fired the dry grass. Again the troops were victorious. Indian casualties are unknown, but the Battle of Spokane Plain forced the tribes to sue for peace. Wright's heavy hand singled out the men who were judged to have committed depredations and led in the Steptoe affair and hanged fifteen. For Captain Ord, the Yakima War marked the close of his service in the Pacific Northwest. In November 1858 his company was dissolved and the officers transferred to the artillery school at Fort Monroe, Virginia.

Captain Ord was now an experienced Indian fighter. At both Four Lakes and Spokane Plain he had distinguished himself, his battalion being cited for gallantry. In earlier operations, especially the Rogue River War, he had also conducted himself creditably. He was now a mature man of forty with a growing family, of average build and military posture, with a head of bushy white hair and a neat white mustache. Ord was dedicated to his profession, aggressive, outspoken, and competent to follow it to its conclusion.

At Fort Monroe's artillery school Ord held the post of superintendent of practical instruction, which in both the field and the classroom was almost the equivalent of school superintendent. School duties were interrupted in October 1859 when John Brown's raid on the Harper's Ferry Arsenal brought orders to march the Fort Monroe troops to the aid of Colonel Robert E. Lee in suppressing the raiders. Lee, however, achieved that before Ord arrived, so Ord returned to Fort Monroe.

CIVIL WAR

The secession crisis following the election of Abraham Lincoln to the presidency in November 1860 plunged Captain Ord into the controversies torturing the country. As a native of Maryland, he considered himself a Southerner: his sentiments rested with the South. Abolitionists angered him, and he regarded black people as fitted for little beyond slavery. As the Fort Sumter crisis evolved, he made his views on proper strategy known in high places. In March 1861, however, orders to take command of his company sent him back to the Pacific. Far from the action in California, he was anxious to be at its center. He mobilized all his influential friends, in the army and out, to seek a promotion. The crucial figure turned out to be an old friend in the Adjutant General's office, Major Julius P. Garesché. Garesché's manipulation led in September 1861 to a commission as brigadier general of Volunteers. He at once gathered his family and headed east.

As a Democrat and an avowed Southerner, whose wife Molly came from a slave-holding family and had relatives in the Confederate Army, General Ord had to endure doubts about his loyalty to the Union. Throughout the

Civil War, as he rose in prominence, newspaper articles, hostile officers, and rumor forced him to defend his loyalty. That proved more aggravating than difficult, because his strong Union record, both in words and in deeds, belied the doubts.

Brigadier General Ord was assigned a brigade in a division holding the right flank of the Union line protecting Washington. On December 21, 1861, he led his men in a probing march west toward the Confederate lines. At Dranesville, Virginia, he collided with a force under Confederate cavalry general J. E. B. Stuart. In the resulting battle Ord's infantry (and especially his artillery) drove the Confederates from the field. The clash was strategically insignificant, but it was the first Union victory in the East. It brought Ord a brevet of lieutenant colonel in the Regular Army (he was already a major) and promotion to major general of Volunteers on May 2, 1862.[4]

Despite his new rank, Ord clashed with his next commander, General Irvin McDowell. McDowell was to march south from Manassas to cooperate with General George B. McClellan in the Peninsular Campaign. Ord commanded a newly organized division and at once came under hostile scrutiny due to McDowell's irascible temperament. When Stonewall Jackson marched down the Shenandoah Valley en route to threaten Washington, Ord's division was diverted to the valley. Ord's feud with McDowell escalated, and Ord asked to be transferred or relieved. When this was denied, he claimed illness and relinquished command of his division. Ord's petulant unmilitary behavior at last led to his transfer in June 1862 to the western theater at Corinth, Mississippi.

Ord reported to Major General Ulysses S. Grant in Corinth and was assigned to command the Second Division of the Army of the Tennessee. In September Ord held the center of Grant's extended line, with his old California friend William T. Sherman on his right at Memphis and General William S. Rosecrans on the left at Corinth. On September 19, 1862, in a complex maneuver designed to trap the army of General Sterling Price, Ord was left out of the fight due to Rosecrans's mistakes. Even so, Grant highly commended Ord for his behavior in the Battle of Iuka, and he received a brevet of colonel.

Absent in Kentucky in early October, Ord learned of vicious fighting swirling around Corinth, with his division fighting under his second-in command, Major General Stephen A. Hurlbut. Ord rushed to join his troops and found them falling back before the retreat of the defeated General Earl Van Dorn.

Ord turned the division around and confronted the Confederates at a bridge across the Hatchie River, where they made a stand. Ord prevailed in a hard-fought contest, driving the Confederates away from the bridge. He was on horseback in full uniform, strangely cloaked in a long white coat and low-cut shoes showing white socks. During the fight a bullet struck Ord's leg, and he was borne from the field. A fellow officer offered his home in Carlisle, Pennsylvania, as a place to recuperate. A belated brevet of brigadier general in the Regular Army on March 13, 1865, recognized his service in the Battle of Hatchie.

Ord's leg had been shattered at Hatchie, and he could not get off crutches until late November. He wanted to return to Grant's command, and Grant and Sherman had both asked for him, but make-work duties detained him until Ord forced the issue. On May 25, 1863, he received orders to report to Grant at Vicksburg.

When Ord arrived at Grant's headquarters on June 18, the Union fight for Vicksburg had progressed to the east side of the Mississippi River; driven Joseph E. Johnston out of the capital at Jackson, although without taking the city; and curled siege lines around Vicksburg's eastern margins. Grant's army numbered about fifty thousand men in three corps, commanded by Generals Sherman, John A. McClernand, and James B. McPherson. McClernand, a political general, had caused Grant serious trouble and failed to keep his siege lines at the same quality and level as those of Sherman on his right and McPherson on his left. On June 18, the very day Ord reported for duty, Grant relieved McClernand of command of Thirteenth Corps and replaced him with Ord. The Thirteenth Corps contained five divisions with fifteen thousand men—infantry, cavalry, and artillery.

Ord pushed his corps to rectify McClernand's failures, advancing his entrenchments to align with the other two corps, preparing proper field works, and mounting an occasional foray in front of his lines. By early July the siege lines had grown close enough, and the debility of the Vicksburg defenses and the hunger of its population had grown so obvious, that Grant planned a major assault on July 6. On June 3, however, Confederate general John C. Pemberton, after tedious negotiations in which Ord took part, surrendered Vicksburg.

Jackson remained in Confederate hands, and General Johnston was still in the field. So Grant assigned Sherman to take three corps and operate against Johnston and the capital. Ord's was one of the three corps. Skirmishing with Johnston's men, the Union formation pushed to the outskirts of Jackson by July 10. Six days of bitter fighting finally drove Johnston from Jackson, with Ord's corps playing a key role in the battle. One of his division commanders, however, disobeyed orders, blundered into an overwhelming defensive position, and got cut to pieces. Furious, Ord extricated the division from its predicament and relieved its commander.

With the Vicksburg campaign triumphantly concluded, Grant's army was broken up. Ord's corps drew assignment to General Nathaniel Banks (another political general) in Louisiana. In October 1863, as Banks opened his ill-fated Red River campaign, Ord fell sick with a respiratory infection and had to yield his command. Returning to duty on February 16, 1864, he learned that General McClernand had been restored to command of the Thirteenth Corps, a severe blow both to the corps and to Ord.

Grant, now lieutenant general commanding the army, brought Ord east and had him operate in the Shenandoah Valley. It went badly, due to incompetent generals, bad weather, and Ord's own dissatisfaction. He asked to be relieved, which did his cause no good. Moreover, Ord was enduring another spate of questions about his loyalty, with Molly's Southern ties thrown into the mix. General Jubal Early's advance down the Shenandoah and into Maryland, however, saved Ord. Almost within sight of the capital, Early halted to fight a weak Union army under General Lew Wallace at Monacacy, Maryland. When President Lincoln lost confidence in Wallace, Grant substituted Ord in early July 1864. When Ord's lines held, Early turned back to the Shenandoah.

As Grant fought his way south and drew siege lines around Petersburg, Virginia, he summoned Ord and on July 21 placed him in command of the Eighteenth Corps. This unit was part of the Army of the James, which formed the extreme right wing of Grant's siege lines, with the right of Ord's corps resting on the Appomattox River. The unfortunate Army of the James was commanded by Benjamin F. Butler, the archetype political general, who had repeatedly demonstrated incompetence. He had built his own loyal command and staff and did not welcome outsider Edward Ord.

On September 29, 1864, Ord's corps, together with Tenth Corps, launched an attack to the northwest in a drive on Richmond. Grant had authorized Butler to undertake this mission, and the assault occurred under his orders.

Ord's corps attacked on the left of Tenth Corps and the cavalry and at once confronted Fort Harrison, the strongest bastion on Richmond's front. Ord attacked with a rapid charge that brought his lead elements to the base of the earthwork. Officers, including Ord, mingled with the troops, urging them on up the base of the fort and over the parapet. As fighting raged inside the fort, a mini-ball hit Ord in the leg, inflicting another serious wound. He continued to fight until the fort fell to him, with three hundred prisoners and twenty cannon. Then an ambulance bore him from the fort.

Fort Harrison had been a major victory, pleasing Grant and advancing the Union lines closer to Richmond. Ord was breveted major general in the Regular Army for "gallant and meritorious" service in the Battle of Fort Harrison. Accompanied by his aide, he traveled to Bellaire, Ohio, to convalesce with Molly and the children. His leave extended to December 1.

Returning from a brief trip to Washington, D.C., on January 8, 1865, Ord learned that Butler had been removed from command of the Army of the James and Ord had been substituted. He now commanded a full army of fifty thousand men. Butler had left behind a civil and military mess, replete with financial irregularities, and a staff still loyal to their political mentor. Ord faced a daunting task in cleaning up the mess and ridding himself of scheming subordinates.

In late January, while acting for Grant on the Petersburg line, Ord tried to act as peacemaker between North and South, a serious indiscretion. One move was to ease the way through the lines of three Confederate commissioners seeking an interview with President Lincoln. Worse was a meeting in late February with Lieutenant General James Longstreet in which he sought to arrange an armistice. Ord's sally into high state affairs embarrassed Grant and the administration in Washington and once more illustrated his potential for bad judgment. He was fortunate to escape adverse consequences.

Ord's most significant Civil War service lay in Grant's spring campaign of 1865: the lunge at Petersburg and Richmond and the pursuit of Lee's army up the Appomattox River. Mobilizing for the assault on Lee's right flank, Grant ordered Ord to send three divisions from his position facing the Confederate left flank to join in the assault on the right. The remainder of his army would continue to menace Richmond.

Ord's divisions, under Major General John Gibbon, were in place when Grant opened the offensive on March 29. General Philip Sheridan commanded in the critical Battle of Five Forks on the following day. Ord's infantry remained in place to Sheridan's right. On April 2, however, Gibbon's infantry joined with those of General Horatio Wright to storm two Confederate bastions, Forts Gregg and Baldwin, which they carried with heavy casualties. Grant's entire line had moved against the Confederate lines, prompting Lee to order the evacuation of both Petersburg and Richmond. The first Union formations to enter both Petersburg and Richmond were black infantrymen of Ord's Army of the James.

As Lee led his army up the Appomattox River in hopes of finding badly needed supplies at Amelia Courthouse, Grant followed the Southside Railway south of the river, riding with Ord's troops. Lee found no supplies at Amelia Courthouse and continued upriver. Sheridan's cavalry rode in advance of his infantry and entrenched in front of Lee. Ord made a forced march in an effort to strengthen Sheridan and on April 6 found the head of Lee's column, under General Longstreet. Ord prepared to attack, but nightfall prevented a battle. Still, Ord had halted Lee's retreat. Lee's army had fought Meade's army vigorously that day and sustained severe losses.

During the night, Longstreet slipped away from Ord's front, but Ord pushed forward on April 7. On this day Grant and Lee exchanged messages, probing the possibility of an armistice, but the fighting continued. Appomattox was the next place where Lee hoped to find trains loaded with rations. Sheridan's cavalry got in front of the gray column but required infantry to bolster their lines. Grant left Ord on April 8 to join Meade, so that he could better control the dispatch riders between himself and Lee. Now the ranking general, Ord continued the march to Appomattox, gathering additional infantry formations as he went. Throughout the night Ord labored to push infantry up to Sheridan's lines and had them in position by the morning of April 9. He had also established his headquarters near Appomattox Courthouse.

Leading the Southern army, General John B. Gordon deployed to overwhelm Sheridan's cavalry. The attack stalled, however, when Gordon glimpsed masses of infantry drawn up behind the cavalry. At 10:00 A.M. a Confederate officer appeared at Ord's headquarters carrying a white flag. It was but one of several white flags borne into the Union lines, but it signified

Lee's willingness to meet with Grant. Neither had arrived, however, and as the senior Union general Ord assumed responsibility for agreeing with Longstreet to suspend hostilities. Not until after 2:00 P.M. did Grant and Lee meet in Wilmer McLean's parlor. Ord was among the handful of Union generals present at the historic surrender of Lee's army, after which he paid McLean forty dollars for the table on which Lee signed the document. General Sheridan bought the Grant table for twenty dollars and presented it to the wife of General George A. Custer. (Both tables are on display at Appomattox Courthouse National Historical Park today.)

Despite his competence and valor, General Ord's Civil War career failed to lift him to the top ranks of Union generals. Only in the Appomattox campaign did he rise to true distinction. His eccentricities and indiscretions harmed his relations with other generals, and his Southern sentiments and connections dogged him throughout the war. His first tour in the western theater was satisfactory but not outstanding; his second, the Vicksburg campaign, earned well-deserved plaudits. In the East his Shenandoah service revealed some of his worst traits and ended in failure. Commanding the Army of the James, he rose above mediocrity and played a significant part in the Petersburg and Appomattox campaigns, but his efforts to encourage a peace between North and South represented another instance of ignoring the chain of command. Nevertheless, Major General Ord emerges from the war one of the better-known Union generals.

POSTWAR COMMANDS

Still in the Volunteers, General Ord commanded the Department of Ohio, a relatively quiet assignment, from July 1865 to August 1866. Mustered out of the Volunteers on September 1, 1866, he had gained the regular rank of brigadier general at the same time as Congress passed the army act of July 28, 1866. He had politicked heavily for the appointment, including a petition on his behalf bearing the signatures of twenty-six senators. After a year in Detroit, Ord drew assignments that sent him South into commands that were hardly routine: the Department of the Arkansas and after a year the Fourth Military District, a Reconstruction command that embraced the states of Arkansas and Mississippi and the Indian Territory. With his Southern sympathies, he related well to the leadership of Arkansas and Mississippi. But it was a hard job, serving both as a military commander and as an officer of the Freedmen's Bureau. In April 1868 he finally drew a more conventional command: the Department of California.

Ord knew California well from his prewar service on the Pacific Coast. The department consisted of California, Nevada, and the Territory of Arizona. Two years of hostilities both in the Department of California and in the Department of the Columbia preceded Ord's arrival, but the vigorous campaigns of Lieutenant Colonel George Crook had ended in conquest of the warlike tribes. Ord's big problems lay with the Apaches in Arizona. Aggressive campaigning by subordinate officers achieved some success, but not much. Like General Sherman, Ord believed that Arizona was not worth the cost and that the citizens were mostly rabble. He seems to have been content to let subordinate officers struggle with the Apaches.

DEPARTMENT OF THE PLATTE

On December 11, 1871, General Ord took command of the Department of the Platte and moved into his headquarters in Omaha, Nebraska. He inherited a department that had been actively engaged with Indian affairs under his predecessor, Christopher C. Augur, and would also be so under his successor, George Crook. That left General Ord little to do except ensure the protection of the Union Pacific Railway. The army forts in the towns spaced along the road needed little oversight and were usually self-regulating. Much as during his years in San Francisco, Ord and his family pursued an easy, pleasant life in Omaha.

In January 1872 Ord enjoyed a bit of diversion, as General Sheridan organized a buffalo-hunting excursion for the Grand Duke Alexei Alexandrovich of Russia on the plains of southwestern Nebraska. The party included Sheridan and his staff, Lieutenant Colonel George Armstrong Custer, Buffalo Bill Cody, James Butler "Wild Bill" Hickock, and other celebrities. The affair was a grand success, thanks in part to Ord's organization of logistics in Omaha.[5]

In 1874 Ord took the initiative in a humanitarian task to relieve the hardships resulting from the drought that had swept the southern plains in summer 1874 and the clouds of grasshoppers that subsequently denuded the crops on which the settlers relied. In winter 1874–75 poverty and acute hunger afflicted the population. Joining with General John Pope, commanding the Department of the Missouri, Ord secured the secretary of war's permission to distribute thousands of blankets, greatcoats, boots, and

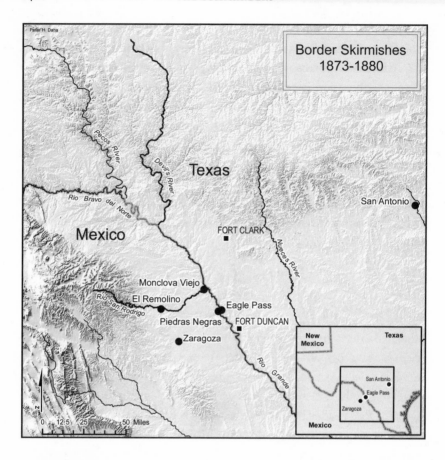

other clothing items to needy settlers. Sheridan opposed food issues, but in February 1875 Congress authorized the army to distribute food, thanks largely to Ord's effective publicity campaign. From February to May 1875 the army issued nearly 2 million rations to 107,535 people in the plains states and territories. However thankful the settlers were, Ord's action did not endear him to General Sheridan.[6]

DEPARTMENT OF TEXAS

Four years of relative tranquillity in Omaha for General Ord would contrast with his next command, the Department of Texas, to which he moved in 1875. Army politics rather than a routine change of assignment governed the transfer, as General Sherman remarked to Sheridan: "You know of course that Ord was sent there without my assent by President Grant, but the immediate motive was of course to make a place for Crook, and also to have Augur at New Orleans."[7] Crook received the Platte in time for the Great Sioux War, and Augur received the Gulf to aid Sheridan, whom President Grant had sent to New Orleans to quell political violence.

Ord moved his family to San Antonio and assumed command of the Department of Texas on April 6, 1875. Under his predecessor, General Augur, Indian hostilities had occurred both in northern Texas and along the Rio Grande frontier. The Red River War of 1874–75 had removed the menace in the north, and Colonel Ranald Mackenzie's bold raid into Mexico in 1873 had quieted the threat to Texas cattle ranchers from Indian raids from Mexico (see chapter 2). Coincident with Ord's arrival, however, the Mexican tribesmen resumed their depredations in Texas and outlaws from both sides of the border plundered the cattle herds.

Ord promptly toured the lower valley and observed the troublesome situation, an inspection that led to a trip to Washington to plead with the secretary of war for more troops. His tour also aroused his contempt for the black infantry regiments that garrisoned the lower Rio Grande. He regarded them as useless and the district commander, Colonel Joseph H. Potter, as physically broken down by age and war wounds. In letters to General Sherman, Ord displayed the racism that he had carried with him into the Civil War. Emphasizing that in Texas the white population was bitterly prejudiced against black soldiers, he appealed to Sherman to withdraw the Twenty-Fourth and Twenty-Fifth Infantry and send him two white regiments. Sherman reminded him that he should address Sheridan, his superior, and quit writing long letters to his old friend at the head of the army. Ord ignored him and continued to write directly to Sherman.[8]

Ord also provoked criticism for his visibly friendly disposition toward former rebels. He attended Confederate veterans' reunions, stood in review of local militias, aided the cause of former generals, and openly cultivated the governor and the Texas congressional delegation. That had a purpose beyond good fellowship. Democrats had seized the House of Representatives in 1875 and were resentful of military employment during Reconstruction. They also resented the use of the army as strikebreakers as well as in the contested election of 1876. As a result, they intended to cut the size of the Regular Army drastically. If Texas Democrats would break with their party, the army might be spared the trauma. Ord's close cooperation with the Texas delegation promoted that end. He enjoyed the support of the people of Texas, moreover, which was not lost on their members of Congress.

Ord quickly jumped to the conclusion that the only way to combat raids across the Rio Grande from Mexico was to pursue the raiders into Mexico as Colonel Ranald Mackenzie had done in 1873. Early in 1876 Ord issued orders for units pursuing raiders on a "fresh trail" to follow it across the Rio Grande. As he later explained in a House hearing, his order was not disapproved when he submitted it for higher approval, so he regarded it as tacitly approved.[9]

Ord had an aggressive like-minded officer at Fort Clark and a uniquely qualified unit for operations against Indians. Lieutenant Colonel William R. Shafter of the Twenty-Fourth Infantry ("Pecos Bill") had a bright reputation as an explorer and Indian fighter, despite a conspicuously well-padded frame. At nearby Fort Duncan was the company of Seminole-Negro Scouts, commanded by First Lieutenant John L. Bullis. A mix of Florida Seminole Indians and escaped slaves, they excelled in every measure of desert campaigning and were devoted to their commander.[10]

Under Ord's order, Shafter and Bullis twice led troops across the Rio Grande, not following fresh trails but in search of marauding Lipan Apaches. In June 1876 Shafter found the Apaches near Zaragoza and struck hard, killing or capturing nineteen Indians and seven horses and destroying the village. A detachment of his command seized two hundred stolen horses. Local authorities, Shafter noted, granted permission to cross.[11]

These local permissions came from officials of the government of President Sebastián Lerdo de Tejada, whose weak regime contended with a revolution led by General Porfirio Díaz. Díaz's coup triumphed in November 1876 and assumed the presidency of Mexico on May 12, 1877. Díaz would rule Mexico for thirty years, and he and his border governors opposed any border crossings by the Americans.

In fact, even as the civil war in Mexico raged on, the governor that Díaz installed in Coahuila, Hipólito Charles, arrested and threatened to hang Shafter's two Mexican guides for treason. Ord reacted at once. His department adjutant general happened to be at Fort Clark, and Ord telegraphed him to join with Colonel Shafter in crossing to Piedras Negras to liberate the guides. At dawn on April 3, 1877, both infantry and cavalry surrounded the town, only to discover that the prisoners had been spirited out during the night. An embarrassed Shafter turned back to the U.S. side, but the incident, carried out on Ord's orders, provoked a diplomatic uproar, as Díaz's foreign office launched undiplomatically worded protests. What happened to the guides is not apparent.[12]

The border incursions as reported by Shafter and Ord stirred up the new administration of President Rutherford B. Hayes. A cabinet meeting supported his determination to take harsh action, especially since Díaz craved American recognition of his legitimacy. The deliberations in Washington led to what became known as the Order of June 1, notifying Mexican border officials that, if the Mexican government continued to neglect its responsibility to prevent border raids, the U.S. government would undertake that task. "You will, therefore," George W. McCrary, secretary of war, wrote to General Sherman, "direct General Ord that in case the lawless incursions continue he will be at liberty, in the use of his own discretion, when in pursuit of them or upon a fresh trail, to follow them across the Rio Grande, and to overtake and punish them, as well as retake the stolen property taken from our citizens and found in their hands on the Mexican side of the line."[13]

The Order of June 1 outraged Díaz, because his foreign minister had informed the American minister in May 1877 that a high-ranking general would be sent to the border with a sufficient force to cooperate in suppressing the problem. On June 15 General Ord crossed to Piedras Negras and met General Gerónimo Treviño. Two days later Treviño and two of his staff crossed to Eagle Pass and were met by Ord. From Fort Duncan they moved up to Fort Clark and conferred for two days. The two generals established a close personal rapport as well as an understanding of mutual obligations pursuant to the Order of June 1.[14]

Treviño and Ord had established a warm and lasting relationship, but they could not make it officially effective because of constraints on the Mexican general. Lacking the troops to quell both Indian and Mexican raiders, Treviño had to rely on locally raised militia that rode stolen American horses and traded for the Indians' plunder. In addition, the Mexican minister of war subjected him to crippling edicts and public opinion opposed cooperation with the Americans. Díaz bitterly resented the Order of June 1.

On July 16 an emissary from Treviño arrived in San Antonio with a letter from the general and the mission of explaining to Ord a directive from the Mexican minister of war. Clearly embarrassed at the peremptory tone of the minister's letter, Treviño had to concede that he would oppose any American border crossings with force. He asked, therefore, that both sides confine their operations to their respective sides of the border until a treaty could be concluded. No treaty was possible, of course, so long as the Order of June 1 remained in effect and the United States declined to recognize Díaz. Ord was directed to continue to be guided by that order.[15]

As directed by Ord, Lieutenant Bullis on August 12, 1877, led a force of ninety-one cavalry and Seminole-Negro Scouts in a reconnaissance out of Fort Clark up the Rio Grande to near the mouth of Devil's River. Here they lay in camp scouting the Rio Grande for an Indian trail to justify crossing into Mexico. Not until September 29 did the lieutenant lead his men into Mexico. On September 30 he found a Lipan Apache camp five miles from Zaragoza. The occupants hastily abandoned their lodges as Bullis crashed among them. The troopers captured fifteen stolen horses and two mules, burned twenty-seven lodges, and made haste to return to the border, where Shafter waited with another command. One hundred Mexican dragoons followed Bullis, who turned and formed a line of battle. The Mexican colonel did the same. Neither side wanted a fight, and Bullis withdrew across the Rio Grande.[16]

Ord's volatile character and his continued correspondence with General Sherman angered General Sheridan, who blamed Ord in part for the border crossing troubles. On November 24, 1877, Sheridan expressed his frustration to Sherman:

> If you will permit me I will say that it is my belief that we cannot have any quiet or peace on the Rio Grande, so long as Ord is in command of Texas. I have lost confidence in his motives, and his management of his department is a confusion which is demoralizing to his subordinates. If he could be sent somewhere else and a good man put in his place, we could bring quiet to that frontier. I am sorry that it is my belief that Ord is the trouble down there.[17]

Sherman agreed:

> I have been conscious for some time that you attribute much of the clamor on the Texas border to General Ord. . . . To change

Ord *now* under pressure might damage him, but I am more convinced that a cool and less spasmodic man in Texas would do more to compose matters on that border than mere increases of cavalry, for which now is the cry.[18]

The cry was answered immediately. Responding to Ord's repeated pleas, Sheridan directed Colonel Mackenzie and part of his Fourth Cavalry to report to Texas for service on the Rio Grande. Mackenzie had led the raid into Mexico in 1873 and stood ready to repeat the performance again.

Aside from his eccentricities, Ord had worked closely with the Texas congressional delegation. His appeals for more troops resonated with Texan members of Congress, as Sherman admitted to Sheridan in November 1877: "The Texas members claim that we of the Army owe them a debt of gratitude for saving the Army Bill this Extra Session, which is true for the Democrats had the power and were resolved to cut us down to 20,000 this session and to 17,000 in the Regular Term. There is some force to this claim, and unless we can reconcile the Texas Democrats in the House, we will be slaughtered this winter."[19] Thanks to the Texas Democrats, the army was not slaughtered during the winter session of Congress. Much of the credit could be attributed to General Ord's amicable relations with the Texas members of Congress.

On April 9, 1878, the Hayes administration extended diplomatic recognition to the Díaz government, but that only slightly alleviated the border tensions because the Order of June 1, 1877, remained in force. Lipan and Mescalero raiders continued to inflame the border, and Mexican military forces did little to prevent them. In summer 1878 Mackenzie determined to demonstrate American resolve. Ord seems not to have been eager for as large an operation as Mackenzie intended but at length provided what the colonel deemed sufficient authorization.

Mackenzie assembled an expedition, consisting of three battalions of infantry under Colonel Shafter, eight troops of cavalry, three batteries of artillery (including one of Gatling guns), Lieutenant Bullis's Seminole-Negro Scouts, and a train of more than forty wagons. Clearly the objective was more than Indian raiding parties. The command crossed above the mouth of Devil's River on June 12, 1878. Twice, near Remolino on June 19 and 21, Mackenzie faced formidable battle lines of Mexican troops drawn up to contest his advance. Both Mexican colonels vowed to resist, but the Mexicans withdrew when Mackenzie pressed forward with Shafter in the center and cavalry on both flanks. Having made his point, Mackenzie returned to the American side of the Rio Grande.[20]

Mackenzie had blatantly violated Mexican sovereignty and provoked public outrage and diplomatic protests. In the months following the Mackenzie operation, however, General Treviño mustered significant forces along the border and made progress in quelling Indian raiding. Also, Treviño and thirteen staff officers crossed the Rio Grande in November 1878, met with Colonel Shafter at Fort Clark, then proceeded to San Antonio to socialize with General Ord. The Ord-Treviño entourage next traveled to Galveston and were richly feted by the city fathers. Treviño's genial personality appealed to Texans and made him immensely popular. The visit further so much cemented his friendship with Ord that in 1880 Treviño married Ord's eldest daughter.

The Mackenzie expedition marked the high point of border troubles. As Generals Treviño and Ord deepened their friendship and cooperation, Treviño's forces brought more and more of the raiding Indians under Mexican control. By October 1879 Ord could report that Mexican officials had demonstrated their intent and ability to suppress the incursions that had led to the Order of June 1, 1877, and recommended that it be suspended.[21] On March 8, 1880, President Hayes withdrew the order.

But Ord still bore Sheridan's animosity, as Sheridan made plain on December 12, 1879:

> General Ord's eccentricity of character and the devious methods he employs to accomplish his ends, some time since forced me to doubt his motives in some of his official actions and so much has this impression gained on me that for a long time I have reluctantly avoided any personal correspondence with him. I have doubted his motives in some of his recommendations for expenditures of public money and even in his calls for and disposition of troops; and the facility with which revolutions, raids, murders and thefts are generated on the Rio Grande border whenever an emergency demands the temporary withdrawal of troops or even a special officer from the Department of Texas is somewhat remarkable.

All of these circumstances have occasioned in my mind a distrust of Ord's management of affairs in Texas and I feel that we want there an officer free from schemes and with such as officer I believe the constant irritation represented as existing on that frontier would be to a great extent modified if not wholly allayed.[22]

This was only the latest—and most damning—of Sheridan's appraisals of his subordinate, which would have doomed most officers. Sherman agreed, at least in part, with Sheridan's indictment and had already conceded that Ord was not a good fit for Texas. But an abiding friendship that extended back to 1847 made it almost impossible for Sherman to act against Ord. Indeed, unexpected events in 1880 compelled him to come to his old friend's defense. On October 18 Ord reached the age of sixty-two. With forty years' service, he was eligible for retirement, but it was not mandatory until age sixty-four. The election of 1880 had ended Rutherford B. Hayes's presidency, but he remained president until inauguration in March 1881. If he wished, he could forcibly retire General Ord and General Irvin McDowell, both of whom were sixty-two. As Sherman wrote to General Alfred Terry:

The moment I heard that the President had called Miles here I saw that Ord's commission was in danger. I was Ord's chum at West Point, served with him side by side ten years in Florida, the South, and California, and am familiar with his career since. He is a rough diamond, always at work, on the most distant frontier; has a far better war record, and is a harder, stronger soldier than McDowell [in] every way; he is as poor as a rat, having been all his life taxed with the care of parents and a large family. I was, therefore, bound as a man to go to his rescue, when I feared that neglect would result in an act of palpable gross injustice. I put it in writing that if the President would retire McDowell and Ord, I and all would say amen, but if Ord alone would be forced out, I believed the Army and the world [would] cry shame.[23]

Much of the army did cry shame, for on the next day, December 6, 1880, President Hayes forcibly retired General Ord and nine days later promoted Colonel Nelson A. Miles to brigadier general. Texans made certain that

Ord received a consolation prize: two days after Miles's promotion, on December 17, Senator Samuel B. Maxey of Texas introduced legislation to place Ord on the retired list as a major general. The bill easily passed both houses on January 28, 1881. As Sherman wrote in thanking the senator, a former Confederate major general: "It actually seems 'funny' that I should be forced to appeal to you, a 'rebel,' to protect my oldest and best friend against the action of the union President; but such is the fact. 'Tempora mutantur'" (The times are changing).[24]

Ord's desperate need for money to sustain his family led him to New York and ultimately a position of surveyor with the Mexican Central Railroad. Docking in Vera Cruz, he was met by the minister of war, Gerónimo Treviño, and his wife, the former Roberta Ord. Ord was feted in Mexico City and pursued his new calling in the Mexican wilderness. In the summer of 1883 he boarded a steamer for New York to deal with company business. While at sea he and other passengers and crew were struck by yellow fever. In Havana, Cuba, Ord was transferred to a hospital, where he died on July 22, 1883. Interred in Oak Hill Cemetery in Washington, D.C., his body was reburied in 1900 in Arlington National Cemetery.

Edward Ord led a checkered military career. As an antebellum subaltern in the West, he distinguished himself as an Indian fighter. During the Civil War, he achieved outstanding performance in the Vicksburg and Appomattox campaigns and as commander of the Army of the James. In the Shenandoah Valley and other operations, however, he displayed a want of judgment and intolerance for inconvenience unbecoming a general. As a department commander in the postwar West, he proved mediocre or worse. The Department of the Platte offered few problems during his tenure. The Department of California demanded attention to Apache Indian hostilities in Arizona, but Ord exercised little influence over subordinate officers. His stature as a department commander rests almost entirely on his five years heading the Department of Texas, 1875–80.

In Texas border troubles constituted Ord's only serious challenge. He handled those principally through his subordinates, Shafter and Mackenzie. Both were competent, and he supported both in their violation of Mexican territory. He deserves credit for gaining popularity with the people of Texas, for his work with the Texas congressional delegation, and above all for cementing consequential friendship with General Gerónimo Treviño. The cross-border operations launched under his orders, (especially the one led by Mackenzie), combined with the cooperation of General Treviño, led to resolution of the border issue.

Ord's eccentricity, however, made his years turbulent. His repeated violation of the chain of command by writing directly to General Sherman, bypassing General Sheridan, kept his headquarters in constant confusion. It also stamped Ord as a maverick general. Sheridan's opinion of Ord as spasmodic, scheming, obstinate, insubordinate, indiscreet, and unpredictable may have exaggerated his flaws but contained some elements of truth. As commander of the Department of Texas, and therefore as a department commander, General Ord emerges as a mediocrity.

Brigadier General John Pope, commanding
Department of the Northwest, 1862–1865;
Department of the Missouri, 1870–1883.
Brady Collection, U.S. Signal Corps (photo BA-230),
National Archives and Records Administration, Washington, D.C.

CHAPTER SEVEN

JOHN POPE

John Pope presents something of an enigma. Until he reached the age of forty, when he began his service against western Indians, he displayed a blazing volcanic temperament. After assuming command of a department in 1862, his volatility subsided. History largely remembers the volcanic John Pope: the arrogant, bombastic, vain, ambitious, opinionated, insubordinate, mendacious, scheming self-promoter. Less well known are the twenty-one years (1862–83) when he commanded a western department and briefly a division. He lost none of his verbosity but commanded effectively and thoughtfully. Perhaps symbolic of the transformation, in 1870 he replaced his large black beard with a neat mustache.

John Pope was born on March 16, 1822, in Louisville, Kentucky. His father and mother were both well educated and transmitted their love of books and learning to young John. Nathaniel Pope represented the new Territory of Illinois in Congress, then served nineteen years as the only federal judge in Illinois. With his firm political alliances, Judge Pope easily secured for his son an appointment to West Point Military Academy. Entering in 1838, John Pope graduated in 1842, seventeenth in his class of fifty-six, a ranking that allowed him to select his branch of service. He chose the elite Corps of Topographical Engineers.[1]

Lieutenant Pope's first postings were in the East, from Florida to Maine. His assignments were uncongenial mainly because he lobbied with politicians to get himself assigned to congenial locations. This angered the chief of the Topographical Corps, Colonel John J. Abert, but the colonel's increasingly ominous reprimands failed to quell Pope's blatant insubordination.

He continued to do as he pleased, despite the growing peril to his career. The Mexican War temporarily saved Pope from Abert's wrath. One of seven topographical officers assigned to General Zachary Taylor's army, Pope distinguished himself through his topographical competence and his battlefield bravery, both at the Battle of Monterey and at the Battle of Buena Vista. The two battles earned him brevets of first lieutenant and captain.

The postwar years focused public interest on the West, especially the southwestern lands acquired from Mexico. The topographical engineers played a dominant role in the West. With the issue of a railroad route to the Pacific hotly debated, Brevet Captain Pope was eager to be sent west with his colleagues. Colonel Abert assigned him to Minnesota instead, where he spent two years making a nuisance of himself and writing pleading letters to politicians. Eventually Abert ordered Pope to New Mexico Territory in 1851 as chief topographical officer.

Pope's first assignment was survey work on the Santa Fe Trail. In his reports he belittled the maps of Captain John C. Frémont, an Abert protégé, and undertook a lengthy treatise on the proper placement of military posts, couched in language that proclaimed himself an expert. Colonel Abert erupted with a severe reprimand, but it had no effect on Pope. With the support of the department commander, he won the post of chief of the topographical survey of the 32nd parallel route for a Pacific Railway. Thereafter he became enamored with the potential of drilling artesian wells on the Texas Staked Plains and won congressional backing to experiment with this technology, which in the end failed.

Yielding to the plight of officers denied promotion for lack of seniority. Congress had enacted legislation that elevated Pope to captain on July 1, 1856, by virtue of fourteen years of continuous service. His artesian project occupied him until 1859, when he was assigned to Cincinnati to design lighthouses for the Great Lakes.

CIVIL WAR

Captain Pope's station in Cincinnati afforded a convenient platform from which to cultivate political connections and led to marriage into a wealthy and prominent family. As the secession winter of 1860–61 unfolded, Pope appointed himself an authority on the crisis. He penned long letters to his fellow Illinoisan Abraham Lincoln, now president-elect living in Springfield.

With characteristic prolixity, Pope told Lincoln what he *had* to do, in both military and civil matters. Rather than openly resenting Pope's audacity, Lincoln invited him to journey to Washington, D.C., aboard the train bearing him to the inaugural. Pope also lectured bombastically on current events. In one lecture, reported in the newspapers, he denounced the still-incumbent President James Buchanan. Publicly maligning his commander-in-chief earned Pope summons to a court-martial, which the president generously rescinded.

After Fort Sumter fell in April 1861, Pope lobbied vigorously for prefer-ment. When the governor of Illinois appointed him mustering officer for the state regiments being formed, he carried out this duty efficiently and pushed hard for high rank. In May, through political friends, he gained appointment as brigadier general of volunteers, but this was not enough. He wanted President Lincoln to grant him a brigadier's commission in the Regular Army. Lincoln declined, stoking Pope's fury and fueling a letter directly to the president accusing him of lying.

Pope's indiscretion could have led to a court-martial, but he was saved by his commander, Major General George B. McClellan, who saved him with orders to proceed to Alton, Illinois, and take command of the six Illinois regiments that he had mustered into the service. The move embroiled Pope in the chaos of Missouri, overrun with guerrilla bands and Confederate partisans. With competence and ingenuity, he achieved a fine record there. At the same time, he wanted senators to see him as a true son of Illinois. He therefore lobbied to bring all Illinois regiments into one command, so large that it would perforce require a major general to command it--and a Regular Army major general at that.

As Pope worked toward this implausible goal, he found himself under the command of Major General John C. Frémont, who imposed martial law and badly mismanaged the Missouri operations. Sensing that Frémont's days were numbered, Pope campaigned to replace him. Instead, on November 19, 1861, Major General Henry Halleck took command of the Department of Missouri. Pope worked well under Halleck during the balance of the fighting in Missouri. He commanded the Union forces in the Battle of Blackwater River on December 19, 1861, a victory that helped clear the southwestern part of the state and opened the way for the decisive Battle of Pea Ridge in April 1862.[2]

While Pope continued his efforts to secure a Regular Army rank of brigadier general and disparaged President Lincoln for not granting it, developments in Halleck's command opened the way for a singular triumph. General Ulysses S. Grant took the Confederate forts Henry and Donelson, prompting a Confederate withdrawal south from Columbus, Kentucky, and fortification of an island in the Mississippi River to prevent Union use of the river. Wanting the river cleared as far south as Memphis, Tennessee, Halleck offered Pope command of an expedition on February 18, 1862, charged with taking Island No. 10 and the nearby town of New Madrid, Missouri, and thus opening the river to Union shipping. Island No. 10 lay upstream from New Madrid but was actually south of town because of the huge southward loop in the river called Kentucky Bend.

Halleck had concentrated troops at Commerce, Missouri, with still more to come, but Pope did not wait. With eight thousand infantry and a contingent of cavalry and artillery, he marched the Army of the Mississippi south from Commerce on February 28. For forty miles a narrow corduroy road to New Madrid cut through flooded fields and spreading swamps. With rain and snow drenching the green infantrymen and the narrow road forcing many to march through mud and swamps, the exhausted mud-caked soldiers reached flat dry land around New Madrid on March 3.

Pope confronted a formidable array of defense works sealing New Madrid against the Mississippi River. Two strong fortresses linked by trenches harbored five Confederate infantry regiments and twenty-one heavy cannon. Supporting the land forces were six enemy gunboats in the river behind the town. Up the river (south) Island No. 10 bristled with nineteen guns and a floating battery of nine guns.

Unwilling to launch a frontal assault against such heavy defenses, Pope sent back to Halleck for heavy siege guns. He then dispatched a brigade south to take position at Point Pleasant, opposite Island No. 10. Shelled by enemy gunboats, the brigade pulled back out of range but then advanced when the vessels left, only to repeat the movement when the gunboats returned.

The siege guns arrived on March 12, and Pope began to bombard New Madrid the next day. Two days of heavy shelling persuaded the enemy to withdraw. After spiking their cannon, they slipped out of their defenses under cover of a rainy night and abandoned New Madrid to Pope.

Flag Officer Andrew H. Foote, commanding the Western Flotilla of six gunboats, was supposed to cooperate with Pope but remained at Cairo, Illinois, repairing damages sustained in the battles against forts Henry and Donelson; Foote therefore refused Pope's pleas by contending that he was not ready. Finally, on March 15, Foote's fleet arrived off Island No. 10. Pope wanted him to slip two or three gunboats past the island at night and proceed to New Madrid to bombard Confederate shore batteries. Pope had adopted a new scheme for getting his army across the Mississippi to attack the island: dig a canal from New Madrid to the river to ferry his units to the east bank of the river and take the island from the rear. Aside from the near impossibility of such a project in a flooded country, Pope needed Foote's guns to neutralize Confederate shore batteries that would hamper construction. Foote refused and settled instead for a steady bombardment of the island.

Despite the terrain obstacles, Pope's engineers prevailed. A day before the canal's completion on March 30, Flag Officer Foote allowed a gunboat to run the island batteries at night. It succeeded, as did a second. Pope summoned a fleet of transports to carry his army through the canal and across the river. When the gunboats destroyed the rebel shore batteries, the prospect of defending Island No. 10 against such odds subdued the Confederates, who surrendered on April 8, 1862.

General Pope could boast—as he did—of a significant victory: opening the Mississippi to Union vessels nearly to Memphis and taking 5,000 prisoners of war, 123 cannon, and huge stores of arms and ammunition, all with only 32 casualties. He had already been promoted to major general of Volunteers, but once more he enlisted his supportive senators to influence the president to reward him with a major general's commission in the Regular Army. Lincoln responded that such commissions "are not as plentiful as blackberries."[3]

Meanwhile General Grant had fought the Battle of Shiloh at great cost and advanced toward Corinth, Mississippi. Halleck himself assumed overall command, leaving Pope's Army of the Mississippi to align with two other armies and form the Union line. Rain and mud slowed the approach to Corinth, but Pope got ahead of the other two armies and fought one engagement. An angry Halleck pulled him back to the line and ordered the entire force to dig in. Pope undertook his own movement with a cavalry raid south of Corinth to tear up the railroad, and on May 31, 1862, the enemy abandoned Corinth.

Pope's role in the Corinth campaign was largely to operate beyond Halleck's instructions, quarrel with fellow generals, and cultivate the press, but the nation and his own troops knew him now as an aggressive fighter. On June 19, on leave with his family, he received a telegram from the secretary of war, Edwin M. Stanton, summoning him to Washington. In the capital the secretary informed Pope that he had been selected to command a newly styled Army of Virginia. Its purpose was to unite the two corps unsuccessfully fighting Stonewall Jackson in the Shenandoah Valley with the corps of General Irvin McDowell to the east, in northern Virginia. The new army's mission was to protect Washington, D.C., defend the valley, and disrupt the vital railroad link to the valley. Unknown to Pope, Stanton and the president had another purpose: they sought a general who would fight, in contrast to General McClellan on the Virginia Peninsula. Pope tried to decline the offer, contending that he would be commanding generals who ranked him and that he wished to retain his army command in the West, but Lincoln decreed that Pope would remain in the East.

Pope's corps commanders not only ranked him but were inept if not incompetent. Franz Sigel, Nathaniel Banks, and Irvin McDowell had all proved their shortcomings on the battlefield. Sigel was a general because he was German and Banks because he was a political power in Massachusetts. Only McDowell, despite his frigid personality, served Pope well. Pope's nemesis, however, was General McClellan, almost inert on the Peninsula because he vastly overrated his opposition and could not have the reinforcements that he demanded. Each detested the other. Pope regarded McClellan as a fool, and McClellan resented Pope's intrusion into his domain.

On July 14, 1862, before leaving Washington, D.C., to take the field himself, Pope issued a proclamation to his army that produced a furious backlash. He had come from the West, he wrote, where the armies had always seen the backs of the enemy and where the aim was attack and not defense. He wanted no talk of lines of retreat, bases of supply, or holding strong positions. His men should study the enemy's lines of retreat. They should regard strong positions as those from which to advance. Look before, not behind, he admonished.

This critique of the eastern armies by a westerner, whose armies were largely from the western states, earned Pope a largely hostile response from an army waiting to follow him into battle. It also produced an angry reaction in the newspapers. General McClellan and his Army of the Potomac were especially wrathful at the implication of their inferiority, but Pope's greatest problem was the alienation of his own Army of Virginia. Poorly equipped and supplied, demoralized by Stonewall Jackson, and badly commanded, that army now had to submit to an alien general who seemed to hold it in contempt.

General Robert E. Lee drew units from the lines facing McClellan east of Richmond and amassed a defense force centered on Gordonsville to screen the Virginia Central Railway, which connected to the Shenandoah Valley. General Halleck, now general-in-chief, instructed McClellan to abandon the Peninsula and join Pope to confront Lee. While waiting for McClellan at Culpepper, Pope was to mark time by keeping Lee engaged but not bringing on battle.

On August 7, however, Lee took the initiative, sending Stonewall Jackson with the left wing of the army to strike Pope's scattered units. Pope learned of Jackson's advance and confronted him at Cedar Mountain. Jackson pushed back his assailants but was in turn pushed back by the arrival of another Union division. On August 12 Jackson withdrew to Gordonsville, where Lee reinforced him with General James Longstreet's right wing.

On August 3 Halleck had directed McClellan to disengage on the Peninsula and begin his march to join Pope. McClellan, adroit at delay and loath to have any association with Pope, began a sluggish movement on August 14. Freed by McClellan's withdrawal, Lee hastened to destroy Pope before McClellan could arrive. Lee sought to steal around Pope's right flank through Thoroughfare Gap and move rapidly east to cut the Orange and Alexandria Railway, the Union supply route. Jackson succeeded and captured the huge Union supply depot at Manassas Junction on August 27. Learning that Longstreet had broken through Thoroughfare Gap and was on the way to join him, Jackson took up defensive positions around the site of the first Battle of Manassas. It remained for Pope's army, and any units arriving from McClellan, to break through the rebel lines and restore communication with Washington.

Pope had erred in not attacking Jackson, and then Longstreet, before they reached Thoroughfare Gap. Reports had reached his headquarters signaling movement by the two corps, but he did not know their destination. He chose to believe that Jackson was headed for the Shenandoah Valley and refrained from moving against him. Instead, anticipating reinforcements from McClellan's army, he held his positions along the Rappahannock River. In fact, the corps of Fitz John Porter and Samuel Heintzelman had reached the field on August 22. Pope dispatched a burst of confusing, contradictory orders to his corps commanders, some written and others verbal, carried by courier. Such orders reflected in part Pope's disorderly mind but also the indecision of General Halleck.

In hopes of trapping Jackson before Longstreet arrived, Pope began to draw his units off the Rappahannock River to unite with the main army at Centreville. One route lay along the Warrenton Pike, which ran parallel to an unfinished railroad grade behind which Jackson had fortified his troops. In late afternoon of August 28 Jackson discovered the lead elements of a Union division, a brigade under General John Gibbon, marching across his front on the pike. Jackson launched an attack that led to a fierce battle with heavy casualties and ended in a stalemate at nightfall.

Pope believed that a vigorous assault against Jackson would capture his corps before Longstreet could arrive. He mistakenly assumed that Jackson was in retreat and discounted the threat of Longstreet. On August 29 Pope ordered the attack to begin with General Franz Sigel's corps to strike Jackson's left, while General Fitz John Porter's corps (from McClellan's army) and McDowell's corps struck against Jackson's right. Now, however, it consisted of Longstreet's corps, which marched into position during the day. Sigel's men attacked several times but were unable to pierce Jackson's lines. Porter and McDowell, halted by a brief skirmish with General J. E. B. Stuart's cavalry, received an order brought by a courier from Pope. It was typical of Pope's obfuscation, leaving the two generals to try to understand what he wanted; nowhere did it order an attack. Pope believed that Longstreet had not arrived and that, despite his muddled order, Porter and McDowell were attacking Jackson's right.

At a council of war on the morning of August 30, Pope still acted on his belief that the Confederates were in full retreat. His generals counseled caution but failed to convince him. He ordered an attack on the "retreating" Southerners. They were not retreating, however, but preparing their own attack with Longstreet's command. And General Lee was now on the scene, commanding the entire Confederate force.

When Porter was thrown back with heavy casualties, Jackson and Long-street threw their divisions against Pope's lines with devastating effect. By evening the truth had finally dawned on Pope: he had to contravene his proclamation and have his men show their backs to the enemy. Unlike the first Battle of Manassas, the withdrawal was orderly but nonetheless a calamitous defeat.

The defeat can be attributed only in part to Pope's egomania, ineptitude, and chaotic command performance. A large share of the blame falls on General Halleck, whose orders to Pope during the battle and its run-up were contradictory, confusing, vague, indecisive, or lacking altogether. General McClellan, who had his own problems with Halleck, seized on any excuse to delay or avoid uniting with Pope. McClellan even advised the president that one of the options to be considered was to "leave Pope to get out of his scrape."[4] Except for the corps of Porter and Heintzelman, this was essentially what happened.

On September 5, 1862, President Lincoln relieved General Pope from command of the Army of Virginia, which was consolidated with the Army of the Potomac under McClellan's command. The problem of what to do with Pope solved itself. On August 17 the Santee Sioux of Minnesota, mistreated for years by settlers and corrupt agents and traders, had launched a reign of terror among the settlements. Militia had taken the field, and the governor petitioned Washington to hold back the recently mustered Minnesota Volunteer regiments. On September 17 Secretary Stanton announced the creation of the Department of the Northwest and the assignment of John Pope to command it.[5]

DEPARTMENT OF THE NORTHWEST

General Pope reached his St. Paul headquarters on September 16, 1862. A week later militia colonel Henry H. Sibley, with four regiments of Minnesota Volunteers, defeated Chief Little Crow at the Battle of Wood Lake. On September 26 Sibley received the surrender of the peace faction of the Indians. The war faction fled west onto the Dakota plains. Pope still would have Indian work to do. Moreover, he was no stranger to Minnesota or its leading citizens, having served there as a topographical engineer before the Civil War.

The Santee uprising, featuring widespread massacre of settlers together with horrid atrocities, had roused the Minnesota population to fury against

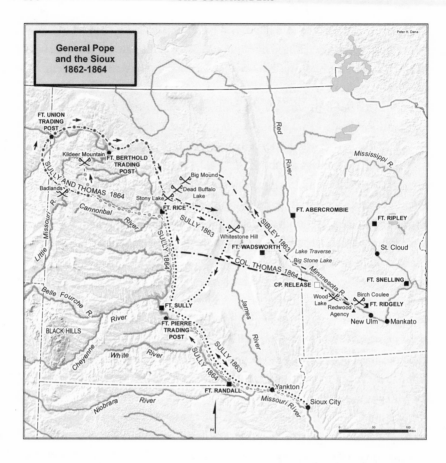

General Pope
and the Sioux
1862-1864

Indians. Colonel Sibley had formed a military commission to deal with
Indians accused of the most heinous barbarities. Ignoring judicial niceties,
the commission quickly condemned 303 warriors to be hanged. President
Lincoln, however, called for the complete records supporting the guilt
of each Indian. Everyone, beginning with Governor Alexander Ramsey,
demanded of Lincoln that the Indians be hanged immediately. So did Pope,
declaring to Lincoln that they were all guilty and that the citizens stood
ready to perpetrate the "indiscriminate massacre of all the Indians—old
men, women and children." He also pointed out that the soldiers guarding the prisoners shared the people's outrage—an assertion reinforced by
the assault of two hundred citizens on the compound in Mankato where

the condemned were held. Pope joined with Governor Ramsey in urging their immediate execution to assuage the citizens. The president, however, refusing to be stampeded, narrowed the list to thirty-eight. Because of the angry populace, Pope imposed tight security on the site of the execution in Mankato. On December 26, 1862, the condemned thirty-eight men were hanged.[6]

While contending with Indians, Pope brooded over his exile from the war zone and over the infuriating defeat at Second Manassas. He believed that he had been the victim of subordinates and superiors alike and especially wanted General Fitz John Porter court-martialed. Without neglecting his local military responsibilities, Pope fired a barrage of outraged letters to senators and the army high command, seeking vindication for Second Manassas and return to the war.

When court-martial proceedings began in December against Fitz John Porter, Pope traveled to Washington, D.C., to testify, then returned to the Northwest. On January 21, 1863, the court found Porter guilty of disobeying an order and misbehavior before the enemy and sentenced him to be cashiered from the army. Pope felt vindicated, although vindication did not earn him a return to the war. Instead Pope returned to the war at hand. To provide better rail and telegraph communication, he moved department headquarters from St. Paul to Milwaukee, Wisconsin.

Pope had no sooner taken command of the department in September 1862 than he discerned that the defeat of the Santees in Minnesota had not ended Indian warfare farther west and began preparing for a campaign against the tribes that had taken refuge in Dakota. They were united with Sissetons and Yanktonais as well as Teton Sioux from the Upper Missouri River, who resented the flocks of gold-seekers using the Missouri River as a path to the Montana and Idaho goldfields. Pope at once began to strengthen Sibley, who had been commissioned brigadier general of Volunteers. In June 1863 Pope alerted Washington about his summer campaign plans. He had succeeded in retaining Minnesota and Wisconsin regiments destined for the South and intended to dispatch Sibley, with three thousand cavalry and infantry as well as artillery, west into Dakota Territory. At the same time, Brigadier General Alfred Sully, who commanded Pope's District of Iowa, would lead two thousand cavalry with a light howitzer battery up the Missouri River, then veer northeast to unite with Sibley.[7]

Pope planned the campaign, but Sibley and Sully carried it out. Both scored significant victories in Dakota east of the Missouri River. On July 24, 1863, Sibley confronted nearly a thousand Sisseton warriors at Big Mound and routed them so decisively that they headed for the British Possessions. On July 27 Sibley camped at Dead Buffalo Lake, only to be assailed by 1,600 Santees united with Tetons who had been hunting bison. Howitzer fire and counterattacks drove the Indians off. The next day the warriors attacked again, at Stony Lake, smashing at both flanks. Again Sibley's howitzers won the day. The Indians raced to cross the Missouri River.

Meanwhile, delayed by low water in the Missouri, General Sully did not reach the battle zone until late August. Sibley had already turned back to Minnesota. On September 3 about a thousand warriors struck a scouting battalion from Sully's command at Whitestone Hill. Surrounded, the battalion held on until a courier who had slipped out brought Sully's entire command to the rescue. The troops drove the attackers into a deep ravine and held them under a heavy fire until nightfall allowed them to escape. About three hundred warriors died in the ravine.[8]

The campaign of 1863 both cost the Indians dearly and roused them to further hostility. Minnesota was now secure, but the Upper Missouri region swarmed with angry Teton Sioux as well as refugees from the Eastern Sioux. Immigration to the Montana goldfields by wagon train and river steamer had increased dramatically, and the gold-seekers and their routes were imperiled by the Sioux. Pope planned a summer 1864 campaign. General Sully would lead his brigade up the Missouri River, establish two military posts, and fight any Sioux inclined to oppose him. Sibley's brigade, now under Colonel Minor T. Thomas, would march to the Missouri River from Minnesota.[9]

The two brigades united on June 29, 1864, even as the various tribes of Tetons coalesced and moved west toward the badlands of the Little Missouri River. With 2,200 men, Sully found trails leading to a large Sioux encampment at the base of Killdeer Mountain that harbored about 1,600 warriors. Sully discovered the sprawling village of tipis on July 28. Dismounting his cavalry and forming a hollow square enclosing his artillery, he launched his attack. Warriors rode forth to contest him, but after heavy fighting they retreated to their lodges to save their women and children. During the night they hastened west into the forbidding Dakota Badlands. The next day the troops burned the Indian camp and all its stores, a grievous loss.[10]

Sully's victory ended Pope's operations of 1864. The Sioux had not been conquered. The army would fight them for another fifteen years, but Pope had planted forts on the Upper Missouri and demonstrated his ability to exercise overall command of military operations against Indians. The experience had led him to thoughtful conclusions about dealing with Indians.

Pope had arrived in Minnesota in 1862 as an advocate of stern measures toward Indians. He even talked of extermination if they did not behave themselves. Two years of campaigning, however, convinced him that war and peace alone were not enough. The whole system of treating Indians was wrong and should be remedied. As with past issues, Pope had the answers and set them to paper in a long treatises. The treaty system and the accompanying practice of paying annuities, which opened the way for unscrupulous traders, should be abolished The "semi-civilized" tribes should be disarmed and moved behind the frontier of settlement, to be educated and Christianized under civilian agents. The "wild tribes" should be placed under military control and gathered around military posts under army authority, to be Christianized and taught to farm. The government should quit paying Indians for lands they supposedly owned, thus allowing them to be robbed by whites and having to fight wars with them. The Indians should be treated as wards of the government. Finally, new trade regulations to be enforced by the military should be drafted (which he himself did).

Pope submitted this proposal to the War Department in April 1864. General Halleck was sympathetic and had it published in the *Army and Navy Journal*. But the nation had a civil war to fight and the Indian Bureau furiously opposed any tampering with Indian policy. Still, Pope embraced his cause and never let go of it.[11]

Pope supposed that the controversy over Indian policy, together with a spat with War Department inspectors over his troop returns, had put him in bad odor in Washington, D.C., so a telegram on November 23, 1864, summoning him there caused worry. At the War Department he was ordered to report at City Point to General Grant, then conducting the siege of Petersburg. Ridding himself of unsatisfactory department commanders, Grant offered Pope the Department of the South. Pope balked, citing the trials of occupation duty and his wish to serve on the frontier. Grant yielded and recommended to the president that the Departments of the Northwest, Missouri, and Kansas be merged into a single Military Division of the Missouri, with Pope commanding

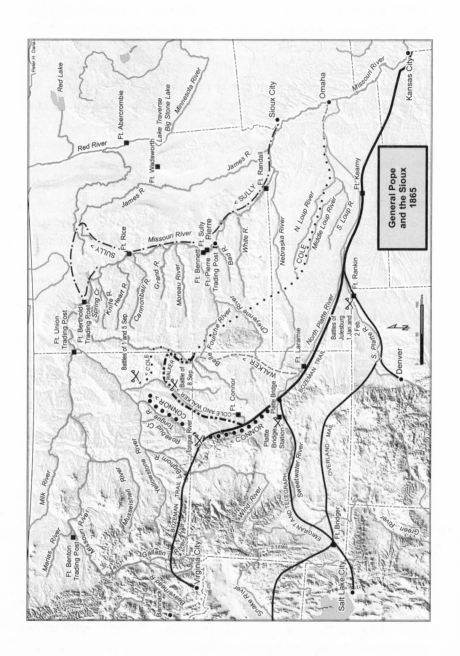

from St. Louis. On February 3, 1865, Pope took command, with a brevet of major general in the Regular Army following on March 13 for "gallant and meritorious service in the capture of Island No. 10."

MILITARY DIVISION OF THE MISSOURI

Pope's new command presented challenges that few other Union generals had to meet. Missouri alone, still swarming with guerrilla bands and freebooters as well as the remnants of Confederate armies, demanded close attention. Fortunately, Major General Grenville M. Dodge commanded the Department of the Missouri, which now included the Department of Kansas after the exile of the inept Samuel R. Curtis to the Department of the Northwest. Dodge was a competent volunteer general and served Pope as well as his meager resources permitted.

Pope's division command lasted only until June 27, when a reworking of military boundaries gave General William T. Sherman division command and relegated Pope to the Department of the Missouri. Even so, he dealt with the same Indian problems he that would have in division command. His most serious challenge, indeed a crisis, lay west of Missouri all the way to the Rocky Mountains. On November 29, 1864, Colorado's rogue militia colonel, John M. Chivington, had perpetrated the Sand Creek Massacre on peaceful Cheyenne Indians. Sand Creek sparked an uprising of the plains tribes from the Arkansas River to the Upper Missouri. Frontier ranches and settlements fell victim to roving war parties as freight trains, stagecoaches, and travelers on the overland trails fought off feathered warriors.

Pope and General Dodge planned a spring 1865 campaign that would have Brigadier General James H. Ford thrust south of the Arkansas River against Cheyennes, Arapahos, Kiowas, and Comanches. Brigadier General Patrick E. Connor would move north from the Platte against the Sioux and Cheyennes. General Sully would push across Dakota and establish a supply base for Connor on Powder River.[12]

Pope and Dodge had hoped to get the three commands in motion by early spring, but bad weather, orders to muster out Volunteer units, and an Indian peace commission in the south frustrated their efforts. General Ford was mustered out even before he could get underway. Brigadier General John B. Sanborn took his place; but the peace commissioners won, and military operations never commenced.[13]

General Connor had modest success although also plagued by regiments that were ordered mustered out and others threatening mutiny. His offensive got underway in early August. Sully had been diverted, but Connor sent three columns to converge on the Powder River country. Connor himself led one, which attacked an Arapaho village on August 29. That was the only success, if it could even be labeled that. In early September the other two columns fought several engagements with the Sioux on the lower Powder, but Sioux aggressiveness only complicated more severe conditions. Exhausted supplies, exhausted men and horses, rain, snow, overflowing rivers, freezing temperatures alternating with broiling heat, and 225 dead horses all contributed to an inglorious finale to Pope's elaborately planned campaign.

After the Connor expedition, Pope was bedeviled by two conditions that froze his plans for military operations. The Civil War was over, and the mutinous troops had to be discharged. Reflecting this necessity, the War Department applied such extreme pressure on Pope to economize that he had to use his much-reduced force solely to garrison the forts and protect the overland trails. The other interference came from the growing power of the Interior Department and its Bureau of Indian Affairs. With Senate backing, the civilians set about making the treaties that Pope so abhorred. As he advised General Sherman, "I must again state to you that I do not consider the treaties lately made with the Sioux, Cheyennes, Arapahos, and Comanches worth the paper they are written on, for reasons I have given you so often that you must be sick of hearing them."[14]

Pope's Indian service was interrupted on September 1, 1866, when he was mustered out of the Volunteers and donned the single star of a Regular Army brigadier general. A month later he took leave of absence for six months, then was assigned to the Reconstruction Third Military District, which consisted of Georgia, Alabama, and Florida. He endured that disagreeable duty from April 1 to December 28, 1867. The more congenial Department of the Lakes returned him to Cincinnati from January 13, 1868, to April 30, 1870. On that date orders sent him back to Indian duty, which occupied him until his retirement in 1886.

DEPARTMENT OF THE MISSOURI

Pope assumed command of the Department of the Missouri on May 3, 1870. Headquartered at Fort Leavenworth, Kansas, the department embraced

Illinois, Missouri, Kansas, the Indian Territory, Colorado, and New Mexico. New Mexico was a separate district whose commander reported to Pope. General Grant's election to the presidency elevated General Sherman to head the army and Lieutenant General Philip H. Sheridan to command the Military Division of the Missouri from Chicago. Pope now reported to Sheridan.

With Cheyennes and Arapahos striking at construction workers on the Kansas Pacific Railway and Kiowas and Comanches raiding south into Texas, Pope at once confronted two of the three issues that would dominate his thinking throughout the years during which he commanded the department. First, the treaties that he had vociferously assailed as terrible policy had created reservations with which he had to deal. In the Indian Territory (moved to the Department of Texas in 1871 and thus out of Pope's jurisdiction), the Kiowa and Comanche Reservation bordered Texas on the south, and the Cheyenne and Arapaho Reservation bordered Kansas on the north. To complicate the military mission, President Grant's Peace Policy placed reservations off-limits to the army. Warriors off the reservations could be pursued and attacked but were safe once on the reservation. Post commanders on the reservations knew who the leaders of the raids were and even when they departed or returned, but they could take no action. Even so, as Pope complained, the army bore some of the blame for the raids. This was especially true, he noted, of Colonel Benjamin H. Grierson at Fort Sill, on the Kiowa-Comanche Reservation. Texans denounced Grierson for not preventing the raids, and even some of the officers in Texas faulted him. Pope called in vain for War Department orders specifying the exact relations between reservation Indians and local commanders. To Pope, this situation reinforced his denunciation of federal Indian policy while he was commanding in the Northwest.[15]

Demonstrating how quickly he grasped the essence of his new command, in six months Pope conceived a strategy that he wanted to apply to Indian operations: concentrate his scattered troops at two large posts for the winter months, then return them to their regular stations in the spring to contend with Indian hostilities. In this manner two posts would replace seven in the winter, and the newly completed Kansas Pacific Railway would facilitate troop movements. Pope thought that his strategy would produce three advantages: a large reduction of expenses; better discipline and morale

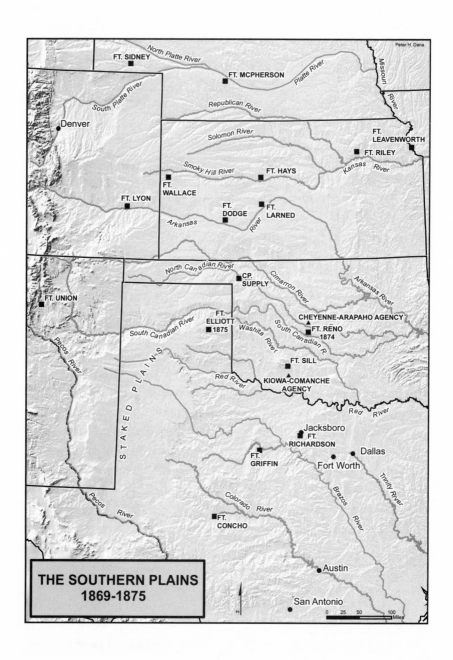

FT. SIDNEY

North Platte River

FT. MCPHERSON

Platte River

Missouri River

Peter H. Dana

South Platte River

Republican River

Denver

Solomon River

FT. LEAVENWORTH

FT. RILEY

Smoky Hill River

FT. HAYS

Kansas River

FT. WALLACE

FT. LYON

FT. DODGE

FT. LARNED

Arkansas River

North Canadian River

CP. SUPPLY

Cimarron River

Arkansas River

FT. UNION

South Canadian River

FT. ELLIOTT 1875

Washita River

South Canadian R.

CHEYENNE-ARAPAHO AGENCY

FT. RENO 1874

Pecos River

S T A K E D   P L A I N S

Red River

FT. SILL

KIOWA-COMANCHE AGENCY

Red River

Jacksboro

FT. RICHARDSON

Dallas

FT. GRIFFIN

Fort Worth

Pecos River

Colorado River

FT. CONCHO

Brazos River

Trinity River

Austin

THE SOUTHERN PLAINS
1869-1875

N

San Antonio

0   25   50   100
Miles

among the troops; and ability to use more of the available force for field service. Concentration would prove his second dominant issue.[16]

Pope and his wife Clara settled into comfortable quarters at the sprawling post of Fort Leavenworth. He was not a field general. He commanded from his desk at department headquarters, occasionally embarking on an inspection tour of his domain. He gave close attention to all the issues arising in the department and reported them verbosely, but without the flamboyant rhetoric of his earlier years. As before, controversy dogged him, but not as intensely as in the past.

In 1874, en route to a new assignment at Fort Wingate, New Mexico, Assistant Surgeon John Vance Lauderdale recorded his impression of General Pope: "Made a call upon Genl Pope and wife in their quarters near the Arsenal. Genl Pope and lady are both very sociable and pleased me very much. The Genl is a man quite well versed in the scientific literature of the day, and when it came my turn to talk with him, we were soon quite deep in Darwinism, evolution and all kindred subjects that came in that range of thought."[17]

Pope's second year commanding the Department of the Missouri was relatively peaceful, in part because the Indian Territory had been transferred to the Department of Texas, a move that Pope himself advocated. He did address a long simmering problem: New Mexican traders journeying to the Staked Plains of Texas to barter arms and ammunition with Kiowas and Comanches for stock and other property seized in Texas. To apprehend the traders, he posted three troops of cavalry on the Canadian River southeast of Fort Union, New Mexico. The summer's mission succeeded in the seizure of many traders, their trains, and large cattle herds, which were turned over to civil authorities in New Mexico. Pope believed that they should be sent to Texas, where owners could more easily retrieve their stolen property. After the same operation the following year, he adopted this change.[18]

Pope still felt strongly about concentration of troops. He repeated verbatim the arguments that he had made a year earlier and added more. General Sheridan disagreed. He considered active operations in Pope's command at an end. Therefore the only remaining mission was to give protection to travel routes and settlements. Garrisoned posts disbursed among the danger points were adequate for that purpose. Sheridan was to be proved badly mistaken in only three years.[19]

In his 1871 annual report Pope hinted at what was to become his third major issue, urged throughout his tenure. Criticizing the Army Regulations, then under revision, he complained of the "concentration of the minutest details of supply and expenditure in the supply bureaus in Washington." This was only the most critical of the flaws in the system of all-powerful staff bureaus in Washington, depriving the army line of control over the many functions that should rest with line commanders.[20]

But concentration of forces remained an obsession for Pope. Never one to be cowed by superior authority, he continued to let Sheridan know how he felt:

> If it were left to my judgment, I would concentrate here [at Fort Leavenworth] all the troops in the department east of New Mexico as winter quarters, and depend altogether on summer camps, thrown out from here in early spring, for all needed military protection of the Kansas frontier. As I have said many times, there is no danger from Indians in this region in the winter, and the summer camps, placed, if judicious, near where the present posts now are, would furnish, and furnish better, and with more efficiency, the military protection now imperfectly supplied by the small posts.[21]

Pope made these same contentions in testifying before the House Committee on Military Affairs in 1874.[22] He succeeded in irritating General Sheridan, who did not take kindly to disagreement. "Pope is a little crazy on staff matters," Sheridan wrote Sherman, referring to Pope's complaint about staff problems, "his mind is in just such a condition that he wants to fight something all the time. I think myself you are the only person who has the best right to complain because Pope can if he wants completely control any & all staff officers in his Dept or any direction they may receive from the Heads of bureaus outside of proper channels."[23]

This was disingenuous and unfair. It was technically true, but in practice the proper channels took so much time that the need had passed before the channels finished working. Moreover, while Pope undoubtedly persisted in fighting for his causes, he was both sincere and thoughtful. His proposals made enough sense that they warranted at least consideration and debate.

As Pope and his fellow department commanders discovered, however, Sheridan's temperament did not brook debate.

The truth hit all the generals in 1874, when Cheyennes raided north into Kansas and Kiowas and Comanches struck for the Staked Plains of Texas. The army was still barred from the reservations. The opening shot of the Red River War took place at the trading post of Adobe Walls, in the Texas Panhandle, on June 27, 1874. The proprietors were bison hide hunters who traded whiskey, arms, and ammunition both with other hunters and with Indians. The warriors' attack on Adobe Walls, fueled by resentment over the slaughter of the herds, was easily repulsed. When the traders applied to General Pope for troops to take station at the trading post, however, he refused: they had proved they could defend themselves, the post was beyond Pope's jurisdiction, and they had not sought protection for their lives but for their illegal business. The traders moved back to Dodge City.[24]

Sheridan objected vociferously to Pope's action. He believed that all U.S. citizens deserved protection, especially these citizens, who were engaged in the valuable work of destroying the Indians' larder. Once the bison vanished, the Indians would do as the government ordered. Sheridan fired off a letter to Sherman, censuring Pope for failing to aid the hide-hunters and for what he labeled a defensive state of mind. Someone leaked the letter to the press, greatly embarrassing Pope, who complained bitterly to Sherman. The affair further roiled the relationship between Pope and Sheridan.[25]

The Red River War began in earnest on July 21, 1874, when Pope received a telegram announcing that the secretary of the interior had opened the Indian reservations to the army. The Cheyennes, Kiowas, and Comanches had taken refuge on the Staked Plains in the Texas Panhandle. Because the area of operations involved both Pope's department and General Christopher C. Augur's Department of Texas, the two generals seem to have evolved the strategy without much oversight from General Sheridan. Five columns converged on the Staked Plains: two from Pope's department and three from Augur's department. Colonel Nelson A. Miles led Pope's main striking force south from Fort Dodge on the Arkansas River. Major William R. Price moved east from New Mexico. Augur launched a command west from Fort Sill, another northwest from Fort Griffin, and a third north from Fort Concho.

On August 30 Miles scored a success against warriors from all three tribes at Tule Canyon, at the northeastern base of the Staked Plain. But lack of supplies, combined with hot, dry weather, forced him to fall back. The principal victory fell to the Fort Concho column under Colonel Ranald S. Mackenzie in a battle in Palo Duro Canyon on September 28. Miles kept to the field, however, after other commands had returned to their bases in the face of winter. By the spring of 1875 all the tribes had given up at their agencies.[26]

The Red River War dramatized Pope's third main cause: the staff's control of events in the field. Colonel Miles's command suffered so much from the failures of supply contractors that on January 23, 1875, Pope wrote a long letter directly to the secretary of war, protesting against a crippling system:

> I assume as a fact which cannot well be disputed, that, being myself responsible for all consequences, and being the person who ought, of all others, to know the needs of the service in the Department and how to meet them, I am the best judge of the sort of contract to be made and the responsibility and ability of the men with whom it is made.
>
> As a matter of fact, I have no control over it, and if the responsibility for whatever may happen from the failure of contractors be assumed by, and enforced against, the Quartermaster General, I am very willing to go on as has been done, but I beg here to protest against being made responsible for the consequences if arrangements which I am not allowed to make and for the failure of the disasters I am not permitted to provide against.[27]

Submerged in his usual drowning verbosity, Pope had identified a basic military maxim: a commander should control his own logistics. When he read the letter, General Sherman understood that too. But he could do little to change the power of the staff bureaus. "We cannot change human nature," he wrote to Pope on April 24, 1876, "or make Congress or the President other than they are; they don't care a cent for the Army, further than that it enables them occasionally to do some favor to a personal friend."[28]

Pope wouldn't give up. In 1876 Ohio judge Alfonso Taft replaced the impeached William Belknap as secretary of war. Taft was more open to needed reforms in the War Department than Belknap had been. Pope therefore urged his wartime comrade, Cincinnati judge Manning F. Force, to press reforms on Secretary Taft. Of the staff bureaus Pope wrote that, "although they absolutely control the supplies of the army to the smallest article, and regulate the manner of its transportation and delivery to the army, they are absolutely without any responsibility for the results at all. Any disaster, dishonor, or suffering occasioned by the failure to furnish an article needed for the soldiers is charged, and naturally charged, upon the military commander, though he has no more power over such matters than the coroner in Cincinnati."[29]

Addressing the House Committee on Military Affairs two years later, Pope provided an illustrative example:

> Even when there was an arsenal here, directly in sight of these headquarters, I could not, with all my authority as department commander, and with the responsibility for supplying the necessities of some thousands of men, procure an arm or a cartridge, nor even a tompion (wooden plug, worth possibly ten cents) to close the muzzle of a piece of artillery to protect the bore from the weather, without forwarding a requisition for it to division headquarters in Chicago, thence to be forwarded to the Adjutant General of the Army for the General-in-Chief; and as neither of these officials had any more authority than I to order its issue, the requisition went to the Secretary of War, from him to the Chief of Ordnance, thence back to me through the same channels.[30]

For all his emphasis on the flaws of the staff system, which would not be remedied until after the turn of the century, Pope never lessened his emphasis on concentration of troops in winter and disbursing them in summer. As late in his tenure as 1881, he was still urging concentration: "I have, however, dwelt on this subject so much in every annual report for a number of years past, that it is superfluous, if not unpleasantly persistent, to repeat the recommendations here."[31] General Sheridan doubtless considered it "unpleasantly persistent."

As early as 1862, when he took command in the Northwest, Pope had embraced the cause of the Indian even when fighting him. His lengthy critique of Indian policy in 1864 provided a base for subsequent years of advocating humane treatment of the Indians. Throughout his career he harbored sympathy for the Indians more pronounced than that of most of his colleagues. His strident opposition to the treaty system was rewarded in 1871 by congressional abolition of treaties. He believed that Indians confined to reservations should receive the full rations and annuities promised by treaties. He wavered on the issue of assimilation into white culture but advocated transforming Indians into farmers and cattle ranchers. He joined with others in an issue that surfaced repeatedly in the Congress: return Indian Affairs to the War Department, where they once were lodged. Opposed by Indian rights groups in the East, these measures repeatedly failed. In short, General Pope earned the sobriquet "humanitarian general," a distinction few other generals merited.[32]

The Red River War of 1874–75 marked the height of Pope's career as an Indian fighter. He had to contend with Ute hostilities in Colorado in 1879–80, but they dimmed in comparison to the Red River hostilities. Instead, beginning in 1878, he became increasingly preoccupied with the case of General Fitz John Porter. Ever since his court-martial in 1862–63, Porter had devoted himself to reversing the findings of the court. With reams of evidence and the support of generals and politicians, Porter succeeded in interesting President Rutherford B. Hayes. Much to Pope's anger and chagrin, Hayes appointed a commission headed by General John M. Schofield to examine the evidence. The Schofield Commission found for Porter, further outraging Pope. He endured continuing strain for five years, however, as his political friends fought the finding and put off the ultimate resolution. In 1882 President Chester Arthur commuted Porter's sentence and restored him to the Regular Army rank of colonel. Then-president Grover Cleveland issued a full pardon in 1884. Pope now bore the full burden of the disaster of Second Manassas.

The blow suffered by the outcome of the Porter case combined with deteriorating health took its toll on Pope, but in 1882 the retirement of General Irvin McDowell opened a vacancy for a major general. As the army's senior brigadier, Pope lobbied vigorously for the appointment. On October 25, 1882, he donned the two stars of a major general.

With the retirement of General Sherman in 1884 and the elevation of General Sheridan to Sherman's place, the Military Division of the Missouri fell vacant. Pope wanted Chicago, but he ended up filling McDowell's vacancy, commanding the Division of the Pacific. Pope and Clara settled in San Francisco in November 1883.

Except for the concluding years of the Apache wars in Arizona, Pope's division was quiet and his duties routine. In Arizona the department commander was first George Crook, then Pope's subordinate from the Red River War, Nelson A. Miles, now a brigadier commanding the department. In his usual arrogant way, Miles directed the final operations against Geronimo without much regard for the chain of command. Pope protested that Miles corresponded directly with General Sheridan in Washington, but to little avail. Sheridan had as little regard for Pope as Miles did.[33]

Even before the surrender of Geronimo, Pope reached the mandatory retirement age of sixty-four. On March 16, 1886, he retired from the army. John and Clara Pope settled in St. Louis, both dogged by declining health. Clara died in June 1888, John on September 23, 1892. They are buried in the Bellefontaine Cemetery in St. Louis.

Aside from John Pope's acerbic temperament, his Civil War career reached its high with the victory at Island No. 10 and plunged to its low with the disaster at Second Manassas. Almost alone, he won Island No. 10. Almost alone, he lost Second Manassas. The exile to Minnesota opened a new and more productive career on the Indian frontier. It also eased his truculent personality. His years of Indian service, 1862–86, quieted his belligerency and steadied his command style. He remained as wedded as ever to his own ideas, however, and expressed them as verbosely as ever. He never used one word when ten would do.

As a department commander, Pope was not a field general. He commanded from his desk at Fort Leavenworth. He conceived the plans but left his subordinates to carry them out without too much interference. He supported them to the extent that he could or thought they deserved. Throughout, in war or peace, he continued to pursue his three basic causes: the iniquity of U.S. Indian policy and its deleterious effect on the Indians; the dispersion of his troops when they should be concentrated at one or two posts in the winter and deployed in the field in summer; and the pernicious consequences of a staff system that deprived line commanders of needed resources. He fought these battles long after he should have understood that he alone could not win them. History judges his causes meritorious and ultimately achieved: Indian policy was reformed, concentration occurred with the close of Indian hostilities, and the staff system underwent radical reform.

John Pope was not only a competent, even superior, department commander but also a noted humanitarian general.

Brigadier General Alfred H. Terry, commanding
Department of Dakota, 1866–1869, 1873–1886.
U.S. Army Military History Institute.

CHAPTER EIGHT
ALFRED H. TERRY

General Alfred H. Terry came into the army as a volunteer without a military education. His way was won without political influence up to an important separate command—the expedition against Fort Fisher in January 1865. His success there was most brilliant and won him the rank of brigadier-general in the regular army and of major-general of volunteers. He is a man who makes friends of those under him by his consideration of their wants and their dues. As a commander, he won their confidence by his coolness in action and by his clearness of perception in taking in the situation under which he was placed at any given time.[1]

Thus General Ulysses S. Grant evaluated Alfred H. Terry. With his usual insight and verbal skill, Grant touched on the essence of Terry: civilian soldier, promoted without political influence, successful in the battle, with a Regular Army brigadier general's commission as a reward, friendly, thoughtful, kind, and generous to his subordinates, and a skilled tactician.

Tall, slender, and full-bearded, Terry had a fine mind and struck people as kind, calm, steady, friendly, and honest. As a military commander, he maintained strict discipline tempered by concern for the well-being of his men. In turn, he earned their loyalty, respect, gratitude, and eventually veneration. He contented himself with doing his duty without ostentation or self-seeking—a modest demeanor that sometimes allowed others to receive credit that should have been his. His career demonstrated that a West Point education was not essential to attaining high rank.

Alfred Howe Terry was born on November 10, 1827, in Hartford, Connecticut, but moved with his growing family to New Haven four years later. He attended Yale University Law School for two years, 1848–49, before withdrawing after being admitted to the bar. While striving to build a law practice, he served as city clerk and then clerk of the state Superior Court.

Attracted from an early age by military affairs, Terry joined the local militia, the New Haven Grays, in 1849, soon after leaving law school. He played an active role in the unit while reading deeply of military history and science. He resigned in 1856 after the governor appointed him a major in the Second Connecticut Volunteer regiment. In 1860 Terry embarked on a European tour, in which he further strengthened his military knowledge by visiting battlefields and museums. He returned early in 1861 to find his military talents in demand.[2]

CIVIL WAR

With the South firing on Fort Sumter, President Lincoln called for three-month volunteers. Connecticut mobilized three such regiments. On May 9, 1861, the governor conferred on Terry the rank of colonel of the Second Connecticut Volunteers. With his self-taught military background, Terry organized, drilled, and quickly gained the respect of his regiment. June 3 found them camped near Vienna, Virginia, where they remained on picket duty until July 16, when they took up the march toward Manassas. The First and Second Connecticut led the advance of Brigadier General Daniel T. Tyler's division, part of Brigadier General Irvin McDowell's hastily assembled army. On July 17, just beyond Vienna, the head of the column encountered Confederate skirmishers. Burdened with an incompetent commander, Terry and his men plunged into the Battle of Bull Run.

Even before the main battle began on July 21, Tyler rashly ignored orders and led his division into a Confederate trap. Fortunately for the Connecticut regiments, they had been replaced in the advance and escaped the artillery fire sweeping the ranks from both flanks. Even worse, on July 21 Tyler's tardiness in carrying out his assignment disordered General McDowell's plan of attack. In the ensuing battle Terry led the Second Connecticut in three assaults on the Confederate lines but was forced back each time by deadly fire. Had General Tyler disposed his forces differently, the Confederate defenses probably would have been taken, but the Battle of Bull Run had already been lost. The Union forces were ordered to retreat. Unlike the panicked flight of most of the army, the Connecticut regiments stood their ground and in one instance turned and shattered a Confederate cavalry charge. They were the last units to leave the battlefield.

Colonel Terry's handling of his regiment at Bull Run drew widespread praise from his superiors, including even General Tyler, and from other ranking officers. He had put his years of preparation to the test and emerged a competent combat commander.

Less than three weeks after Bull Run, the Second Connecticut was mustered out in New Haven. A month later, on September 13, Colonel Terry began organizing and training the Seventh Connecticut, a regiment enlisted for three years or the duration of the war. He shaped it into a well-trained, well-led, highly disciplined body of infantrymen who would serve him loyally even after he ascended above the grade of colonel. Both Terry and the regiment would pass the rest of the war largely operating in tandem with the navy against the Confederacy's South Atlantic coastal defenses, which for most of the time were commanded by General P. G. T. Beauregard.

Port Royal, South Carolina, was the first objective. It gave access to Beaufort, North Carolina, which lay between Charleston and Savannah and was connected by railroad to both cities. The large guns of two forts, Walker and Beauregard, commanded the entrance to the harbor from islands on either side. The campaign fell under command of Flag Officer Samuel Du Pont and was almost entirely a naval operation. A division of infantry under Brigadier General Thomas W. Sherman lay in transports offshore ready to support the navy. Terry's Seventh Connecticut was part of one of Sherman's three brigades.

On November 7, 1861, Du Pont launched his armada: a column of nine gunboats and another of five gunboats. They were to move in an elliptical formation, bringing both forts under continuous fire as they circled. For five hours the gunboats battered the two forts, sustaining little damage in the process. Running low on powder, the Confederate commanders abandoned Forts Walker and Beauregard. Small boats bore Sherman's soldiers from the transports to the shore below the two forts. Terry and the Seventh Connecticut waded ashore in advance of the troops assigned to occupy Fort Walker.

Port Royal provided a staging area for the next operation: an offensive to close the port of Savannah, Georgia, to Confederate blockade-runners.

Fort Pulaski, a formidable prewar brick fortification, commanded the mouth of the Savannah River. The plan for taking the fort was devised by General Sherman's chief engineer, Captain (soon to be General) Quincy Gillmore. He believed that the newly invented rifled cannon and mortars alone could bombard the fort into submission. Batteries would be planted on Tybee Island, across the river from the fort on the south, and Jones and other islands on the north shore. To Colonel Terry's Seventh Connecticut fell the task of preparing the swampy areas on Tybee Island where the batteries would be placed. This labor—building roads, hauling stores, and preparing bomb-proof emplacements for the artillery—had to be carried out silently at night to conceal it from the notice of the fort. The effort continued through January and February 1862, but the hardest work took place in March and April, after the heavy ordnance arrived and the men had to snake the cannon and mortars through mud and water and build bomb-proof platforms for mounting them.

By April 10, when the bombardment began, acerbic General Sherman had been replaced by Major General David Hunter. For two days Hunter's big guns pounded the fort, gradually breaking down the walls and finally imperiling the powder magazine. Early in the afternoon of April 11 the Confederate commander surrendered the wrecked Fort Pulaski.

Although the Gillmore plan had its skeptics—including the disliked General Sherman—the siege had proved Gillmore right: rifled cannon could prevail over a heavily defended fort without the need for an infantry assault.

Fort Pulaski remained in Union hands for the rest of the war, but Savannah itself did not fall to the Union until December 1864, when General William T. Sherman completed his march from Atlanta to the sea. Even so, the Union blockade and the guns of Fort Pulaski denied the port to Confederate shipping.

Three weeks after the fall of Fort Pulaski, on April 26, 1862, the Senate confirmed the promotion of Alfred H. Terry to brigadier general of Volunteers. The promotion rewarded merit that his superiors had long recognized. As summarized by Terry's biographer: "Coolness and bravery under fire, care and consideration for the well-being of his fellow soldiers, skill in organizing and directing the activities of his men, dependability under all conditions, and the willingness to sacrifice himself for the general good: these are the key themes of Terry's early military career."[3]

After Terry's promotion, he was placed in command of an area along the coast from Beaufort north to the islands marking the approach to Charleston Harbor, with his headquarters on Hilton Head Island, South Carolina. Charleston was the next major operation after Fort Pulaski, but in June 1862 costly battles on James Island and at Simon's Bluff stalled the Union advance. Terry's administrative burdens, including a long inspection tour of Florida and court-martial duty, freed him from the mishandled combat operations of summer 1862.

Terry's first combat as a brigadier came in October 1862, when he commanded a brigade in an effort to destroy railroad works near the village of Pocotaligo, South Carolina. Carried from Hilton Head by naval vessels, two brigades landed and advanced on the objective. Severe fighting took place, but the Union forces failed to overcome the Confederate opposition. Terry handled his regiments well both in combat and in the retreat to the ships to return to Hilton Head.

Terry took a long leave of absence, then returned to Hilton Head to participate in the planning for an offensive against Charleston. Plans and concentration of troops and naval vessels extended into the spring of 1863. Admiral Samuel Du Pont led the first assault on the forts that guarded Charleston Harbor, but his ironclads failed to do much damage. The second effort involved both the navy (now under Admiral John A. Dahlgren) and the army (under Major General Quincy Gillmore).

Union forces faced formidable obstacles. The heavy cannon of the Confederate forts swept all the harbor approaches. The main Union objectives were Fort Wagner on Morris Island and Fort Sumter on the northwestern tip of James Island. In this offensive General Gillmore gave Terry command of a full division. Beginning in April 1863, Terry's regiments labored to erect gun emplacements on Folly Island, opposite Morris Island, to support troops when they landed on the island. By July Gillmore was ready to move.

While a brigade went ashore on Morris Island, Gillmore ordered Terry to move his division up the Stono River to a landing on James Island, where he was to distract the enemy and prevent reinforcements from reaching Fort Wagner. On July 8 Terry's division went ashore, to find a Confederate force drawn up to oppose him. He forbore to attack, however, because he was already accomplishing his mission by tying down potential reinforcements. On July 16 the Rebels launched a vigorous attack on Terry at Grimball's Landing. Marshy ground disorganized the assault, and Terry's artillery halted them before they came into musket range. Ordered by Gillmore to abandon James Island and come to Morris Island, Terry moved his division down the Stono River.

In Terry's absence, Gillmore, supported by the artillery on Folly Island, landed a brigade of his second division on Morris Island on July 10. Commanded by Brigadier General George C. Strong, the brigade encountered fierce resistance but continued the advance and on July 11 assaulted Fort Wagner. Met by heavy cannon and musketry fire, the brigade faltered. Terry's old regiment, the Seventh Connecticut, seized a line of rifle pits, but the brigade was repulsed.

Before Terry's division reached the field of action, Gillmore threw three brigades against Fort Wagner on July 18. After a day-long bombardment, the brigades advanced at dusk. Under heavy fire, several regiments reached the slopes of the bastion and one regiment, the fabled black Fifty-Fourth Massachusetts, surmounted the parapet. Nightfall and stubborn defenders ended the second Battle of Fort Wagner.

Arriving with fresh troops, Terry discovered the Union troops reeling from the chaos of the battle, the Fifty-Fourth Massachusetts having sustained 45 percent casualties. Gillmore placed Terry in command of Morris Island and, instead of mounting another bloody assault, began digging siege lines. As the lines angled forward, Terry and Gillmore arranged heavy artillery for barrages against both Fort Wagner and Fort Sumter, across the inlet. While the bombardment of Fort Wagner continued, Terry and Gillmore worked heavy artillery into position to bring Fort Sumter under fire. On August 17 the big guns erupted, and by August 23 the fort was a pile of rubble. Under occasional fire, however, Confederates remained in the ruins until the end of the war.

With Fort Sumter disintegrating, Gillmore increased the pressure on Fort Wagner with continuous heavy bombardment from both land and sea even as Terry's men worked on the siege trenches. On September 6 Gillmore ordered Terry to prepare a full-bore assault on the fort with his division. Before he could signal the advance on September 7, a Confederate deserter brought word that the fort had been evacuated. Terry occupied Fort Wagner and other Confederate strong points.

The seizure of Charleston's harbor defenses had been costly and fatiguing but had succeeded. Charleston lay open to a direct assault. Bickering between army and navy, however, stalled further efforts, and the offensive ended in a stalemate. Charleston did not fall to the Union until February 1865.

The offensive against Charleston offered General Terry no opportunities for battlefield distinction. In all his division's missions, however, he performed efficiently and effectively and made no mistake that would have invited censure.

Terry and his division occupied Morris Island until the spring of 1864, cleaning the island of the debris left by months of bloody conflict. It was boring, tiring work, made more difficult by the sandy character of the terrain. In late October and early November Terry enjoyed a three-week respite in New Haven. In April 1864 orders arrived transferring Terry and his division north, to the command of Major General Benjamin Butler in Virginia.

Two corps formed Butler's Army of the James, one under Quincy Gillmore, the other under Major General William F. "Baldy" Smith. Terry's division remained under Gillmore's command. Butler's army was to operate against Richmond from the southeast while Grant, with the Army of the Potomac, plunged into the Wilderness and aimed at Richmond from the northwest. In early May 1864, as Grant began to battle Confederates in the Wilderness, the Army of the James steamed up the James River to the village of Bermuda Hundred, at the confluence of the James and Appomattox Rivers. Here the army debarked on May 5 and set about digging entrenchments and positioning artillery.

On May 9 both corps advanced into the peninsula between the two rivers. Terry's division set about tearing up the Richmond and Petersburg Railway, clearing a line of Confederate entrenchments in the process. The next day, while destroying the railway, firing from the north alerted Terry that his rear guard of three regiments was under fire. He marched rapidly to the rescue, arriving in time to save the regiments. In a furious three-hour fight, his force of 3,250 infantrymen and an artillery battery beat off three determined charges by a Southern force with twice their number. Sustaining heavy casualties, the attackers withdrew from the field.

On May 12, from the Union entrenchments, both Gillmore and Smith advanced their corps north toward Richmond. At Drewry's Bluff they faced General Beauregard's heavily manned entrenchments. The ensuing battle swirled around the defenses, with Union forces seeking to penetrate and flank the lines. Terry's division held firm as other elements began to fall back. Still, only confusion among Beauregard's commanders saved the Army of the James from destruction. With 4,500 casualties, the Union corps fell back to Bermuda Hundred.

After the failed move against Beauregard, the Army of the James settled into its entrenchments. Even before the Bermuda Hundred campaign, Butler and his generals had carried on a rancorous feud. Butler, Gillmore, and Smith detested one another. In part, Drewry's Bluff had failed because of the faults and controversies of the three generals. In the months following the battle Butler found cause to relieve both Gillmore and Smith, but Terry remained loyal under Butler's command. Under a reorganization directed by General Grant, the Army of the James consisted of the Twenty-Fourth and Twenty-Fifth Corps, one white, the other black. Major General Edward O. C. Ord took command of the Twenty-Fourth, which included Terry's division.

Butler's next mission, in December 1864, was Fort Fisher, at the mouth of the Cape Fear River, which gave blockade-runners access to Wilmington, North Carolina. A massive fortification constantly improved and enlarged for the past four years, Fort Fisher was known as the "Gibraltar of the Confederacy." It was the South's last major coastal bastion.

The campaign against Fort Fisher was again a combined army-navy expedition. Rear Admiral David D. Porter commanded sixty gunships and a fleet of transports to carry the infantry. Grant assigned Major General Godfrey Weitzel to lead the expedition, but General Butler dominated Weitzel, without the knowledge of Grant, who thought Butler went merely as an observer. These troops constituted only part of the Army of the James. Terry and his division were not included.

The first Battle of Fort Fisher took place on December 24, 1864. Naval bombardment failed to neutralize the fort's batteries, and the infantry attack encountered such strong resistance that Butler concluded that the fort could not be taken. He called off the expedition and returned to Bermuda Hundred. In response, Grant relieved Butler and replaced him with General Ord.

An incensed Admiral Porter wrote to General Grant: "Send me the same soldiers with another general, and we will have the fort."[4] Grant selected another general: Alfred Terry. He was assigned selected elements of three divisions in a "Provisional Corps" of nine thousand infantry. On January 6, 1865, Terry's expedition embarked from Bermuda Hundred to join Admiral Porter's squadron of more than fifty vessels in another assault on Fort Fisher.

Cooperating closely with Porter, Terry landed his entire force on the river side of the peninsula on January 13 and went into camp, without taking any fire from the fort. On January 15, following a naval bombardment that ravaged the fort's guns, Porter landed two thousand sailors and marines on the opposite (ocean) side of the peninsula, while Terry launched his infantry from the other side. For five hours the battle raged, with attacks and counterattacks and heavy casualties on both sides. The fight continued into the night, with naval guns still active even as the infantry swarmed into the fort's interior. Terry scaled the parapet and took personal command as the two sides struggled. Bursts of musketry felled men by the dozen. By 10:00 P.M. Fort Fisher had been taken. But the senior Confederate officer, General W. H. C. Whiting, and other top officers had taken refuge in a small shore-side redoubt named Battery Buchanan. Terry led a brigade to attack the fort, but before they opened fire a white flag appeared. It was Terry who received General Whiting's surrender.

Terry's victory was a triumph, and accolades showered the victor of Fort Fisher. Grant ordered a one hundred–gun salute fired along the Petersburg line and promptly recommended Terry for appointment as brigadier general in the Regular Army. President Lincoln and Secretary Stanton sent their congratulations, and a formal resolution conveyed the thanks of Congress to the general. The nation's press praised Terry lavishly.

With the fall of Fort Fisher, the Confederacy's last remaining outlet to the sea was closed. Eager to occupy Wilmington and provide reinforcements for General Sherman, then advancing from the west, General Grant brought Major General John M. Schofield and his corps from the west to work with Terry and Admiral Porter in breaking down the remaining Confederate defenses on the Cape Fear River. Schofield arrived in mid-February 1865 and took command even as Confederate general Braxton Bragg was placed in charge of defending Wilmington. With Terry's Provisional Corps and Schofield's corps, aided by Porter's gunships, the Union force fought three engagements as it advanced up the Cape Fear River. In less than a week Bragg began evacuating Wilmington. On February 22 Terry and Schofield's subordinate General Jacob D. Cox entered the city.

After marching his corps northwest to Goldsboro and linking up with General Sherman's army, Terry took station briefly in Raleigh, North Carolina. In May, after war's end, he went to New Haven on leave but resolved to stay in the army. In June he was assigned to Reconstruction duty in Virginia, with headquarters in Richmond. After a year in this assignment, he was mustered out of the Volunteers on September 1, 1866, as a full major general. Secretary Stanton gave him his choice of a new assignment in his Regular Army grade of brigadier general. He chose St. Paul, Minnesota, headquarters of the newly created Department of Dakota.

DEPARTMENT OF DAKOTA

Terry's new command, subordinate to the Military Division of the Missouri, encompassed Minnesota and most of Dakota and Montana. Headquarters varied between Fort Snelling and St. Paul, Minnesota. A seasoned general at thirty-nine, Terry arrived in St. Paul at the end of October 1866 ignorant of the northern Great Plains and their Indian inhabitants. From his predecessor, General John Pope, he inherited ongoing warfare with the Teton Sioux and the responsibility of protecting gold-seekers using the Missouri River to access the goldfields of western Montana and Idaho. The other route, the Bozeman Trail from Fort Laramie to the goldfields, had been assigned to the adjoining Department of the Platte.

Terry quickly organized his department into districts and traveled widely in Dakota, inspecting existing forts and authorizing two new ones, Totten and Stevenson. In June 1867, as instructed by General Sherman, Terry traveled by horse and steamer to Helena, Montana, where he found the settlers frightened by Sioux aggressions. The acting governor had called out volunteers and urged that they be placed in federal service. Terry refused, but the militia rampaged across the country anyway. The Gallatin Valley, where citizen anxiety was justified, posed a special problem. He authorized the erection at Bozeman of Fort Ellis. By the end of the year Terry could report that his department was organized into four districts containing fourteen posts garrisoned by four infantry regiments. He also conferred with General Sherman on measures to make peace with or fight the Indians, mainly the Teton Sioux. Within two years Terry had mastered the intricacies of his new command, in which he would pass most of his remaining career.[5]

As Terry acquainted himself with the Department of Dakota, forces gathered to shape the course of U.S. Indian policy. In December 1866 the Fetterman disaster at Fort Phil Kearny, on the Bozeman Trail from Fort Laramie to the Montana mines, sparked vigorous controversy over how to respond both to the Teton Sioux perpetrators and to the larger question of how to deal with all the plains tribes. The Indian Bureau and its friends in the Senate urged a peaceful approach that depended on treaties and reservations to lead the tribes into "civilization." The army and its congressional friends favored military conquest as the first objective before pursuing more moderate measures. The army also lobbied for transfer of the Indian Bureau from the Interior Department to the War Department.

To resolve the issues Congress created a commission on July 20, 1867, to go among the tribes of both the northern and southern plains and attempt to conclude peace treaties establishing reservations. The commission consisted of both humanitarian peace advocates and three generals—Sherman, Terry, and retired general William S. Harney—appointed by President Andrew Johnson. With Sherman absent in Washington most of the time, Brigadier General Christopher C. Augur sat in for him. Augur commanded the Department of the Platte, adjoining Terry's department on the south.[6]

The Peace Commission gave Terry a broad view of the Indian tribes, their homeland, and the politics of Indian policy. The first stop was Fort Laramie, where Red Cloud of the Teton Sioux declined to leave his hunting grounds. Kansas was the next stop, where the commissioners succeeded in negotiating the Medicine Lodge Treaty with the southern plains tribes. Meeting in St. Louis in January 1868, the members signed a report boasting of the Medicine Lodge Treaty but leaving unresolved the Teton Sioux. Another visit to Fort Laramie still failed to lure Red Cloud into the fort. Eventually, after the commission left, he came in and made his mark on the Treaty of 1868, which would have significant consequences in future years, with which General Terry would have to deal.

The final meeting occurred in Chicago on October 7, 1868. War had broken out on the southern plains, and the generals easily outvoted the peace proponents. Sitting in on the meeting was General Grant, who clearly stood to be the next president of the United States. Terry and Augur readily voted with the generals. The Peace Commission did not solve the dilemma of war versus peace, but it marked a significant event in the history of Indian affairs.

For General Terry, the Peace Commission had been a major learning experience, which had equipped him to approach the affairs of the Department of Dakota with a wide perspective but had kept him away from his department headquarters. Back in St. Paul, however, he was afforded only seven months before he was transferred on May 17, 1869, to command the Department of the South in Atlanta, still in the throes of Reconstruction chaos. His legal knowledge and his success in similar duty in Virginia probably played a part. Terry was replaced in St. Paul by Major General Winfield S. Hancock, who took up President Grant's Peace Policy of coaxing the tribes onto reservations while protecting the travel routes from those who refused to submit. Not until January 2, 1873, could Terry free himself from the demanding assignment in Atlanta and return to command the Department of Dakota.

The department that Terry left in 1868 roiled with Sioux troubles. The Treaty of 1868 had created a Great Sioux Reservation covering all of what is now the state of South Dakota west of the Missouri River, including the Black Hills. To gain Red Cloud's assent, the treaty had also promised to abandon the Bozeman Trail forts and authorized an "unceded Indian territory" west of the reservation. This territory, the rugged country drained by the Tongue and Powder Rivers, was for Indian use only; all whites were barred. Here Lakotas and Cheyennes who scorned reservation life could follow the bison as long as they existed. "Winter roamers" under Sitting Bull, Crazy Horse, and other Teton chiefs followed the old life. Reservation Indians drew rations at their agencies on the reservation, but many rode west to the unceded territory to join their kin for a summer spent reliving the old life. Further agitating affairs, many winter roamers slipped into the agencies in the winter to share in the rations issued the agency Indians. Nor did bold young men always respect boundaries, and settlements and ranches along the Platte River suffered from Indian raids.

Motivated by the principles of President Grant's Peace Policy, General Terry believed the Indians in his department should be led into the paths of self-supporting "civilization." This was also the task of the civilian Indian agents. Two factors inhibited Terry from pursuing his thinking: many of the agents were corrupt and incompetent; and his superior in division headquarters in Chicago, Lieutenant General Philip Sheridan, held warlike views at odds with his own. Another complication was the Northern Pacific Railway. Halted at the Missouri River by the Panic of 1873, it nevertheless enjoyed the vigorous support of both Sheridan and Sherman, who had replaced Grant when he became president. The railway also promised to antagonize the Sioux when it resumed construction westward. Still another irritant was the Black Hills, part of the Great Sioux Reservation but coveted by whites because of rumors of gold in its streams. Sheridan took great interest in the Hills despite their being guaranteed to the Sioux by treaty. Confronted by Sheridan, a domineering, volatile superior, Terry settled in at St. Paul largely as a desk general, overseeing the wishes of Sheridan in the Department of Dakota.

Even before the Northern Pacific Railway declared bankruptcy in 1873, Sheridan had ensured that the railroad's surveying expeditions worked with military escorts. Surveys as far as Montana's Yellowstone River in 1871 and 1872 encountered Sioux resistance, indicating that the railroad would be hotly contested. Anticipating the survey of 1873, therefore, Sheridan brought Lieutenant Colonel George A. Custer and the Seventh Cavalry from the South to provide the escort. Although commanded by Colonel David S. Stanley, Custer and his cavalry engaged and routed Sitting Bull's Lakotas on two occasions. At the conclusion of the expedition, the Seventh Cavalry settled into the new post of Fort Abraham Lincoln, on the west bank of the Missouri River, three miles south of Bismarck. These measures seem to have been undertaken with little or no consultation with General Terry after his arrival in 1873.

In 1874, after three years of consideration, Sheridan determined to explore the Black Hills and fix a site for a military post to prevent the Sioux from raiding along the Platte. He consulted the president, the secretaries of war and the interior, and General Sherman. After gaining their assent, Sheridan visited Fort Lincoln in June, talked with Custer, and returned to Chicago, where he issued orders to Terry to organize the expedition. Terry endorsed Sheridan's orders with a detailed analysis of the legality of penetrating the Black Hills, all of which supported Sheridan's orders. Again, however, Terry had been ignored in forming the plans, as indicated in his annual report the following year: "The Black Hills expedition was organized pursuant to orders of General Sheridan issued while he was at Fort Lincoln in June 1874."[7]

Custer's Black Hills expedition, revealing a largely unknown land of timbered mountains and lush valleys, gained widespread publicity. What caught the public eye, however, was the discovery of gold, which obscured the purpose of the expedition. Custer did fix a site for a military post, but it would not be built until 1878. More immediately, the Sioux regarded the intrusion into their domain as a violation of the Treaty of 1868 (but it wasn't) and the inevitable flood of gold-seekers as a more serious violation (it was).

Lieutenant Colonel George A. Custer, Seventh Cavalry.
Little Bighorn National Battlefield Monument.

No sooner had Custer returned to Fort Lincoln than General Sheridan directed Terry to use his troops to intercept gold-seekers, destroy their wagons and outfits, and arrest the leaders. As the *New York Tribune* pointed out, however, "If there is gold in the Black Hills, no army on earth can keep the adventurous men of the west out of them, and the Government should lose no time in extinguishing the Indian title to the auriferous lands." Recognizing this reality, the government did indeed move to extinguish Indian title. The secretary of the interior appointed a commission headed by Senator William B. Allison to persuade the Sioux either to grant mining rights or to sell the Hills outright. General Terry was a member of the commission and played an active role, possessing more knowledge of the Indians than most of the other members. The negotiations with Red Cloud and other Sioux chiefs took place at the Red Cloud Agency in September 1875. A month's deliberations, often raucous, failed to overcome Lakota resistance.[8]

The failure of the Allison Commission focused official attention on the winter roamers who occupied the unceded territory. They had disrupted the proceedings of the Allison Commission, raided both in Montana and along the Platte River road, and stirred up the agency Indians. On November 3, 1875, President Grant met with the secretary of war, the secretary of the interior, the commissioner of Indian Affairs, and Generals Sheridan and George Crook. A saber-rattling report by an Indian bureau inspector, almost certainly engineered for the purpose, provided a pretext for ordering all Indians in the unceded territory to report to their agencies by February 1, 1876, or be considered hostiles subject to military action.

The Indians did not report. For one thing, moving their villages in a northern plains winter was a daunting undertaking. For another, they probably did not understand the message delivered by runners to be an ultimatum, if they even knew what an ultimatum was. General Sheridan began organizing a three-pronged winter offensive into the Powder and Yellowstone River country. Brigadier General George Crook would move north from Fort Fetterman. Two columns under Terry's command would form a pincer on the Yellowstone River: Colonel John Gibbon east from Fort Ellis, and Colonel Custer west from Fort Lincoln. Severe winter weather confounded Crook's thrust and prevented Terry's columns from marching until spring advanced, nudging the winter campaign into a summer campaign.

Terry's strategy was sound: turn Custer loose. Sheridan had done that on the southern plains in 1868, and Custer delivered. Terry would remain in his St. Paul headquarters while Custer and Gibbon struck the Sioux. Politics intervened, however. A staunch Democrat, Custer had quietly provided material to eastern newspapers that accused Grant administration officials of corruption. With the impeachment of Secretary of War William W. Belknap, congressional investigations advanced. Custer was summoned as a witness and further angered President Grant by implicating his brother, Orvil. When Custer hastened back from Washington to lead his command west, he failed to gain permission and was halted in Chicago. Grant ordered that another officer lead the expedition. Sheridan ordered Terry to take the field himself. Responding to appeals from Terry and Sheridan, Grant relented insofar as to allow Custer to go, under Terry, in command of his own regiment.[9]

Thanks to his reckless subordinate and an angry president, General Terry embarked on his only postwar field command. He approved of the objective: round the Indians up and force them to settle on their reservation and become civilized.

With Gibbon already on the Yellowstone with his infantry and Major James Brisbin's cavalry, Terry assumed command of the Dakota Column, which comprised Custer's entire Seventh Cavalry and assorted infantry units. It departed Fort Lincoln on May 17, 1876. The long, plodding march to the Yellowstone, with frequent rain, snow, and cold dogging the troops, was aimed at finding the Indians. It also tested Terry's relations with Custer. Twice in his field diary Terry hinted at irritation with his subordinate, but it is improbable that he ever treated him sternly.[10] Custer ranged widely, following his own inclinations rather than Terry's; in fact, he had boasted to a fellow officer that once in the field he intended to cut loose from Terry. But the general issued enough orders to establish his status as expedition commander. If he disliked or distrusted Custer, he kept his opinion to himself. Notably, when he later joined with Colonel Gibbon, he maintained the same benign attitude, even though during the Civil War he had often recorded his dislike of Gibbon.

On June 8 the Dakota Column reached the Yellowstone at the mouth of the Powder River. Here Terry met Captain Grant Marsh's river steamer *Far West* bearing supplies and established a supply base. Boarding the *Far*

Colonel John Gibbon, Seventh Infantry.
Author's collection.

THE SIOUX WAR
OF 1876

Peter H. Dana

FT. TOTTEN 1867

FT. STEVENSON
1867

FT. A. LINCOLN
FT. RICE
FT. YATES

STANDING ROCK
AGENCY

Heart River
Cannonball R.
Grand R.

Slim Buttes
9 Sep.

Moreau R.

FT. SULLY 1866

CHEYENNE RIVER
AGENCY

River

White River

Belle Fourche R.

Cheyenne River

CP. SHERIDAN

Niobrara River

RED CLOUD
AGENCY

CP. ROBINSON

FT. BUFFORD
1866

Little Missouri River

Yellowstone River

Redwater Cr.

Redwater
1 Dec.

Cedar Creek
21 Oct.

Big Dry C.

FORT PECK
AGENCY

Missouri River

Musselshell River

Pumpkin Cr.

Tongue R.

Rosebud

Powder River

Wolf Mtn. Powder River
18 Jan. 17 Mar.

Rosebud
17 June

Dull Knife
26 Nov.

North Platte R.

War Bonnet Creek
17 July

FT. FETTERMAN
1867

FT. LARAMIE

Platte River

FT. ELLIS
1867

Little Bighorn
25 June

Bighorn R.

Little Big Horn R.

Yellowstone River

→	Crook March 1876
•••••	Gibbon April–June 1876
– – –	Terry and Custer May–June 1876
▲▲▲	Crook May–June 1876
✦✦✦✦	Custer June 1876
○○○○○	Terry and Crook August 1876
▢▢▢▢	Crook September 1876

N

0   50   100
Miles

West, he steamed up the river until spotting Gibbon's Montana Column on the north bank. Meeting with the colonel, Terry ordered him to march back to the mouth of the Rosebud and await further orders. On June 10 Terry ordered a sweeping scout south of the river by Major Marcus A. Reno aimed at trying to locate the Indian village. Reno's scout bore fruit: a large Indian trail led up the Rosebud and, as Terry's scouts noted, almost certainly turned west to the Little Bighorn. On June 21, at the mouth of the Rosebud, Terry convened a conference aboard the *Far West* to outline his strategy to Gibbon, Custer, and Major James Brisbin of Gibbon's command. Although the officers discussed the strategy at length, it was conceived by Terry himself.[11]

Terry's orders, committed to paper by his adjutant general, were handed to Custer the next morning. They explicitly outlined Terry's thinking: Custer would lead the Seventh Cavalry up the Rosebud, follow the Indian trail when it was found, then continue up the Rosebud when the trail turned west to the Little Bighorn as assumed until reaching the headwaters of the Tongue River. From there Custer would turn down the Little Bighorn, enabling him to strike the village from the south and driving it against Gibbon's infantry, which would be advancing up the valley from the north. The two forces would be approaching each other on the afternoon of June 26. But the orders also provided the basis for endless argument: Terry placed too much confidence in Custer's "zeal, energy, and ability" to burden him with precise orders that might hamper him when nearly in contact with the enemy. However, Custer should follow them unless he saw "sufficient reason" for departing from them, which, of course, Custer did find. Whether the reason was sufficient or not fuels a controversy enduring to this day.[12]

On the morning of June 22, at the mouth of the Rosebud, Terry, Gibbon, and Brisbin watched the departure of the Seventh Cavalry as it began the march up the Rosebud. They then boarded the *Far West* and returned to the north bank of the Yellowstone. Gibbon and Brisbin joined their troops for the march up the river, while Terry remained on board. On June 24 the steamer ferried the troops to the south bank. Terry's plan called for the column to turn up the Bighorn to the mouth of the Little Bighorn and follow that river upstream until encountering the village or Custer. At the mouth of the Bighorn Terry took to his horse with his staff and joined the advance on the right bank of the Bighorn, while the *Far West* maneuvered up that river to the mouth of the Little Bighorn.

Scouts brought word of increasing signs of Sioux. On June 26, the day appointed for the junction with Custer, Terry and Gibbon reached the mouth of the Little Bighorn and turned up the valley. Lieutenant James H. Bradley and his Crow scouts ranged ahead of the column. Camping on the night of June 26, the command continued the march up the valley on June 27. Four miles from camp they discovered the great Sioux village, abandoned. Proceeding through the vacated village, they met two officers of the Seventh Cavalry. The two men and Terry burst out with the same question: "Where is Custer?"

Lieutenant Bradley brought the answer. He and a mounted infantry detachment had been probing the rugged hills east of the valley. They had discovered the stripped and mutilated remains of Custer and 197 cavalrymen. The balance of the regiment, Terry learned, was entrenched atop high bluffs across the river. Major Reno commanded, backed by Captain Frederick W. Benteen.

Although Terry had to remain in the field to continue the campaign against the Sioux, recriminations flared at once. Who was to blame for such a horrid disaster? Terry? Custer? Reno? Benteen? Unpredictably overwhelming numbers of Indians? As soon as word reached the East, controversy erupted.

Unwittingly, Terry contributed to the controversy. In his official report, dated June 27, he cast no aspersions on Custer and took full responsibility for the disaster. Delayed en route, however, the telegraphic dispatch did not reach Sheridan until after a second report, dated July 2 and marked "confidential," arrived and mysteriously appeared in the press as the official version. In this dispatch Terry outlined his plan and informed Sheridan that he believed it would have succeeded had not Custer departed from it. Typically, Terry had sought to screen his dead subordinate from blame but had failed.

Never thereafter did Terry openly ascribe the catastrophe to Custer. The controversy continued decade after decade, growing ever more vehement, and rages to this day. Distressed by the blame heaped on Terry, in 1896 his longtime aide and brother-in-law, Colonel Robert P. Hughes, published a long treatise arguing the case against Custer in immense detail. It only fueled the conflict.

Perhaps more telling than the military argument was Hughes's assessment of Terry the man, which was bolstered throughout his life by the opinion of others: "I have been thoroughly conversant all these years with the noble and generous sacrifice, the complete abnegation of self that General Terry knowingly made for the avowed purpose of shielding a dead man from public blame. I have seen him receive thrust after thrust, year after year, on this matter, and quietly ignore it with some such remark as 'Blinder Eifer schadet nur'" (blind zeal only does harm).

Terry had more immediate concerns. Custer's dead had to be buried and Major Reno's wounded cared for. On June 28 the Seventh buried its dead while the infantry rigged mule-borne stretchers to carry Reno's wounded. With their cargo, Gibbon's men and Reno's battered remnant of the Seventh Cavalry moved laboriously down the Little Bighorn to its mouth, arriving on June 30. Here Captain Grant Marsh had anchored the *Far West*. With the wounded bedded on its decks, the steamer moved down to the mouth of the Bighorn. Terry and Gibbon followed by land. On July 3 Marsh ferried the command to the north bank of the Yellowstone and began his voyage of 710 miles down the Yellowstone and Missouri to Fort Lincoln.

The Sioux and Cheyennes who had destroyed Custer were now even more the objective of the troops in the field. The six camp circles had moved up the Little Bighorn and crossed to the Rosebud, then turned east toward the Tongue and the Powder. Beyond that they were uncertain.

Terry spent most of July bringing fresh supplies upriver on the *Far West* and the *Josephine*. Also, he strove to find out where General Crook and his command were. He had no knowledge of Crook's setback at the Battle of the Rosebud on June 17 or what Crook's plans were. Moreover, in the wake of a disaster such as Custer's defeat, he awaited reinforcements. Low morale and petty feuding rocked the camp, and Terry himself seemed dispirited and uncertain. Scouts finally made contact with Crook. The Sioux village was thought to be on the middle Rosebud and might be caught between Terry and Gibbon. They agreed that Terry would march up the Rosebud and Crook down. If they were right about the location of the enemy, they could strike it from two directions. Late in July Terry moved his command down the Yellowstone and camped opposite the mouth of the Rosebud. Steamers brought reinforcements.

On August 8 the Terry column began its march up the Rosebud. On August 10 the two columns met, but they were too late. The trail pointed east, inviting the generals to give chase.

Terry was the senior brigadier, but Crook was the experienced Indian fighter. Terry offered Crook command of the combined outfit. Crook refused. The two had not only striking differences of character and personality but different ideas about strategy. Crook, heading the Department of the Platte, believed that the Sioux would turn south toward the Black Hills in his Department of the Platte. Terry, concerned for his Department of Dakota, thought that the Sioux would head north toward Canada. To counter this possibility, he detached the Fifth Infantry and sent it back to the Yellowstone with the supply wagons. This move had been suggested by the Fifth's colonel, Nelson A. Miles, as always aggressively ambitious for an independent command. Miles would patrol the river by steamer to ensure that the Sioux did not try to cross and head north. The combined commands of Terry of Crook, relying on pack mules, would follow the Indian trail eastward.

The campaign was doomed from the start. More than three thousand infantry and cavalry, burdened by pack mules, hardly constituted a force with the mobility to overtake and defeat the Sioux. Weather proved a formidable deterrent. Cold rains turned the hills and valleys, roiled by so many feet, into mud and took severe toll on the health and morale of the troops. Terry's infantry constantly slowed the march because of inexperienced mule tenders. Both generals had their full staffs, which did not get along well. After a week of floundering in the Tongue and Powder valleys, the expedition went into camp at the mouth of the Powder on August 17. Fresh supplies alleviated some of the distress, but the men were demoralized.

So were the two generals. They could not agree on the proper strategy, whether to operate against Sitting Bull to the north or head east and south on the Indian trail. At length, on August 24, Crook simply marched east without alerting Terry. Terry followed and overtook him, but after further discussion he accepted the separation and returned to the Yellowstone.

Terry now turned his attention to the Yellowstone, where Colonel Miles had established himself with orders from Sheridan to build two posts: one at the mouth of the Tongue, the other at the mouth of the Little Bighorn. Miles would remain on the Yellowstone all winter to fight with Sioux if they intruded (they did, so he did). On September 5 Terry disbanded his army and ordered the components back to their stations. In St. Paul he returned to his life as a desk general.

For Terry, the summer operations had been a failure. He had lost five companies of the Seventh Cavalry and their flamboyant commander. His campaign with Crook had demonstrated the futility of sending large columns into a remote country where logistics overrode mission. Crook demonstrated this reality in his famous "mud march" to the Black Hills.

With Terry comfortably in his St. Paul headquarters, Colonel Miles had the independent command he so anxiously sought. In October, as Terry had foreseen, Sitting Bull and a large aggregation of Sioux crossed the Yellowstone and headed north. Miles handled the situation expertly, both fighting and negotiating with the Sioux and forcing some chiefs to surrender and return to the reservation. Miles's infantry erected a "cantonment" at the mouth of the Tongue River and settled in for a brutal winter. Crazy Horse and his following had remained south of the Yellowstone, however, and aggressively attracted Miles's attention. A winter campaign led to a successful battle with the chief and his warriors. Afterward Miles competed with General Crook, to the south, in trying to coax the Indians to surrender. Crook gained most of them; Crazy Horse gave up to Crook in the spring of 1877. Miles received what he deemed less than his fair share of surrenders. Throughout all the winter operations, Terry remained in his headquarters devoting himself to supporting Miles. Ungrateful, Miles constantly complained of lack of support from department headquarters.

Miles, and to a lesser extent Crook, overseen by Sheridan, brought the Great Sioux War of 1876–77 to a successful conclusion. Throughout, public and official attention centered on them. Terry shared in none of the laurels but quietly performed his departmental duties from his headquarters—except for one more field mission.

After negotiating and battling with Miles, Sitting Bull and his following took refuge in Canada, where they made friends with Major James M. Walsh of the North-West Mounted Police. But they were troublesome to the police and to the U.S. government, which foresaw raiding across the border. Therefore a peace commission headed by General Terry journeyed to Canada to persuade Sitting Bull to bring his people back to their reservation. The meeting took place at Fort Walsh on October 17, 1877. Sitting Bull heaped scorn on Terry and refused even to talk about surrender. He would stay with his red-coated friends.

Indian hostilities in Montana continued for five more years after 1876. Terry quietly issued the orders for a series of operations, but Colonel Miles took the initiative and proceeded in his own way. Striving to be free of Terry, he wrote to his wife's uncle, General Sherman: "I am satisfied that there is criminal neglect of duty at St. Paul or there is a determination that I shall not accomplish anything." Therefore he wanted a command separate from Terry's.[13] In fact he already proceeded independently and repeatedly prevailed. All the acclaim attached to him.

Despite Miles's successes, Sitting Bull remained safely distant in Canada. Faced with starvation, however, he crossed the border in 1881 and surrendered at Fort Buford. This event marked the formal close of hostilities with the Sioux. Six months earlier Nelson A. Miles had donned the star of a brigadier.

From St. Paul Terry oversaw the readjustment of his system of forts to reflect the end of Sioux hostilities. He abandoned old stations and created new ones. His department's relative tranquillity was interrupted in 1877, however, by the flight of the Nez Perces from Idaho toward Canada. General Oliver O. Howard pursued but failed to overtake them. From his base at the mouth of Tongue River, now named Fort Keogh, Miles dashed northwest and headed off the fugitives. In the Battle of Bear Paw Mountains he added another victory to his record. The Northern Pacific resumed construction, and again military escorts protected workers.

After Sitting Bull's surrender, Terry pursued a routine life in his department headquarters. This lasted until 1886, when he received the two stars of a major general. Sherman had retired, and Sheridan replaced him as head of the army. Terry moved into Sheridan's former command, the Division of the Missouri with headquarters in Chicago. With the Indian wars subsiding, the division no longer dealt with such large issues as in Sheridan's time. Moreover, Terry's health had been declining even while he still in St. Paul. He had Bright's disease, a kidney disorder that added to other ills, including gout and heart disease. At sixty-one, three years shy of the mandatory retirement age, he asked to be retired in 1881 for medical disability.

A lifetime bachelor with inherited wealth, well educated and with wide-ranging interests, Terry passed his declining years with his three sisters in New Haven. He died on December 16, 1891, and was buried in the Grove Street Cemetery in New Haven, Connecticut.

As a soldier, Alfred Terry displays a paradox. His Civil War career was exemplary. He exercised command quietly, competently, and with due regard for the welfare of his troops. Terry demonstrated his leadership at the regimental, division, and corps levels. His setbacks were few, and those occurred when he was not exercising independent command. His victory at Fort Fisher, although subjected to controversy over who deserved the credit after the war, truly merited the accolades showered on him and justified his appointment to the Regular Army. He won the respect and friendship of his peers and the adulation of his subordinates. He gained promotion without the politicking so common among others. He did not boast of his achievements. In short, Terry was one of the most successful and admirable Union generals.

Terry's record in the West after the Civil War stands in marked contrast to his Civil War career. He cannot be classified a failure but was not a success. He ran his department competently from his desk in St. Paul but seems to have lacked the initiative to advance his beliefs as other department commanders did. Terry did nothing to stir trouble with either Sheridan or his subordinates. His subordinate field commanders ran their domains largely on their own, reporting their activities and receiving logistical support from headquarters. His membership on the Peace Commission of 1867–68 was substantial but was more a learning experience than a contribution. His one field experience, forced on him by President Grant and General Sheridan, turned out calamitously. He bears much of the blame, which he shares with General Crook. History has been kinder to both than was General Sheridan, whose remark at the end of the campaign of 1876 strikes the right note: "The fact of the case is, the operations of Genls. Terry and Crook will not bear criticism, and my only thought has been to let them sleep. I approved what was done, for the sake of the troops, but in doing so, I was not approving much, as you know."[14]

Terry's competence as an administrator and his likable demeanor spared him harsh criticism. Compared to his colleagues heading departments, however, he emerges as a mediocre though extremely well-liked brigadier. The memorial plaque fixed to the wall of the United Church in New Haven, Connecticut, well phrases the legacy of Alfred H. Terry: "Honored by his countrymen for his unsullied patriotism, and his devoted service to the nation in war and in peace. Loved for the purity of his life, and the nobility of his character. 1827–1890."

CHAPTER NINE

EVALUATING THE COMMANDERS

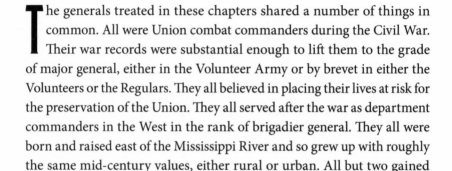

The generals treated in these chapters shared a number of things in common. All were Union combat commanders during the Civil War. Their war records were substantial enough to lift them to the grade of major general, either in the Volunteer Army or by brevet in either the Volunteers or the Regulars. They all believed in placing their lives at risk for the preservation of the Union. They all served after the war as department commanders in the West in the rank of brigadier general. They all were born and raised east of the Mississippi River and so grew up with roughly the same mid-century values, either rural or urban. All but two gained their education at the U.S. Military Academy at West Point, thus fostering a uniformity of military thought and ambition. One of these two was educated in the law, while the other educated himself. Of the seven, four served in the West before the war as junior officers, three in line combat units, and one in a staff position. These officers ventured west after the Civil War with insights denied to their colleagues.

The generals approached the West and its Indian inhabitants with attitudes more or less typical of their time. Those who had not served in the West before the war thought of the West, if they thought of it at all, as a romantic land of adventure; those who had served there knew it for what it was: a hard land of beauty and sterility. All viewed the Indians as most easterners did: as exotic savages who disrupted the legitimate westward movement of the American people, who should be compelled or led to yield their lands to the "civilized race" and work to elevate themselves. To be sure, most generals sympathized with the Indians' plight and believed that white people caused most Indian hostilities. Still, frontier officers of all ranks knew where their duty lay and harbored little hesitation in carrying it out.

The generals represented their generation in believing that the nation's destiny lay in uniting East and West in one political and economic polity. Exploiting land for agriculture, livestock grazing, minerals, and commerce took precedence over the rights of Indians. Settlements and travel routes—trails, roads, and railways—commanded high priority among the generals. Such manifestations of white culture both provoked and tempted the affected Indians. The generals faced Indian hostilities, ranging from minor skirmishes to full-scale Indian wars as they took station in the West. Their adaptation to the new environment, so in contrast to Civil War operations, influenced the course of events and whether they gained a second star in the postwar army.

Did the commanders treated in this volume shape the West, and if so how?

They were department commanders, the most influential component of frontier military geography. The department was the shock absorber insulating the field units from the division commander. The way in which they carried out their function determined how their subordinates performed. And how their subordinates performed helped shaped the West that emerged at the end of the nineteenth century. Many other factors—economic, political, environmental, demographic—combined to shape the postwar West, but the department commanders must be counted among the shapers. They and their troops helped open the West to settlement, helped subdue the Indians, helped protect westerners from Indians, pioneered wagon roads, aided the advance of railroads, erected telegraph lines, and fortified white citizens' morale by their proximity. They also had a huge impact on the Indian peoples with whom they or the subordinates under their orders engaged.

History holds the generals partly accountable for the tragedy of the American Indian. But like all other expansionists, they were products of their times. They were bound by the military code of obedience to orders—as men of their times they could not have acted otherwise. They should be judged within the context of their times—in this accounting as Indian fighters.

A department commander's measure of success lay in four major factors. First, smooth relations with his division commander ensured a healthy working atmosphere. Antagonism on the part of either superior or subordinate disturbed military order in the department. Second, a department commander's administrative ability governed how smoothly the large and small complexities of a sprawling department functioned. Administrative competence, as revealed to superiors and to all subordinate personnel, was an imperative quality in anyone who commanded people and managed systems. Third, interaction with department staff officers influenced subsistence, personnel, paper flow, transportation, medicine and hygiene, ordnance, and other functions critical to a military organization. Often staff officers had loyalties divided between their staff chiefs in Washington and division headquarters and their immediate commanding general. Dealing with such conflicts when they occurred affected the working relationships and morale of the department headquarters. Especially revealing was the quality of logistics, the feature most vital to a functioning military organization. Finally, for the twenty-five years after the Civil War all the departments contended with Indian warfare. How well a department commander performed in fighting Indians, either in the field or from a desk in headquarters, defined his standing in the military hierarchy.

Only one of the seven generals—George Crook—grasped the essence of Indian warfare and devised unconventional techniques to cope with it. As a field general rather than a desk general, Crook pioneered reliance on pack mules rather than wagon trains for logistical purposes. This enhanced his mobility and allowed him to operate in terrain unsuited for wagons. Another Crook hallmark was extensive use of Indian scouts, preferably from the tribe against which he was operating. Not only did the scouts know the country and the adversary, but their employment devastated the morale of their kin. Crook's tactical approach was to operate with small commands and, once on the trail, follow it despite obstacles until he overtook the quarry. Crook's methods proved effective against Apaches in the Southwest in 1872–73 and 1882–86. On the northern plains in 1876–78, however, he largely failed. Indian scouts gave way to Crow and Shoshone auxiliaries, pack mules replaced wagons for only part of his operations, his command was far too large, the expanses of the terrain were too great, the weather was brutal, and his decisions reflected poor judgment.

Crook's relations with his division commander, General Philip Sheridan, were ostensibly amicable. Smoldering beneath the surface, however, was

Colonel Ranald S. Mackenzie, Fourth Cavalry.
Brady Collection, U.S. Signal Corps (photo SC-87407),
National Archives and Records Administration, Washington, D.C.

Crook's bitter resentment of a perceived Civil War wrong inflicted by Sheridan. It manifested itself in the 1876 Sioux campaign, when Sheridan berated Crook's performance, and again in the Apache campaigns of 1883–86, when Sheridan's dissatisfaction led to Crook's relief from command. Crook's headquarters seems to have functioned smoothly largely because his staff adored him. As an Indian fighter, he reveled in the public reputation as the army's best. He was not.

The best Indian fighter was Nelson A. Miles, although he achieved this record as a colonel rather than as a brigadier. His role in the Red River War of 1874–75, in the operations against the Sioux after the Custer disaster of 1876, and in the Nez Perce War of 1877 all record a chain of successes without parallel in the Indian fighting army. Although Colonel Ranald S. Mackenzie is regarded by many authorities as the best, his victories fail to match Miles's. As a brigadier commanding the Department of Arizona in 1886, Miles brought the Apache wars to a close, although he did this by covertly resorting to Crook's method while heaping public credit on the Regulars. Miles conducted this campaign mainly by traveling by rail around his department and leaving field operations to subordinates. The Apache campaign was Miles's only Indian action as a department commander rather than as a regimental colonel.

Miles's first command as a brigadier had been the Department of the Columbia, where he served from 1881 to 1885. No Indian troubles disturbed the department during his tenure. It fared well in routine duties and received little scrutiny from the chief. His only notable achievement was in dispatching exploring expeditions to Alaska. Miles preferred a less remote station, however, where he could better seek preferment. The Department of the Platte in 1885–86 afforded a more visible headquarters, from which he shortly departed for his Arizona assignment and the campaign against the Apaches.

In 1888, still a brigadier, Miles took command of the Division of the Pacific and began his ascent to the top rank in the U.S. Army. The only basis for judging Miles as a department commander, other than Indian combat, lies in his four years in the Department of the Columbia and two years after the Apaches surrendered in 1886. No viable evidence bears on his headquarters composition at Fort Vancouver. General Sherman retired in 1883, which deprived Miles of his conduit to influence. He grew restless enough largely to ignore routine department duties. He spent most of his time traveling, revisiting old controversies, and lobbying for his own preferment. As an Indian fighter, therefore, Miles ranks at the top; as a department commander he sinks below mediocrity.

General Oliver O. Howard had long experience as a department commander, four years in the Department of the Columbia and four in the Department of the Platte. In the Nez Perce War of 1877 he functioned as an Indian-fighting combat commander. His reputation rests almost entirely on that experience. He handled it so badly in the early phases that he came close to being relieved. Afterward he fought a victorious battle at the Clearwater but failed to follow up, leaving the Nez Perces to trudge across the Bitterroot Mountains in search of refuge in Montana or Canada. Howard's pursuit so exhausted him and his command that he had resolved to turn back when General Sherman humiliated him into continuing. To compound the humiliation, Colonel Nelson A. Miles won the final victory. Considering the obstacles, Howard probably did as well as other generals might have, but his mistakes detract from his record. Using the Nez Perce War as the only basis for judging him as an Indian fighter, the verdict would be barely satisfactory. However, his operations in 1878 against the Bannocks, Paiutes, Shoshones, Umatillas, and Sheepeaters were so successful that they should have redeemed his reputation. They didn't.

General Howard's departmental headquarters seems notable for one thing: his extreme Christian faith. In Portland he spent much of his time in biblical pursuits, such as faithfully attending church, teaching a Bible class, and lecturing in various venues. His staff seems to have functioned adequately and probably, as in all other of Howard's stations, bridled at overt piety in headquarters. He traveled extensively in his department, including Alaska. As for his relations with his division commander, Major General Irvin McDowell joined General Sherman in scolding Howard for wanting to call off the pursuit of the Nez Perces and had not objected to the president's proposal to relieve Howard at the beginning of the campaign. That hardly promoted harmonious relations. Transfer to the Department of the Platte in 1882 brought Howard under the command of General Sheridan; but the department was quiet, and he and Sheridan seem not to have experienced any friction.

Both as a field general and as a headquarters general, Oliver O. Howard may be judged a moderate success.

Alfred H. Terry presents a strange case. He was a desk general who administered his department quietly and competently. His staff worked smoothly because he was such a kind and considerate superior. He got along with General Sheridan simply by carrying out Sheridan's orders. Yet on one occasion he became a field general not by choice but by Sheridan's orders. Because of Custer's political indiscretions, Terry had to lead the command that he had intended for his subordinate. Thus he headed the Dakota column in the Sioux War of 1876. In that capacity he invites scrutiny as an Indian fighter.

Terry did not intend to become an Indian fighter. He was content to oversee any such operations in his department from his St. Paul headquarters. In the Sioux expedition, however, his command suffered the loss of five troops of the Seventh Cavalry. Whether he shares blame for that is still highly controversial. More obvious is his joint operation with General Crook, which, as Sheridan noted, was an abject failure for both Crook and Terry. No other field service fell to Terry, who retained the respect and affection of the army's top ranks.

As a department commander, Terry rates low marks as an Indian fighter and high marks as a headquarters general.

The remaining three department commanders—Augur, Pope, and Ord— were headquarters generals who oversaw Indian operations conducted by subordinates.

Christopher C. Augur held command of the Department of the Platte from 1867 to 1871 but devoted two years of that time to the Indian Peace Commission. That experience gave him opinions on Indian affairs, which General Sherman characterized as "forbearance and moderation." Even so, Augur organized and oversaw from headquarters Major Eugene A. Carr's successful Republican River Expedition of 1869 against the Sioux and Cheyennes. In the Department of Texas from 1871 to 1875 Augur dealt with more compelling Indian hostilities. He contended with raids against Texas ranchers by tribesmen living in Mexico. Colonel Ranald S. Mackenzie's thrust across the border in 1873, however, was carried out under General Sheridan's personal direction. More directly, Augur organized two of the five converging columns that conquered the Cheyennes and Comanches in the Red River War of 1874–75. Even though he was a desk general, his Indian record deserves high marks.

Augur's headquarters appears to have been tranquil both in Omaha and San Antonio. He administered it efficiently, maintained excellent relations with General Sheridan, and endeared himself to the army top command by gaining the affection of Texans who had only recently fought for the South. This in turn translated into Texan political support for the army in Congress.

C. C. Augur's quiet, modest demeanor deprived him of public visibility, but even so he ranks as one of the best department commanders.

Despite his failed Civil War career, John Pope did well as a department commander in the Indian country. First on the northern plains and then on the central plains, he redeemed his Civil War reputation as a competent, if sometimes difficult, leader. Like others, he was a desk general. He organized and oversaw operations in his jurisdiction and closely monitored the conduct of his subordinate commanders. His Sioux campaigns of 1863 and 1864 achieved success, in large part because of competent field commanders. The campaign of 1865 failed because of conditions beyond his control. His two field columns in the Red River War of 1874–75 also performed well and won two important victories. As a headquarters Indian fighter, John Pope prevailed. At the same time, his efforts on behalf of the Indians earned him the sobriquet of "humanitarian general."

Commanding the Department of the Northwest in the waning days of the Civil War, Pope performed well as an administrator and avoided friction with superiors, largely because the Civil War focused attention elsewhere. As the longtime commander of the Department of the Missouri, however, he made such a nuisance of himself by prodding General Sheridan to adopt unwanted measures that he suffered a rocky relationship with his division commander. His proposals made sense, which only exacerbated the friction. During the Red River War, logistics presented a severe problem and strained staff relations as well as relations with both Sheridan and his field commander Nelson Miles. Both Pope and Miles, of course, were prolific wordsmiths, whose verbal outpourings contributed to logistical as well as strategic difficulties.

Edward O. C. Ord commanded the Departments of California, the Platte, and Texas. California and the Platte offered little challenge, either in the field or in headquarters. Texas, however, was apparently another matter. To his credit, Ord continued the effort of his predecessor, General Augur, to befriend Texans and help mobilize the support of the state's congressional delegation to save the army from drastic cuts. He succeeded admirably.

Citizen friendship for Ord derived in large part from his aggressive offensives against tribal raids across the Mexican border into Texas. His border commanders were Colonel Ranald S. Mackenzie and Lieutenant Colonel William R. Shafter. Both violated the border with expeditions taunting Mexico as much as seeking Indian raiders. The invasions did succeed in alleviating the cross-border raids, although at the price of damaged relations with Mexico. The Hayes administration fostered such incursions, which Ord loyally supported. In the process, however, Ord repeatedly addressed letters to his prewar comrade and friend General Sherman. Bypassing the chain of command angered General Sheridan, whose enmity deepened as he discovered faulty departmental administration, what he and Sherman labeled "eccentricity," and Ord's tendency to follow his own instincts, however unwise. Both Sheridan and Sherman felt so strongly about Ord's unfitness for the Texas command that they wished to move him quietly aside. That was not possible, and the problem only vanished when the president forcibly retired Ord.

Although General Ord's tenure in the Departments of California and the Platte passed quietly, his record in Texas is a more accurate basis for judging him. His performance there does not stamp him as a satisfactory department commander.

Evaluating the seven generals treated in this book calls for ranking them on their merits as department commanders. This requires judging them only in that capacity and disregarding their combat records in lower ranks, both prewar and postwar. It also requires judging them on the other elements of command—smooth relations with the division commander, administrative ability, and a harmonious staff. Fighting Indians was not their only mission. Based on those criteria, I offer the following ranking:

1. Christopher C. Augur
2. George Crook
3. John Pope
4. Alfred H. Terry
5. Oliver O. Howard
6. Nelson A. Miles
7. Edward O. C. Ord

Basing the ranking exclusively on their combat record as department commanders, whether in the field or at headquarters, the order could change to Crook, Augur, Pope, Howard, Ord, and Miles. Despite Miles's successful campaigns as a colonel, he rates the bottom slot only by virtue of the Apache campaign of 1886.

Finally, in a larger sense than the strictly military, all the generals played a part in "shaping" the American West. By virtue of their military role, they impacted the western tribes. Crook takes first rank, for his direct interaction, both in war and in peace, with Apaches, Sioux, Crows, Shoshones, and Poncas. Beyond his influence on Indians, Crook yields the issue of seeking to advance western settlement to Augur and Pope. Both Augur and Pope consciously aimed at protecting and aiding the civilian population and favored opening the West. In his 1896 book Nelson Miles created a sense of awe at the great West and the opportunities that it held for all white Americans. He influenced the settlement of the West far less than his grand hyperbole would suggest. General Howard, in association with Colonel Miles, effectively reduced the Nez Perce to a hapless tribe scattered beyond unity. As a department commander, Ord did much to make the Texas border habitable for whites.

In short, the commanders, with varying impact, influenced what the West had become by the beginning of the twentieth century.

NOTES

Abbreviations

AGO   Adjutant General's Office
NARA   National Archives and Records Administration
OR   *Official Records of the Union and Confederate Armies*
RG   Record Group
Stat.   *U.S. Statutes at Large*, vols. 14–18

Chapter 1. The Postwar U.S. Army

1. 14 *Stat.* 332–38 (July 28, 1866).
2. 14 *Stat.* 223 (July 25, 1866).
3. 15 *Stat.* 315–18 (March 3, 1869); 16 *Stat.* 315–21 (July 15, 1870); 18 *Stat.* 72 (June 16, 1874).
4. James B. Fry, *The History and Legal Effect of Brevets in the Armies of Great Britain and the United States* (New York: D. Van Nostrand, 1877). Throughout this book, when an officer is awarded a brevet (whether in quotation marks or not) the source is Francis B. Heitman, comp., *Historical Register and Dictionary of the United States Army*, vol. 1 (Washington, D.C.: GPO, 1903; facsimile, Urbana: University of Illinois Press, 1965). Officers' names are arranged alphabetically.
5. Col. John Gibbon, 7th Infantry, to Sherman, Fort Shaw, Mont., March 15, 1877, U.S. House Misc. Doc. No. 56, 45th Cong., 2nd sess., pp. 124–28.
6. Sherman to Sheridan, Washington, October 7, 1872, Sherman-Sheridan Papers, Library of Congress.
7. Ibid., April 1, 1876.
8. Special Session Message of President R. B. Hayes, October 15, 1877, in James D. Richardson, comp. *A Compilation of Messages and Papers of the Presidents, 1789–1897*, 10 vols. (Washington, D.C.: Bureau of National Literature and Art, 1897), 7:452–54.
9. *Army and Navy Journal* 14 (May 12, 1877): 640.
10. In U.S. Secretary of War, *Annual Report* (1872), p. 53.

NOTES TO PAGES 10–25

11. William A. Dobak and Thomas D. Phillips, *The Black Regulars, 1866–1898* (Norman: University of Oklahoma Press, 2001).
12. Quoted in *Army and Navy Journal* 14 (August 12, 1876): 4.
13. Lansing B. Bloom, "Bourke on the Southwest," *New Mexico Historical Review* 9 (1934): 52.
14. Charles Braden, "The Yellowstone Expedition of 1873," *Journal of the U.S. Cavalry Association* 16 (1905): 240–41.
15. Throughout his journal, Dr. John Vance Lauderdale has much to say about both sanitation and women. Robert M. Utley, ed., *An Army Doctor on the Western Frontier: Journals and Letters of John Vance Lauderdale, 1864–1890* (Albuquerque: University of New Mexico Press, 2014).
16. *Army and Navy Journal* 15 (September 8, 1877): 73.
17. U.S. House Misc. Doc. No. 56, 45th Cong., 2nd sess., p. 34.

Chapter 2. Christopher C. Augur

1. Sherman to S. F. Tappan, St. Louis, September 26, 1868, Sherman Papers, vol. 89, Library of Congress.
2. I derive this characterization from Augur's official correspondence and the observations of his superiors, Generals Sherman and Sheridan. Of the generals treated in this volume, Augur and Terry are the only ones lacking a biography. Augur's papers are archived in the Newberry Library in Chicago.
3. I treat the Battle of Big Meadows in *Frontiersmen in Blue: The United States Army and the Indian, 1848–1865* (New York: Macmillan, 1967), pp. 183–86.
4. U.S. Senate Executive Doc. No. 13, 40th Cong., 1st sess., p. 27.
5. Sherman to Assistant Adjutant General Hq. of Army, St. Louis, March 13, 1867, U.S. Senate Ex. Doc. No. 7, 40th Cong., 1st sess., 1867, pp. 1–3 (response to the Senate Resolution of March 11 asking for information about armed expeditions against western Indians).
6. I treat these commissions in *The Indian Frontier, 1846–1890* (rev. ed., Albuquerque: University of New Mexico Press, 2003), pp. 106–10.
7. Annual Report of Bvt. Maj. Gen. C. C. Augur. Augur to Bvt. Maj. Gen. W. A. Nichols, Assistant Adjutant General Military Division of the Missouri, Hq. Dept. of the Platte, Omaha, October 14, 1868, in U.S. Secretary of War, *Annual Report* (1868), pp. 21–24; Statement of campaigns, expeditions, and scouts made in the Department of the Platte during the year ending September 30, 1868, Hq. Dept. of the Platte, Omaha, October 17, 1868, sgd Bvt. Brig. Gen. George D. Ruggles, in ibid., pp. 25–29.
8. Report to the President by the Indian Peace Commission, January 7, 1868, House Ex. Doc. No. 97, 40th Cong., 2nd sess., pp. 1–22.
9. Untitled essay (thoughts on Indian wars) by Augur on stationery of Department of the Platte in the late 1860s, Christopher C. Augur Papers, Newberry Library, Chicago.
10. Ibid.

11. Annual Report of Bvt. Maj. Gen.1 Augur, Augur to Hartsuff, Dept. of the Platte, Omaha, October 23, 1869; U.S. Secretary of War, *Annual Report* (1869), pp. 70–75. See also my book *Frontier Regulars: The United States Army and the Indian, 1866–1891* (New York: Macmillan, 1973), pp. 156–57.

12. Annual Report of Brig. Gen. Augur, Augur to Adjutant General E. D. Townsend, Hq. Dept. of the Platte, Omaha, October 25, 1870; U.S. Secretary of War, *Annual Report* (1870), pp. 31–35. See also Utley, *Frontier Regulars*, p. 241.

13. U.S. Senate Ex. Doc. No. 89, 41st Cong., 2nd sess., Message of the President, May 23, 1870, in response to Senate Resolution of May 12, 1869; Encroachments upon Indians in Wyoming Territory, Annual Report of Brig. Gen. Augur, Augur to Adjt. Gen. E. D. Townsend, Hq. Dept. of the Platte, Omaha, October 25, 1870; U.S. Secretary of War, *Annual Report* (1870), pp. 31–35.

14. Annual Report of Brig. Gen. Augur, Augur to Lt. Col. J. B. Fry, Asst. Adjt. Gen. Hq. Military Division of the Missouri, Chicago, Hq. Dept. of the Platte, Omaha, October 10, 1871; U.S. Secretary of War, *Annual Report* (1871), pp. 31–33.

15. Both Augur's and Merritt's reports are printed in *Army and Navy Journal* 9 (May 25, 1872): 653.

16. *Indian Frontier*, pp. 140–44, on the City of Refuge.

17. Annual Report of Brig. Gen. Augur, Augur to Fry, Asst. Adjt. Gen. Military Division of the Missouri Chicago, Hq. Dept. of Texas, San Antonio, September 28, 1872; U.S. Secretary of War, *Annual Report* (1872), pp. 54–60.

18. I treat this episode and the operation that followed in "Border Showdown," *MHQ: The Quarterly Journal of Military History* 23 (Spring 2011): 98–104. See also Paul Andrew Hutton, *Phil Sheridan and His Army* (Lincoln: University of Nebraska Press, 1985), pp. 221–25; R. G. Carter, *On the Border with Mackenzie: or, Winning West Texas from the Comanches* (New York: Antiquarian Press, 1961), pp. 422–23; and A. M. Gibson, *The Kickapoos: Lords of the Middle Border* (Norman: University of Oklahoma Press, 1964), pp 239–54.

19. Mackenzie to Augur, Fort Clark, April 20, 1873, Christopher C. Augur Papers, Newberry Library, Chicago.

20. Mackenzie to Assistant Adjutant General Department of Texas, Fort Clark, May 23, 1873, in Ernest Wallace, ed., *Ranald S. Mackenzie's Official Correspondence Relating to Texas, 1871–1875*, 2 vols. (Lubbock: West Texas Museum Association, 1967), 1:167–72. The report was at once endorsed by Sheridan, Sherman, and Belknap but not by Augur.

21. Sherman to Sheridan, June 3, 1873, Sherman-Sheridan Letters, Sheridan Papers, Library of Congress; Sheridan to Sherman, June 5, 1873, Sherman Papers, vol. 35, Library of Congress.

22. Many monographs treat the Red River War. See in particular my *Frontier Regulars*, chap. 13; *Indian Frontier*, pp. 171–74; and "The Red River War: Last Uprising in the Texas Panhandle," *MHQ: The Quarterly Journal of Military History* 20 (Autumn 2007): 74–83; and Hutton, *Phil Sheridan and His Army*, chap. 11.

23. Hutton, *Phil Sheridan and His Army*, chap. 12, deals with this interlude.

24. Letter of 138 Texas citizens to Augur, San Antonio, March 12, 1875, Christopher C. Augur Papers, Newberry Library, Chicago.

25. Report of Brig. Gen. C. C. Augur. Augur to Adjt, Gen. Military Division of the Missouri Chicago, Hq. Dept. of Texas, San Antonio, September 27, 1881; U.S. Secretary of War, *Annual Report* (1881), pp. 128–30.

26. Report of Brig. Gen. Augur, Augur to Adjt. Gen. Military Division of the Missouri Chicago, Hq. Dept. of Texas, San Antonio, September 21, 1883; U.S. Secretary of War, *Annual Report* (1883), p. 146.

Chapter 3. George Crook

1. Two biographies authoritatively treat Crook the Indian fighter. Charles M. Robinson III covers Crook's entire life in *General Crook and the Western Frontier* (Norman: University of Oklahoma Press, 2001). The second biography is a projected three-volume work, of which the first two have been published: Paul Magid, *George Crook: From the Redwoods to Appomattox* (Norman: University of Oklahoma Press, 2011), and *The Gray Fox: George Crook and the Indian Wars* (Norman: University of Oklahoma Press, 2015). The first volume treats Crook's service in the Pacific Northwest before the Civil War and his service during the war itself, while the second volume deals with his postwar career to the surrender of Crazy Horse in 1877. Presumably the final volume will deal principally with Crook's Arizona service. I have relied heavily on both of Magid's excellent volumes. Useful in understanding Crook is the hagiographic memoir by his longtime aide Captain John G. Bourke, *On the Border with Crook* (New York: Charles Scribner's Sons, 1891).

2. Many of these characteristics are described by all who knew and wrote about Crook. Others are my own judgment based on a comparison of his official reports with what actually happened as revealed by reliable sources. Magid states some and implies others.

3. Martin F. Schmitt, ed., *General George Crook: His Autobiography* (Norman: University of Oklahoma Press, 1946), pp. pp. 17–20. Magid, in *George Crook: From the Redwoods to Appomattox*, pp. 54–55, describes this event better than Crook does.

4. Schmitt, *General George Crook*, p. 21.

5. Crook describes these events in detail in ibid., pp. 35ff.

6. Crook describes this operation in ibid., pp. 57–68. I treat the march in the larger context of Indian warfare in Washington Territory in *Frontiersmen in Blue*, pp. 203–204.

7. Crook's Civil War career is detailed in his autobiography (Schmitt, *General George Crook*, chaps. 3 and 4), and in Robinson, *General Crook*, chaps. 3–6. See also Warner, *Generals in Blue*, pp. 102–104.

8. In his autobiography Crook expressed his resentment in blunt terms: Schmitt, *General George Crook*, p. 127.

9. Ibid., p. 134n7.

10. Ibid., p. 141.

11. Both engagements are noted in Special Order 32, Hq. Dept. of the Columbia, Portland, November 1, 1867, By command of Bvt. Maj. Gen. F. Steele, in U.S. Secretary of War, *Annual Report* (1868), pp. 770–72. Crook's operations in this campaign and all that followed are described in great detail in Magid, *The Gray Fox*. As previously noted, this volume is the second of three by Magid, with a third still to come. I relied extensively on the first volume in recounting Crook's Civil War career. This volume carries the story to 1877, at the close of Crook's 1876 campaign against the Sioux. In addition, consult Robinson, *General Crook*; and Schmitt, *General Crook*.

12. The battle is noted in Special Order 32 in U.S. Secretary of War, *Annual Report* (1868), pp. 771–72. See also Magid, *The Gray Fox*, pp. 32–35, and Robinson, *General Crook*, pp. 96–101.

13. Magid, *The Gray Fox*, p. 42.

14. Crook to Assistant Adjutant General, Dept. of the Columbia, Camp Warner, Oregon, August 22, 1868, in U.S. Secretary of War, *Annual Report* (1868), pp. 72–73.

15. Halleck to Adjutant General, Hq. Military Division of the Pacific, San Francisco, September 22, 1868, in U.S. Secretary of War, *Annual Report* (1868), p. 44.

16. The details of Crook's march from Tucson and his interaction with the White Mountain Apaches are recounted by a correspondent of the *Army and Navy Journal* who accompanied the command: *Army and Navy Journal* 9 (August 8, 1871), 816; 9 (October 7, 1871): 120.

17. Schmitt, *General George Crook*, p. 169.

18. Both Magid and Robinson, of course, deal with this operation in detail. I treat it in *Frontier Regulars*, pp. 195–98.

19. Crook explains his agreement with the miners in his annual report for 1875 and emphasizes the provocation of the Sioux raiders. September 15, 1875, in U.S. Secretary of War, *Annual Report* (1875), pp. 69–70.

20. The definitive history of this campaign is Paul L. Hedren, *Powder River: Disastrous Opening of the Great Sioux War* (Norman: University of Oklahoma Press, 2016). I deal with the Great Sioux War in *Frontier Regulars*, chaps. 14–15.

21. Crook to Assistant Adjutant General, Military Division of the Missouri, Chicago, Hq. Department of the Platte, Omaha, May 7, 1876, in U.S. Secretary of War, *Annual Report* (1876), pp. 502–503.

22. Reynolds to Sherman, Fort D. A. Russell, Wyo., April 11, 1876, Sherman Papers, vol. 43, Library of Congress.

23. Crook's report of the battle, demonstrating more than a touch of dissimulation, is found in Crook to Assistant Adjutant General, Military Division of the Missouri, Hq. Big Horn and Yellowstone Expedition, Camp Cloud Peak, Base Big Horn Mountains, June 20, 1876, in U.S. Secretary of War, *Annual Report* (1876), pp. 504–505.

24. Crook tells of Slim Buttes in Telegram, Crook to Sheridan, Camp on Owl River, D.T., September 10, 1976, in U.S. Secretary of War, *Annual Report* (1876), pp. 506–507.

25. Sheridan to Sherman (confidential), February 10, 1877, Sherman Papers, vol. 45, Library of Congress.

26. Annual Report of General Crook, Crook to Assistant Adjutant General, Military Division of the Missouri, Chicago, Hq. Department of the Platte, Omaha, August 1, 1877, in U.S. Secretary of War, *Annual Report* (1877), pp. 84–86.

27. Brig. Gen. George Crook to Assistant Adjutant General, Military Division of the Missouri, Chicago. Hq. Department of the Platte, Omaha Bks, December 6, 1877, in U.S. Secretary of War, *Annual Report* (1878), pp. 91–92.

28. Report of Brig. Gen. George Crook, Crook to Assistant Adjutant General, Military Division of the Missouri, Chicago, Hq. Department of the Platte, Fort Omaha, September 27, 1879, in U.S. Secretary of War, *Annual Report* (1879), pp. 77–78; Annual Report of Lt. Gen. P. H. Sheridan, Sheridan to Townsend, Hq. Military Division of the Missouri, Chicago, Oct. 22, 1879, in ibid., pp. 42–46.

29. Paul Magid ends the second volume of his three-volume biography of Crook with the surrender of Crazy Horse in 1877, so he does not treat the Ponca affair. Crook ceased to compile his biography at the same time; but his editor, Martin Schmitt, compiles a thorough history of the episode. See Schmitt, *General George Crook*, pp. 231–35. I have relied heavily on Robinson, *General Crook,* chap. 14, for the Ponca affair.

30. Sheridan to Sherman (strictly confidential), January 22, 1879, Sherman Papers, vol. 49, Library of Congress.

31. General Order 43, Hq. Department of Arizona, Whipple Barracks, October 5, 1882, by command of Brig. Gen Crook, in U.S. Secretary of War, *Annual Report* (1883), pp. 170–71.

32. Memorandum of a council at San Carlos, November 2, 1882, between General Crook and the Indians on the White Mountain Reservation, in U.S. Secretary of War, *Annual Report* (1883), pp. 172–73.

33. I treat Crook's Arizona tenure, 1882–1886, in *Geronimo* (New Haven: Yale University Press, 2012).

34. Crook's summary is found in Crook to Assistant Adjutant General Military Division of the Pacific, [Hq. Department of Arizona, Whipple Bks., n.d., c. 9/84,] in U.S. Secretary of War, *Annual Report* (1884), pp. 131–34.

35. Annual Report of Lieutenant General Sheridan, October 10, 1886, in U.S. Secretary of War, *Annual Report* (1886), p. 72.

36. George Crook, "The Apache Problem," *Journal of the Military Service Institution 7,* no. 27 (October 1886): 266.

37. I recount this complex story in detail in *Geronimo,* chap. 21 (quotation on p. 182).

38. Originals of all the telegrams are found in Record Group 94, Letters Received, Office of the Adjutant General, 1881–1889, 1066 AGO 1883, National Archives and Records Administration (hereinafter NARA).

39. This is my own analysis, as set forth in *Geronimo,* p. 190.

Chapter 4. Oliver O. Howard

1. This is the portrait provided by his biographer: John A. Carpenter, *Sword and Olive Branch: Oliver Otis Howard* (New York: Fordham University Press, 1999, first published

in 1964). My own essay draws heavily on this book. For Howard's Civil War career, see, in addition, Warner, *Generals in Blue*, pp. 237–39.

2. Howard quoted in Carpenter, *Sword and Olive Branch*, p. 60.

3. Sherman quoted in ibid., p. 65 (the following Sherman quotation is also from this source).

4. Paul S. Peirce, *The Freedmen's Bureau: A Chapter in the History of Reconstruction* (Iowa City: State University of Iowa, 1904), pp. 111, 170.

5. I treat the Howard peace mission in *Geronimo*, chap. 8.

6. Quoted in Carpenter, *Sword and Olive Branch*, pp. 232–33.

7. Sherman to Howard, Washington, D.C., November 12, 1872, Sherman Papers, vol. 90, p. 220, Library of Congress.

8. Sherman to Howard, Washington, D.C., November 29, 1873, Sherman Papers, vol. 90, pp. 301–302.

9. An abundance of helpful books describe the Nez Perce War. The most valuable is Jerome A. Greene, *Nez Perce Summer, 1877: The U.S. Army and the Nee-Me-Poo Crisis* (Helena: Montana Historical Society Press, 2000). See also Utley, *Frontier Regulars*, chap. 16; and Carpenter, *Sword and Olive Branch*, pp. 246–64.

10. U.S. Secretary of War, *Annual Report* (1877), pp. 12–14.

11. U.S. Secretary of War, *Annual Report* (1878), p. 235.

12. Sherman to Howard (at Ebbitt House), December 7, 1880, Sherman Papers, vol. 91, pp. 545–46, Library of Congress.

13. My account of the Whittaker affair is drawn entirely from an online article in Black-Past.org. Strangely, although Carpenter, in *Sword and Olive Branch*, pp. 272–77, deals with Howard's two years at West Point, he ignores the Whittaker court-martial and dismissal entirely, failing even to note that Howard ordered the court-martial. A century later a Mississippi professor unearthed Whittaker's story. It was made into a television movie. President Bill Clinton posthumously commissioned Johnson Whittaker a second lieutenant in the army on July 24, 1995.

Chapter 5. Nelson A. Miles

1. Robert Wooster, *Nelson A. Miles and the Twilight of the Frontier Army* (Lincoln: University of Nebraska Press, 1993), p. 273. My work relies heavily on this definitive biography.

2. Besides Wooster's biography, consult Ezra J. Warner, *Generals in Blue*, pp. 322–24.

3. Flaws in the officer corps are clearly set forth in Frank D. Baldwin to My Darling Little Wife, Hq. Indian Territory Expedition, Camp on Wolf Creek, Tex., October 22, 1874, and Baldwin to My Darling Wife, Camp on Red River, Tex., November 4, 1874: Baldwin Papers, Box 11, Henry E. Huntington Library, San Marino, California.

4. All official reports and correspondence of the Red River War are set forth in Joe F. Taylor, ed., *The Indian Campaign on the Staked Plains, 1874–1875: Military Correspondence from War Department Adjutant General's Office, File 2815–1874* (Canyon, Tex.: Panhandle-Plains Historical Society, 1962). An especially graphic description of

the fight is found in the Journal of Frank D. Baldwin, August 30, 1874, Box 1, Folder A3c, Baldwin Papers, Huntington Library.

5. Journal of Frank D. Baldwin, November 8, 1874, Box 1, Folder A3c, and Baldwin to My Darling Wife, Camp on Red River, Tex., November 4, 1874,, Box 11: Baldwin Papers, Huntington Library. This letter was continued on December 18 after the battle.

6. Baldwin's journals are in Box 1, Folder A3f, his letters in Box 11, Frank D. Baldwin Papers, Huntington Library.

7. Telegram, Terry to Sheridan, Camp on Rosebud, August 10, 1876, received in Chicago on September 4, Record Group (hereinafter RG) 393, Records of U.S. Army Continental Commands, Special Files, Military Division of the Missouri, M1495, Roll 4, Frame 39, NARA.

8. Sheridan to Terry, Hq. Military Division of the Missouri, Chicago, August 18, 1876, RG 94, Office of the Adjutant General Letters Received (Main Series), 1871–1880, File 4163 AGO 1876 (Sioux War Papers), M666, Roll 278, Frame 219, NARA.

9. Miles to Assistant Adjutant General Department of Dakota, Camp opposite Cabin Creek on Yellowstone River, October 25, 1876 (Frame 431), and Miles to Terry, Camp on Bad Route Creek, October 28, 1876 (Frame 413), RG 94, Office of the Adjutant General Letters Received (Main Series), 1871–1880, File 4163 AGO 1876 (Sioux War Papers) M666, Roll 279, NARA. I treat these events in my book *The Lance and the Shield: The Life and Times of Sitting Bull* (New York: Henry Holt, 1993), chap. 13. For the entire campaign, see Jerome A. Greene, *Yellowstone Command: Colonel Nelson A. Miles and the Great Sioux War, 1876–1877* (Lincoln: University of Nebraska Press, 1991; paperback: Norman: University of Oklahoma Press, 2006).

10. Miles to Assistant Adjutant General Department of Dakota, Cantonment at Tongue River, December 17, 1876 (Frame 593), and telegram, Miles to Terry, Dec. 20, 1876 (Frame 573), RG 393, Records of U.S. Army Continental Commands (Special Files), Hq. Military Division of the Missouri, M1495, Roll 4, NARA; Miles to Assistant Adjutant General Department of Dakota, December 21, 24, 1876, in U.S. Secretary of War, *Annual Report* (1877), pp. 493–94. The movements of Miles's command and Baldwin's command in more detail are recorded in Baldwin's journals, diaries, and letters to his wife: Box 1, Folder A3f, and Box 11, Frank D. Baldwin Papers, Huntington Library.

11. Miles to Sherman, Opposite Fort Peck, Mont., November 18, 1876, Sherman Papers, vol. 45, Library of Congress.

12. Miles to Assistant Adjutant General, Department of Dakota, Cantonment at Tongue River, December 17, 1876, RG 393, Records of U.S. Army Continental Commands, Special Files, Hq. Division of the Missouri, M1495, Roll 4, Frame 593, NARA.

13. Miles to Assistant Adjutant General, Department of Dakota, Hq. Yellowstone Command, Cantonment on Tongue River, January 23, 1877, RG 94, Office of the Adjutant General Letters Received (Main Series), 1871–1880, File 4163, AGO 1876 (Sioux War Papers), M666, Roll 280, Frame 88, NARA.

14. Miles to Sherman, Cantonment on Yellowstone, January 20, 1877, Sherman Papers, vol. 45, Library of Congress.

15. Miles to Sherman, Tongue River, March 29, 1877, Sherman Papers, vol. 46, Library of Congress.

16. The official report is Miles to Assistant Adjutant General, Department of Dakota, Cantonment at Tongue River, May 16, 1877, RG 94, Office of the Adjutant General Letters Received (Main Series), 1871–1880, File 4163, AGO 1876 (Sioux War Papers) M666, Roll 281, Frame 536, NARA. The anonymous participant's letter is in *Army and Navy Journal* 14 (June 16, 1877): 723.

17. Sherman to McCrary, Cantonment on Tongue River, Mont., July 16, 1877, RG 94, Office of the Adjutant General Letters Received (Main Series), 1871–1880, File 4163, AGO 1876 (Sioux War Papers), M666, Roll 282, Frame 184, NARA. In 1867 Canada was a dominion within the British Empire. London conducted foreign affairs on behalf of the dominion, which is why the Sitting Bull negotiations were handled by England. I deal with Sitting Bull's Canadian episode in *The Lance and the Shield*, chap. 15.

18. Miles's official reports are found in U.S. Secretary of War, *Annual Report* (1877), pp. 74–76 and 514–16. I treat this battle in *Frontier Regulars*, pp. 311–14.

19. Sherman to Sheridan, Headquarters of the Army, February 9, 1878, RG 94, Office of the Adjutant General Letters Received (Main Series), 1871–1880, File 4163 AGO 1876 (Sioux War Papers), M666, Roll 284, Frame 190, NARA.

20. Telegram, Miles to Ruggles (in St. Paul), Fort Keogh, February 24, 1878 (with Sherman endorsement of March 11), RG 94, Office of the Adjutant General Letters Received (Main Series), 1871–1880, File 4163, AGO 1876 (Sioux War Papers), M666, Roll 284, Frame 329, NARA.

21. Telegram (via Fort Buford), Miles to Assistant Adjutant General Department of Dakota, Camp opposite Frenchman's Creek, July 18, 1879, RG 393, Records of U.S. Army Continental Commands: Special Files, Hq. Military Division of the Missouri, M1495, Roll 5, Frame 305 telegram (via Fort Buford), same to same, Camp on Trail immediately south of line, July 24, 1879, RG 393, Records of U.S. Army Continental Commands: Special Files, Hq. Military Division of the Missouri, M1495, Roll 5, Frame 346, NARA; Utley, *Frontier Regulars*, 287.

22. Telegram, Sherman to Sheridan, July 24, 1879 (Frame 311), and telegram, McCrary to Sheridan, July 23, 1879 (Frame 269), RG 393, Records of U.S. Army Continental Commands: Special Files, Hq. Military Division of the Missouri, M1495, Roll 5, NARA.

23. Telegram, Sheridan to Miles at Fort Leavenworth, April 3, 1886, RG 94, Letters Received, Office of the Adjutant General, 1881–1889, M689, 1066 AGO 1883, Roll 182, NARA. I treat the story of Miles's Arizona command in *Geronimo*, chap. 22.

24. General Order 58, by order of Col. W. B. Royall, Fort Huachuca, May 4, 1886, in U.S. Secretary of War, *Annual Report* (1886), pp. 176–77.

25. Lawton's official report of his expedition, September 9, 1886, in RG 94, Letters Received, Office of the Adjutant General, 1881–1889, M689, 1066 AGO 1883, Roll 186, NARA. The most detailed accounts of Lawton's Mexican campaign are in his letters to his wife, Papers of the Order of the Indian Wars, Misc. Coll., Box 1, folder

Personal Letters, U.S. Army Military History Institute, Carlisle Barracks, Pa.; and Leonard Wood, *Chasing Geronimo: The Journal of Leonard Wood, May–September 1886*, ed. Jack C. Lane (Albuquerque: University of New Mexico Press, 1970).

26. Miles to Assistant Adjutant General, Division of the Pacific, Presidio, Fort Apache, June 7, 1886, RG 94, Letters Received, Office of the Adjutant General, 1881–1889, M689, 1066 AGO 1883, Roll 184, NARA.

27. Louis Kraft, *Gatewood and Geronimo* (Albuquerque: University of New Mexico Press, 2000), p. 133; Morris E. Opler, "A Chiricahua Apache's Account of the Geronimo Campaign of 1886," *New Mexico Historical Review* 13 (October 1938): 371–73.

28. Thompson [Miles's aide] to Lawton, Fort Bowie, April 29, 1886; Lawton to Miles, San Bernardino, August 30, 1886; and Miles to Lawton, Fort Bowie, August 31, 1866, Miles Papers, Box 3, Folder 6, U.S. Army Military History Institute, Carlisle Barracks, Pennsylvania. Lawton's state of mind is captured in a letter to his wife, August 26 and 27, 1886, Lawton Papers, Box 3, Folder 6, U.S. Army Military History Institute, Carlisle Barracks, Pennsylvania.

29. Several eyewitness accounts describe the meeting, although differently. These are cited and discussed in my book *Geronimo*, p. 310n9.

30. I treated the story of the Ghost Dance and Wounded Knee in *The Last Days of the Sioux Nation* (1963; 2nd ed., New Haven: Yale University Press, 2004).

31. The literature on Wounded Knee is immense. I have relied heavily on my own *Last Days of the Sioux Nation*, chap. 12; and, in my judgment, the most authoritative book: Jerome A. Greene, *American Carnage: Wounded Knee, 1890* (Norman: University of Oklahoma Press, 2014).

32. Miles to Forsyth, January 4, 1891, Special Orders, No. 8, Hq. Div. of the Missouri in the field, Pine Ridge, RG 94, Wounded Knee Investigation Report, NARA.

33. Endorsements by Schofield and Proctor, February 4 and 13, 1891, Microfilm 983, NARA.

Chapter 6. Edward O. C. Ord

1. An excellent biography, on which this chapter relies heavily, is Bernarr Cresap, *Appomattox Commander: The Story of General E. O. C. Ord* (San Diego: A. S. Barnes, 1981).

2. In addition to ibid., chap. 4, I deal with the Pacific Northwest Indian wars in *Frontiersmen in Blue*, chap. 9.

3. General Orders 14, Hq. of the Army, Nov. 13, 1857, in U.S. Secretary of War, *Annual Report* (1857), pp. 51–52.

4. My reconstruction of Ord's service in the Civil War is drawn mainly from Cresap, *Appomattox Commander*. See also Warner, *Generals in Blue*, pp. 349–50.

5. The hunt is well described in Hutton, *Phil Sheridan and His Army*, pp. 212–16.

6. Gilbert C. Fite, "The United States Army and Relief to Pioneer Settlers, 1874–1875," *Journal of the West* 6 (1967): 99–107.

7. Sherman to Sheridan, November 29, 1877, Washington, D.C., Sherman-Sheridan Letters, Sheridan Papers, Library of Congress.

8. Ord to Sherman, San Antonio, July 6, 1875, Sherman Papers, vol. 39; Sherman to Ord, St. Louis, July 14, 1875, Sherman Papers vol. 40l, Sherman to Sheridan, July 14, 1875, Sherman-Sheridan Letters, Sheridan Papers, Library of Congress; Ord to Sherman, San Antonio, October 5, November 1, 1875, Sherman Papers, vol. 41, Library of Congress.

9. Testimony of Ord, December 6, 1877, before House Committee on Military Affairs on Texas border problems, in U.S. House Misc. Doc. 64, 45th Cong., 2nd sess., p. 103.

10. Kenneth W. Porter, "The Seminole-Negro Indian Scouts, 1870–1881," *Southwestern Historical Quarterly* 55 (1951–52): 358–77.

11. Testimony of Lt. Col. William R. Shafter before House Committee on Military Affairs on Texas border troubles, January 6, 1878, in U.S. House Misc. Doc. 64, 45th Cong., 2nd sess., pp. 58–59.

12. Telegram, Col. S. H. Taylor, Assistant Adjutant General Department of Texas, to Ord, Fort Duncan, April 3, 1877, Rec'd 10:30 A.M. in San Antonio, p. 11; Ord to M. M. Morales, Consul of Mexico in San Antonio, Hq. Department of Texas, San Antonio, April 14, 1877, pp. 58–59; Mexican Minister Ignacio Masical to Secretary of State William M. Evarts, Mexican Legation, Washington, D.C., April 28, 1877, pp. 56–57: all in U.S. House Ex. Doc. 13, 45th Cong., 1st sess.

13. Secretary of War G. W. McCrary to Gen. W. T. Sherman, June 1, 1877, in U.S. House Ex. Doc. 13, 45th Cong., 1st sess., pp. 14–15, transmitted to U.S. Minister in Mexico by secretary of state, June 4, 1877, p. 14. Further explanation of the order of June 1 is contained in Testimony of Secretary of War McCrary before House Committee on Military Affairs investigating Mexican border crossings, November 22, 1877, p. 7; and Testimony of General Ord, December 6, 1877, p. 94: U.S. House Misc. Doc. 64, 45th Cong., 2nd sess.

14. U.S. Minister Foster to Secretary of State Evarts, Mexico City, May 28, 1877, rec'd June 8, p. 14;. Ord to Sheridan, Fort Clark, June 19, 1877, in Sheridan to Adjutant General E. D. Townsend, June 20, 1877, 159; Treviño to Minister of War, Constitutional Army, Hq. Line of the North, Monterey, June 30, 1877, 264: U.S. House Ex. Doc. 13, 45th Cong., 1st sess.

15. Ord to Adjutant General, San Antonio, July 16, 1877, pp. 172–73; telegram, Ord to Adjutant General, July 13, 1877, p. 174; Adjutant General T. M. Vincent to Ord, Washington, D.C., July 14, 1877, p. 175: U.S. House Ex. Doc. 13, 45th Cong., 1st sess.

16. 1st Lt. John L. Bullis to 1st Lt. Helenus Dodt, Post Adjutant Fort Clark, October 12, 1877, Shafter Papers, Stanford University; telegrams, Sheridan to Adjutant General, October 2 and 3, 1877, transmitting telegrams from Ord,, pp. 240–41, and Gen. Francisco Naranjo, commanding Río Grande frontier, to Minister of War, Monterey, October 9, 1877, pp. 53–54: U.S. House Ex. Doc. 13, 45th Cong., 1st sess.

17. Sheridan to Sherman, November 24, 1877, Sherman Papers, vol. 47, Library of Congress.

18. Sherman to Sheridan, November 29, 1877, Washington, D.C., Sherman-Sheridan Letters, Sheridan Papers, Library of Congress.

19. Ibid.

20. Mackenzie's report, dated Fort Clark, June 23, 1878, is in Record Group 94, Box 1127, NARA. I treat this episode in *Frontiersmen in Blue*, 354.

21. Ord's annual report, October 1, 1879, in U.S. Secretary of War, *Annual Report* (1879), p. 93.

22. Sheridan to Sherman (confidential), December 12, 1879, Sherman Papers, vol. 51, Library of Congress, pp. 541–66.

23. Sherman to Terry in St. Paul, December 5, 1880, Sherman Papers, vol. 91, pp. 541–44.

24. Sherman to Senator S. B. Maxey of Texas, December 17, 1880, Sherman Papers, vol. 91, pp. 562–63, Library of Congress.

Chapter 7. John Pope

1. This sketch draws heavily on the excellent biography of Pope by Peter Cozzens, *General John Pope: A Life for the Nation* (Urbana: University of Illinois Press, 2000).

2. For Pope's Civil War career, see Warner, *Generals in Blue*, 376–77.

3. Quoted in Cozzens, *General John Pope*, p. 65.

4. Quoted in ibid., p. 161.

5. Stanton to Pope, September 6, 1862, in *Official Records of the Union and Confederate Armies* (hereinafter *OR*), ser. 1, vol. 13, p. 617.

6. Lincoln to Pope, November 10, 1862, *OR*, ser. 1, vol. 13, p. 787. Governor Alexander Ramsey to Lincoln, in *OR*, p. 787, and Pope to Lincoln, November 10, 1862, November 11, 1862, in *OR*, p. 788; Sibley to Brig. Gen. Elliott, December 6, 1862, in *OR*, ser. 1, vol. 22, pt. 1, p. 815.

7. Pope to Assistant Adjutant General John C. Kelton, Milwaukee, June 1, 1863, in *OR*, ser. 1, vol. 22, pt. 2, pp. 304–305.

8. Sibley's official reports are printed in *OR*, ser. 1, vol. 33, pt. 1. For Sully, see *OR*, ser. 1, vol. 22, pt. 1, pp. 555–68.

9. Instructions for conduct of summer campaign, by Maj. Gen. John Pope, March 15, 1864, in *OR*, ser. 1, vol. 34, pt. 2, pp. 622–64.

10. Expedition against Sioux Indians in Dakota Territory, Reports of Sibley, Sully, and subordinate officers, July 25 to October 8, 1864, in *OR*, ser. 1, vol. 44, pt. 1, pp. 131–74.

11. Richard N. Ellis, *General Pope and U.S. Indian Policy* (Albuquerque: University of New Mexico Press, 1970), chap. 2.

12. *OR*, ser. 1, vol. 48, pt. 1, pp. 1212, 1295–96; pt. 2, pp. 162–63, 237–38.

13. I treat the campaigns of 1865 in *Frontiersmen in Blue*, chap. 15. See also Ellis, *General Pope and U.S. Indian Policy*, chap. 4.

14. Pope to Sherman, Fort Union, New Mexico, August 11, 1866, in U.S. Secretary of War, *Annual Report* (1866), p. 30.

15. Annual Report of Bvt. Maj. Gen. John Pope, Pope to Lt. Col. G. L. Hartsuff, Adjutant General, Military Division of the Missouri, Hq. Department of the Missouri, Fort Leavenworth, October 31, 1870, in U.S. Secretary of War, *Annual Report* (1870), pp. 6–10.

16. Ibid., pp. 11–13.

17. Robert M. Utley, ed., *An Army Doctor on the Western Frontier: Journals and Letters of John Vance Lauderdale, 1864–1890* (Albuquerque: University of New Mexico Press, 2014), p. 64.

18. Annual Report of Brig. Gen. Pope, Pope to Fry at Military Division of the Missouri, Chicago, Hq. Department of the Missouri, Fort Leavenworth, October 2, 1871, in U.S. Secretary of War, *Annual Report* (1871), p. 43.

19. Annual Report of Lt. Gen. Sheridan, Sheridan to Adjutant General, Hq. Military Division of the Missouri, Chicago, November 4, 1871, in U.S. Secretary of War, *Annual Report* (1871), p. 24.

20. Annual Report of Brig. Gen. Pope, Pope to Fry at Military Division of the Missouri, Chicago, Hq. Department of the Missouri, Fort Leavenworth, October 2, 1871, p. 44.

21. Annual Report of Brig. Gen. Pope, Pope to Fry, Assistant Adjutant General Military Division of the Missouri, Chicago, Hq. Department of the Missouri, Fort Leavenworth, September 28, 1872, in U.S. Secretary of War, *Annual Report* (1872), p. 48.

22. U.S. House Report 384, 43rd Cong., 1st sess., *Reduction of the Military Establishment*, January 17, 1874, p. 189.

23. Sheridan to Sherman (ca. November 1872), Sherman Papers, vol. 34, Library of Congress.

24. Annual Report of Bvt. Maj. Gen. John Pope. Pope to Col. R. C. Drum, Assistant Adjutant General Military Division of the Missouri, Hq. Department of the Missouri, Fort Leavenworth, September 7, 1874, in U.S. Secretary of War, *Annual Report* (1874), p. 29.

25. Pope to Sherman, Fort Leavenworth, September 16, 1874, Sherman Papers, vol. 37, Library of Congress; Hutton, *Phil Sheridan and His Army*, pp. 245–48.

26. All official reports and correspondence of the Red River War are set forth in Taylor, *The Indian Campaign on the Staked Plains*. I treat the Red River War in *Frontier Regulars*, chap. 13.

27. Pope to Belknap, Fort Leavenworth, January 23, 1875, Sherman Papers, vol. 90, pp. 409–18, Library of Congress.

28. Sherman to Pope, Washington, D.C., April 24, 1876, Sherman Papers, vol. 90, pp. 409–18, Library of Congress.

29. Pope to Judge M. F. Force, Fort Leavenworth, March 13, 1876, quoted in James A. Garfield, "The Army of the United States," *North American Review* 136 (1878): 445–48.

30. Pope to House Committee on Military Affairs, Hq. Department of the Missouri, Fort Leavenworth, January 2, 1878, U.S. House Misc. Doc. No. 56, 45th Cong., 2nd sess., p. 28.

31. Annual Report of Brig. Gen. John Pope, Pope to Assistant Adjutant General, Military Division of the Missouri, Hq. Department of the Missouri, Fort Leavenworth, September 22, 1881, in U.S. Secretary of War, *Annual Report* (1881), pp. 123–24.

32. Ellis, *General Pope and U. S. Indian Policy*, chap. 12.

33. I treat Pope's involvement in the Geronimo operations in *Geronimo*, chaps. 22–24.

Chapter 8. Alfred H. Terry

1. Ulysses S. Grant, *Personal Memoirs of U. S. Grant* (New York: Century, 1885), p. 540.

2. For Terry, I draw heavily on Carl W. Marino, "General Alfred Howe Terry: Soldier from Connecticut" (Ph.D. dissertation, New York University, 1968). Marino covers Terry's Civil War years thoroughly but only summarizes his postwar career.

3. Ibid., p. 192.

4. Ibid., p. 415. In addition to Marino's dissertation, see Richard B. McCaslin, *The Last Stronghold: The Campaign for Fort Fisher* (Abilene, Tex.: McWhiney Foundation Press, 2003).

5. Annual Report of Bvt. Maj. Gen. Alfred H. Terry, Hq. Department of Dakota, St. Paul, September 27, 1867, in U.S. Secretary of War, *Annual Report* (1867), pp. 49–52. Terry's postwar career is treated in John W. Bailey, *Pacifying the Plains: General Alfred Terry and the Decline of the Sioux, 1866–1880* (Westport Conn.: Greenwood Press, 1970). I have relied heavily on this work.

6. I treat the Peace Commission in *The Indian Frontier, 1846–1890* (rev. ed., Albuquerque: University of New Mexico Press, 2003), pp. 106–10. See also chapter 2 in the present book.

7. Terry's statement is found in his annual report, Hq. Department of Dakota, St. Paul, September 9, 1874, in U.S. Secretary of War, *Annual Report* (1874), p. 37. Sheridan's role is covered in his annual report, Military Division of the Missouri, Chicago, October 3, 1874, in ibid., 22–29. Terry's legal analysis is laid out in Bailey, *Pacifying the Plains*, 95–97.

8. Sheridan's orders to Terry, September 3, 1874, are set forth in the *Army and Navy Journal* 12 (September 12, 1874): 70. The excerpt from the *New York Tribune* is cited in the *Army and Navy Journal* 12 (April 10, 1875): 555. The report of the Allison Commission is found in U.S. Commissioner of Indian Affairs, *Annual Report* (1875), pp. 184–200.

9. I recount this story in *Cavalier in Buckskin: George Armstrong Custer and the Western Military Frontier* (rev. ed., Norman: University of Oklahoma Press, 2001), chap. 7.

10. Terry's field diary briefly describes each day's march but records little more. Michael J. Koury, ed., *The Field Diary of General Alfred H. Terry: The Yellowstone Expedition—1876* (Bellevue Nebr.: Old Army Press, 1970).

11. Official records of the Sioux war of 1876 are contained in U.S. House Ex. Doc. 184, 44th Cong., 1st sess., vol. 17, 1876: *Expedition against the Sioux Indians*.

12. Col. Robert P. Hughes, "The Campaign against the Sioux in 1876," *Journal of the Military Institution of the United States* 18 (January 1896): 1–44 (the following orders and quotations on Terry are also from this source). I set forth my own conclusions in *Cavalier in Buckskin*, chap. 9.

13. Miles to Sherman, Cantonment on Yellowstone, January 20, 1877, Sherman Papers, vol. 45, Library of Congress.

14. Sheridan to Sherman (confidential), February. 10, 1877, Sherman Papers, vol. 45, Library of Congress.

BIBLIOGRAPHY

Manuscripts and Archival Collections

Augur, Christopher C., Papers, Newberry Library, Chicago.

Baldwin, Frank D., Papers, Henry E. Huntington Library, San Marino, California.

Lawton, Henry W., Papers, U.S. Army Military History Institute, Carlisle Barracks, Pennsylvania.

Marino, Carl W. "General Alfred Howe Terry: Soldier from Connecticut." Ph.D. dissertation, New York University, 1968.

Miles, Nelson A., Papers, U.S. Army Military History Institute, Carlisle Barracks, Pennsylvania.

Papers of the Order of the Indian Wars, U.S. Army Military History Institute, Carlisle Barracks, Pennsylvania.

Sheridan, Philip H., Papers, Library of Congress, Washington, D.C.

Sherman, William T., Papers, Library of Congress, Washington, D.C.

Government Documents

National Archives. RG 94, Office of the Adjutant General Letters Received (Main Series), 1871–1880, File 4163 AGO 1876 (Sioux War Papers), M666.

———. RG 94, Office of the Adjutant General, Letters Received (Main Series), 1881–89, 1066 AGO 1883.

———. RG 393, Records of U.S. Army Continental Commands, Special Files, Military Division of the Missouri, M1495.

Official Records of the Union and Confederate Armies, ser. 1, vol. 13; vol. 22, pts. 1, 2; vol. 34, pt. 2; vol. 44, pt. 1; vol. 48, pts. 1, 2. Washington, D.C.: GPO.

U.S. Commissioner of Indian Affairs. *Annual Reports.* Washington, D.C.: GPO, 1866–90.

U.S. House Ex. Doc. No. 88, 39th Cong, 2nd sess. 1866. *Commissioners to Indian Tribes.*

U.S. House Ex. Doc. No. 97, 40th Cong., 2nd sess. 1867. *Report of Indian Peace Commissioners.*

U.S. House Ex. Doc. No. 184, 44th Cong., 1st sess., vol. 17, 1876. *Expedition against the Sioux Indians.*

U.S. House Misc. Docs. No. 56, 45th Cong., 2nd sess., 1877, *Reorganization of the Army.*

U.S. House Report No. 384, 43rd Cong., 1st sess., 1874. *Reduction of the Military Establishment, Jan. 17, 1874.*

U.S. Secretary of War. *Annual Reports,* Washington, D.C.: GPO, 1866–90.

U.S. Senate Ex. Doc. No. 13, 40th Cong., 1st sess., 1867. *Indian Hostilities.*

U.S. Senate Ex. Doc. No. 7, 40th Cong., 1st sess., 1867. *Expeditions against the Indians.*

U.S. Senate Ex. Doc. No. 89, 41st Cong., 2nd sess., 1870. *Encroachments on Indians in Wyoming.*

U.S. Statutes at Large. Vols. 14–18. Washington, D.C.: GPO, 1874–75.

Articles and Periodicals

Army and Navy Journal 9 (August 8, 1871); 9 (October 7, 1871); 9 (May 25, 1872); 14 (May 12, 1877); 14 (June 16, 1877), 15 (September 8, 1877).

Bloom, Lansing B. "Bourke on the Southwest." *New Mexico Historical Review* 9 (1934): 33–77, 159–83, 273–89, 375–437.

Braden, Charles. "The Yellowstone Expedition of 1873." *Journal of the U.S. Cavalry Association* 16 (1905): 218–41.

Crook, George. "The Apache Problem." *Journal of the Military Service Institution* 7, no. 27 (October 1886): 257–69.

Fite, Gilbert C. "The United States Army and Relief to Pioneer Settlers, 1874–1875." *Journal of the West* 6 (1967): 99–107.

Garfield, James A. "The Army of the United States." *North American Review* 136 (1878): 445–48.

Hughes, Col. Robert P. "The Campaign against the Sioux in 1876." *Journal of the Military Institution of the United States* 18 (January 1896): 1–44.

Opler, Morris E. "A Chiricahua Apache's Account of the Geronimo Campaign of 1886." *New Mexico Historical Review* 13 (October 1938): 371–73.

Porter, Kenneth W. "The Seminole-Negro Indian Scouts, 1870–1881." *Southwestern Historical Quarterly* 55 (1951–52): 358–77.

Utley, Robert M. "Border Showdown." *MHQ: The Quarterly Journal of Military History* 23 (Spring 2011): 98–104.

———. "The Red River War: Last Uprising in the Texas Panhandle." *MHQ: The Quarterly Journal of Military History* 20 (Autumn 2007): 74–83.

Books

Bailey, John W. *Pacifying the Plains: General Alfred Terry and the Decline of the Sioux, 1866–1880.* Westport Conn.: Greenwood Press, 1970.

Bourke, John G. *On the Border with Crook.* New York: Charles Scribner's Sons, 1891.

Carpenter, John A. *Sword and Olive Branch: Oliver Otis Howard* (1964). New York: Fordham University Press, 1999.

Carter, R. G. *On the Border with Mackenzie: or, Winning West Texas from the Comanches*. New York: Antiquarian Press, 1961.

Cozzens, Peter. *General John Pope: A Life for the Nation*. Urbana: University of Illinois Press, 2000.

Cresap, Bernarr. *Appomattox Commander: The Story of General E. O. C. Ord*. San Diego: A. S. Barnes, 1981.

DeMontravel, Peter R. *A Hero to His Fighting Men: Nelson A. Miles, 1839–1925*. Kent, Ohio: Kent State University Press, 1998.

Dobak, William A., and Thomas D. Phillips. *The Black Regulars, 1866–1898*. Norman: University of Oklahoma Press, 2001.

Ellis, Richard N. *General Pope and U.S. Indian Policy*. Albuquerque: University of New Mexico Press, 1970.

Fry, James B. *The History and Legal Effect of Brevets in the Armies of Great Britain and the United States*. New York: D. Van Nostrand, 1877.

Gibson, A. M. *The Kickapoos: Lords of the Middle Border*. Norman: University of Oklahoma Press, 1964.

Grant, Ulysses S. *Personal Memoirs of U. S. Grant*. New York: Century, 1885.

Greene, Jerome A. *American Carnage: Wounded Knee, 1890*. Norman: University of Oklahoma Press, 2014.

———. *Nez Perce Summer, 1877: The U.S. Army and the Nee-Me-Poo Crisis*. Helena: Montana Historical Society Press, 2000.

———. *Yellowstone Command: Colonel Nelson A. Miles and the Great Sioux War, 1876–1877*. Lincoln: University of Nebraska Press, 1991. Reprinted, Norman: University of Oklahoma Press, 2006.

Hutton, Paul Andrew. *Phil Sheridan and His Army*. Lincoln: University of Nebraska Press, 1985.

Koury, Michael J., ed. *The Field Diary of General Alfred H. Terry: The Yellowstone Expedition—1876*. Bellevue, Nebr.: Old Army Press, 1970.

Kraft, Louis. *Gatewood and Geronimo*. Albuquerque: University of New Mexico Press, 2000.

Magid, Paul, *George Crook: From the Redwoods to Appomattox*. Norman: University of Oklahoma Press, 2011.

———. *The Gray Fox: George Crook and the Indian Wars*. Norman: University of Oklahoma Press, 2015.

McCaslin, Richard B. *The Last Stronghold: The Campaign for Fort Fisher*. Abilene Tex.: McWhiney Foundation Press, 2003.

Miles, Nelson A. *Personal Recollections and Observations of General Nelson A. Miles* (1896). Reprint, New York: Da Capo, 1969.

——— *Serving the Republic: Memoirs of the Civil and Military Life of Nelson A. Miles, Lieutenant General, United States Army*. New York: Harper & Bros., 1911.

Richardson, James D., comp. *A Compilation of Messages and Papers of the Presidents, 1789–1897*. 10 vols. Washington, D.C.: Bureau of National Literature and Art, 1897.

Robinson, Charles M., III. *General Crook and the Western Frontier*. Norman: University of Oklahoma Press, 2001.

Schmitt, Martin F., ed. *General George Crook: His Autobiography.* Norman: University of Oklahoma Press, 1946.

Taylor, Joe F., ed. *The Indian Campaign on the Staked Plains, 1874–1875: Military Correspondence from War Department Adjutant General's Office, File 2815–1874.* Canyon, Tex.: Panhandle-Plains Historical Society, 1962.

Utley, Robert M. *Cavalier in Buckskin: George Armstrong Custer and the Western Military Frontier.* 1988. Revised ed., Norman: University of Oklahoma Press, 2001.

———. *Frontier Regulars: The United States Army and the Indian, 1866–1891.* New York: Macmillan, 1973.

———. *Frontiersmen in Blue: The United States Army and the Indian, 1848–1865.* New York: Macmillan, 1967.

———. *Geronimo.* New Haven: Yale University Press, 2012.

———. *The Indian Frontier, 1846–1890.* 1984. Revised ed., Albuquerque: University of New Mexico Press, 2003.

———. *The Lance and the Shield: The Life and Times of Sitting Bull.* New York: Henry Holt, 1993.

———. *The Last Days of the Sioux Nation* (1963). 2nd ed. New Haven: Yale University Press, 2004.

Utley, Robert M., ed. *An Army Doctor on the Western Frontier: Journals and Letters of John Vance Lauderdale, 1864–1890.* Albuquerque: University of New Mexico Press, 2014.

Wallace, Ernest, ed. *Ranald S. Mackenzie's Official Correspondence Relating to Texas, 1871–1875.* 2 vols. Lubbock: West Texas Museum Association, 1967.

Warner, Ezra J. *Generals in Blue: Lives of the Union Commanders* (1964). Baton Rouge: Louisiana State University Press, 1999.

Wood, Leonard. *Chasing Geronimo: The Journal of Leonard Wood, May–September 1886.* Edited by Jack C. Lane. Albuquerque: University of New Mexico Press, 1970.

Wooster, Robert. *Nelson A. Miles and the Twilight of the Frontier Army.* Lincoln: University of Nebraska Press, 1993.

INDEX

Kiowa Indians, 24, 27, 28, 31, 32, 98, 99, 100, 165, 167, 169, 171
Klamath River, 36
Ku Klux Klan, 96
Knoxville, Tenn., 72

Lame Deer, 106–7
Lapwai Agency, Ida., 78
Lauderdale, John Vance, 169
Lawton, Henry W., 114, 115, 116, 117
Lee, Robert E., 19, 40, 43, 69, 70, 73, 93, 95, 132, 137–38, 157, 158
Leeds, Me., 69
Lewisburg, Battle of, 39
Lincoln, Abraham, 19, 39, 70, 74, 132, 135, 136, 152–53, 154, 156, 159, 160, 178, 185
Lincoln, Robert T., 87
Lipan Apache Indians, 27, 30, 142, 144, 145
Little Bighorn, Battle of, 7, 10, 54, 56, 102, 195–96
Little Bighorn River, 54, 195, 197, 198
Little Crow, 159
Little Missouri Badlands, 162
Little Missouri River, 162
Little Wolf, 56, 58, 59
Logan, John A., 72, 73
Lolo Trail, 81, 82, 83
Longstreet, James, 136, 137, 157, 158
Looking Glass, 81, 82
Los Angeles, Calif., 129
Louisiana, 32, 135
Louisville, Ky., 151
Lyman, Wyllys, 99

Mackenzie, Ranald S., 29–31, 32, 56, 58, 98, 100, 106, 112, 141, 142, 145–46, 148, 172, 206, 208, 210
Maine, 70, 73, 151
Malheur River, 45
Man-Afraid-of-His-Horses, 20
Manassas, First Battle of. *See* Bull Run, Battle of
Manassas, Second Battle of, 157–59, 161, 174, 175

Manassas, Va., 178
Manassas Junction, Va., 157
Mankato, Minn., 160, 161
Marsh, Grant, 192–93, 197
Martine, 115, 116
Maryland, 40, 43, 70, 127, 132, 135
Massachusetts, 20, 93
Maus, Marion P., 63, 65
Maxey, Samuel B., 148
McClellan, George B., 18, 40, 69, 92, 133, 153, 156, 157–59
McClellan Creek, Battle of, 100–101
McClernand, John M., 134, 135
McCrary, George W., 108, 111, 143
McDowell, Irvin, 6, 77, 78, 84, 112, 133, 147, 156, 174, 178, 207
McIntosh, Archie, 46, 48, 49
McKinley, William, 124
McLaughlin, James, 119
McLean, Wilmer, 138
McPherson, James B., 74
Meade, George G., 71, 93, 95, 96, 137
Medical Department, 5
Medicine Lodge Treaty, 24, 28, 187
Memphis, Tenn., 133, 154
Merritt, Wesley, 28, 84, 87
Mescalero Apache Indians, 27, 30, 145
Mexican Central Railroad, 148
Mexican War, 15, 17, 127, 152
Mexico, 27, 29–32, 61–63, 113, 114, 141, 142, 152, 208, 210
Mexico City, Mexico, 148
Miles, Nelson A., 4, 32, 33, 55–56, 57, 64, 87, 88, 112, 118, 175, 198, 200, 210, 211; ambition, 93, 96, 104, 105, 111, 117, 123, 200, 209; and Apache campaign, 63, 114–18, 206; and Bear Paw battle, 85, 109–10, 206, 207; called Bear Coat, 103; Canadian border operations, 108–11, 199; in Civil War, 91–96; as colonel in Fifth Infantry, 96; commands Department of Arizona, 114–18; commands Department of the Columbia, 112–13, 206, commands